THE FAMILIES OF WORDS

OTHER BOOKS BY MARIO PEI

Published by Harper & Brothers

The *Holiday* Magazine Language Books for the Traveler
  Getting Along in French (with John Fisher)
  Getting Along in German (with Robert Politzer)
  Getting Along in Italian
  Getting Along in Portuguese (with Alexander R. Prista)
  Getting Along in Russian (with Fedor I. Nikanov)
  Getting Along in Spanish (with Eloy Vaquero)
  Talking Your Way around the World

Published by J. B. Lippincott Co.

The Story of Language
All About Language
The Story of English

Published by The Devin-Adair Co.

Language for Everybody
One Language for the World

Published by The John Day Co.

Swords of Anjou

Published by Henry Holt & Co., Inc.

First Year French (with E. Méras)

Published by Philosophical Library, Inc.

The Sparrows of Paris
Dictionary of Linguistics (with F. Gaynor)

Published by Lothrop, Lee & Shepard Co., Inc.

The Book of Place Names (with E. Lambert)
Our Names (with E. Lambert)

Published by Crown Publishers, Inc.

The Consumer's Manifesto

Published by Vanni Publications

The Italian Language
The Language of the Eighth-Century Texts in Northern France
The World's Chief Languages

The Families of Words

by

Mario Pei

Professor of Romance Philology, Columbia University

HARPER & ROW, PUBLISHERS
New York and Evanston

ACKNOWLEDGMENTS

The author wishes to acknowledge his indebtedness to his colleagues who assisted him in the compilation of this work, and particularly to Professor Elliott V. K. Dobbie, of Columbia University, who went over a great deal of the Germanic material and supplied numerous valuable suggestions; and Professor Robert Fowkes of New York University, who performed the same service for the Celtic material.

ABBREVIATIONS MOST FREQUENTLY USED

AF—Anglo-French
Ar.—Arabic
AS—Anglo-Saxon
Celt.—Celtic
Dan.—Danish
Du.—Dutch
Eng.—English
Fr.—French
Gaul.—Gaulish
Ger.—German
Goth.—Gothic
Gk.—Greek
Heb.—Hebrew
HG—High German
Hind.—Hindustani
IE—Indo-European
II—Indo-Iranian
Ir.—Irish
It.—Italian
Jap.—Japanese
Lat.—Latin
LG—Low German

Lith.—Lithuanian
ME—Middle English
MHG—Middle High German
MLG—Middle Low German
NF—Northern French
    (Norman-Picard-Walloon)
OF—Old French
OHG—Old High German
OIr.—Old Irish
ON—Old Norse
OPers.—Old Persian
Osc.—Oscan
Prov.—Provençal
Pt.—Portuguese
Rum.—Rumanian
Russ.—Russian
Scand.—Scandinavian
Sem.—Semitic
Skt.—Sanskrit
Sl.—Slavic
Sp.—Spanish
VL—Vulgar Latin

CONTENTS

THE FAMILIES OF WORDS

CHAPTER 1

The Background of Indo-European

How many words are there in the world's 2,796 spoken languages? This is an idle question, to which no one has the answer.

Estimates of the number of words in individual languages often appear. One such estimate for English, based on the entries in the New English Dictionary, the most comprehensive lexicological tool at our disposal, places the total number of English words at somewhere in the neighborhood of 600,000, exclusive of such variants as *dogs* from *dog*, or *takes, took, taking, taken* from *take*. But even the New English Dictionary misses many of the words in actual use—slang or dialectal forms, new technological expressions, new acceptances for old words, brand-new coinages that appear every day. Each language is in a state of flux, each adds to its wordstock at the rate of dozens, perhaps hundreds, of words each day. The task of listing all the words in the language (any language) is a hopeless one, because by the time you have completed your list a new list is needed.

Yet it is a fact that all these hundreds of thousands of words, in English as in all other tongues, have a way of grouping themselves under common ancestors which are relatively few in number. Anyone who gives the matter even fleeting thought will realize at once that there must be something which *receive, deceive, conceive, perceive* hold in common, a root word which in English assumes the form *-ceive*. Any dictionary that gives etymologies will inform us that this *-ceive*, as well as the *-cept* of *intercept, concept*, the *-cipate* of *participate*, the *cap-* of *capable* and *captive*, goes back to a Latin word, *capio*, which may also assume the form *-cipio* in compounds, that means "to seize, take" and the like. What the dictionary does not ordinarily tell us is that this Latin word stems from the same original root that produces *have, haven, heave* and *heft*. The Latin *capio* and the English *have* are members of the same word-family, and go back to a single common root-word.

1

This may cause a little surprise, because anyone knowing some Latin and German would rather naturally assume that the Latin *habeo* corresponds to both the German *haben* and the English *have*, all the more since *habeo* means exactly "to have", while *capio* means "to seize". Yet this apparently simple and logical assumption is wrong. It can be proved wrong, and the proof will be forthcoming a little later.

Again, it will rather naturally be assumed that English *day* and Latin *dies* (or Spanish *dia*, or French *-di* of *lundi*, *mardi*) are the same original word. Again, this assumption is wrong.

In English we speak of a *rare* occurrence and *rare* meat. Is it the same word? Not at all. The first is Latin, the second is Anglo-Saxon, and they have nothing in common save that in modern English they have fallen together in pronunciation and spelling.

On the other hand, there are cases where our elementary etymological instinct, based on similarities of sound and meaning, does not deceive us. Does there not seem to be a relationship of some sort between *deep* and *dip*, and could this not carry on even to *dimple* and *dump*? The answer is yes. Does not the link between *just* and *justice* carry on to *juror*, *jury*, even *conjure*, *injure* and *perjury*? It does. Is it not natural to assume a kinship between *beard* and *barber*, and when someone who has studied Russian informs us that the Russian word for "beard" is *boroda*, do we not have the feeling that it is a related form?

The real fact of the matter is that words, in English as in other languages, come in families, not as individuals. The word that has no relatives is as rare as the man who tells you that he is entirely alone in the world. In fact, there are no such words, and there are no such men. He may not know it, but the mere fact that he is alive is clear indication of the existence of cousins and other kinsmen, however far removed, however much unknown to him.

We are going to present English words (with occasional words that are not English, but with which most readers are acquainted) in their family groupings. Some of them will be small and quite simple groups, others extremely large and seemingly far-fetched, like *water*, *whiskey*, *hydrant* and *vodka*, or *rule*, *royal*, *right* and *rajah*.

But first something must be said of the conditions that led to the formation of these word-families and the way in which they started.

Do all of the world's languages, past and present, stem from a single original tongue? Or did they originate in various spots, with the evolution of different groups of human beings?

This question has interested linguists since linguists began to exist. But it has far more than linguistic implications. If it could be proved that all languages come from a single source, it would be a very strong element of proof that all human beings likewise come from a single source. It would be highly improbable that men, arising in unrelated groups and in various regions of the earth without speech, would later fasten upon a single form of speech. It is perfectly true that speech can be acquired; but if we postulate, as some anthropologists do, one human group arising in northern Europe, a second around the Gulf of Guinea, and a third in the valley of the Yellow River in China, we would then have to suppose that one of these three groups began to speak, and that speech was spread by later contacts to the other two groups. This is not altogether impossible, but at a period when there was little migration or intermingling, it seems not too likely.

If, on the other hand, three or more races of mankind had arisen separately, and each had separately evolved its own form of speech, then we would expect these forms of speech to be different from the outset and show no common link save to the extent that the races later came in contact.

The Biblical account describes all men as having a common origin, and a single original form of speech, later differentiated as a result of the Tower of Babel episode. This belief predominated throughout the Middle Ages and well into the Renaissance, with the Hebrew of the Old Testament assumed to have been the original tongue from which all others stemmed.

It was not until the voyages of discovery began to bring to light a vast number of hitherto unknown languages that this point of view began to change. Many of the newly discovered tongues were so utterly different from the familiar ones of the older period that those who studied them were in spite of themselves forced to doubt that all could stem from the same source. Eventually there came attempts at classification, and by the eighteenth century most language scholars were convinced that the relationship of all the world's languages supposed at an earlier period was a figment of the imagination.

Numerous errors were made when classification was first attempted, and it was not until the dawn of the nineteenth century that the languages were finally placed in some sort of satisfactory pigeon-hole arrangement (for a good many of the more obscure tongues, the pigeon-holes are quite tentative even today).

Of one thing, however, the language scholars felt more and more certain. These languages that were becoming ever more numerous and diverse could not possibly all belong to the same family, or have any sort of universal origin. Throughout the nineteenth century, which was the great period of language classification, the possibility of common origin was hushed up, and when the Italian linguist Trombetti brought it up again in 1905 and presented a daring series of comparisons among all the languages of the world designed to prove their monogenesis, or unity of origin, his attempt met with skepticism and barely veiled scorn.

Today the linguists are not so sure. Many of them admit the possibility of links among language families that were formerly considered altogether distinct and unrelated. The question of monogenesis, with its far-flung implications concerning the single origin of the human species, is still a highly debatable one.

What is not debatable is the very evident link among *certain* languages, to the exclusion of others. No linguist denies the relationship and common origin of Latin, Greek, Sanskrit, German, Russian and Welsh; or of Arabic and Hebrew; or of Finnish and Hungarian. What some linguists (perhaps still a majority) deny is the common origin of all three groups.

The general classifications that were established in the nineteenth century still hold, save for minor shifts. The present-day language expert can state with almost absolute assurance, backed by undeniable evidence, that certain tongues are related; beyond that, for lack of irrefutable proof, he is unwilling to commit himself.

Among the major language classifications that have been established beyond the shadow of a doubt is one called Indo-European (often abbreviated in writing to IE), from the fact that its members extend from northern India across Europe. Another name for it is Indo-Germanic, which is justified by the fact that the name includes the easternmost and westernmost members of the family (the Indian branch, represented by Sanskrit, and the Germanic branch, represented by Icelandic); but this name also seems to give those two members undue prominence, leaving the others out in the cold. A third name is Aryan, which is even more objectionable because of its use in racial rather than linguistic connotations.

The Indo-European language family has a demonstrable common origin, but the original parent tongue is unknown, because writing had not yet been invented at the time when it was spoken. The common origin is shown by the vast number of word-roots which the member languages hold in common, though they may use them in different ways and with different meanings, and also by the fact that the different branches show in their use of these root-words certain highly consistent sound-shifts and sound correspondences. One of the most elementary examples of the latter is that where Sanskrit, Greek and Latin have an initial p, the members of the Germanic branch have an initial f (Latin *pater, ped-, piscis*, vs. English *father, foot, fish*).

The original speakers of Indo-European are supposed to have lived in northern Europe, around the shores of the Baltic, though of that we do not have absolute proof. An earlier theory was to the effect that they lived on the Iranian plateau, in western Asia, and moved westward in successive waves, save for the group that moved southeastward into India. What led people to prefer north central Europe as a hypothetical original habitat for the early speakers of Indo-European was the fact that all or most of the branches hold in common certain words for plants, animals, and minerals that exist in north central Europe, but not other words denoting objects existing on the Iranian plateau or in northern India. For example, most of the early Indo-European languages show native developments of the same original root for *birch, beech, willow, ash, wolf, bear, goose, horse, dog, gold, silver*, but not for *palm, olive, vine, laurel, tiger, elephant, lion, leopard*.

Whichever way the migration may have gone, as groups of these speakers wandered away in various directions, they lost touch with one another, and their once identical speech began to develop differences, until finally a number of separate dialects emerged. Many of these disappeared in the course of history, their speakers dying out or being absorbed by other groups. (Two important extinct groups were the Hittite and the Tokharian.) Eight of them have come down to the present day, and have modern representatives in the tongues of most of Europe and southwestern Asia.

These eight living Indo-European groups, with their major sub-divisions, are:

1. Indo-Iranian; this includes the ancient and modern languages of what is today northern India, Pakistan, Afghanistan, and Iran. The Indian sub-branch takes in ancient Sanskrit, ancient and medieval languages called Prakrits, of which Pali is one, and modern languages like Hindi, Urdu, Bengali, and numerous others. The Iranian division comprises the Old Persian of Darius and Artaxerxes, the Avestan used by Zoroaster, and the official tongues of present-day Iran and Afghanistan (Persian, Pashtu, Kurdish, etc).

2. Armenian; this is a small and isolated branch, appearing in ancient, medieval , and modern times around the border region of present-day Turkey and the Soviet Union.

3. Albanian; another small and isolated branch, spoken in Albania and near-by regions.

4. Greek; in ancient times Greek was subdivided into several dialects, and was spoken not merely in Greece, but in most of Asia Minor, the islands of the Aegean, and in numerous Greek colonies along the shores of the Black Sea and the Mediterranean. Today it is restricted to Greece and near-by islands, including Cyprus and Crete.

5. Balto-Slavic; here, as with Indo-Iranian, we have two sub-branches: the Baltic, including Lithuanian and Latvian, and the Slavic, which takes in Russian, Ukrainian, Polish, Czech, Slovak, Serbo-Croatian, Slovenian, and Bulgarian.

6. Italic; in ancient times this had two branches, Oscan-Umbrian and Latin-Faliscan. Latin, however, absorbed all its kindred tongues, and from Latin come all the modern Romance languages: French, Italian, Spanish, Portuguese, Catalan, Provençal, Sardinian, Rheto-Rumansh, Rumanian.

7. Germanic; in ancient times, this had three branches; an eastern one, represented by Gothic, which disappeared; a northern, which gave rise to the Scandinavian tongues (Old Norse, modern Swedish, Norwegian, Danish, Icelandic); and a western, which further sub-divided itself into a High German and a Low German variety; Old High German, with some admixtures from the Low German dialects, forms the basis of modern literary German; the chief Low German varieties were, in the early Middle Ages, Old Saxon, Anglo-Saxon

(which ultimately turned into English) and Old Frisian, which gave rise to Dutch (with closely related Flemish, Frisian, and Afrikaans).

8. Celtic; here again antiquity shows three subdivisions: a continental one, represented by ancient Gaulish, which vanished; a Goidelic, whose modern descendants are Irish, Scots Gaelic, and Manx; and a Brythonic, represented by Welsh, Cornish, and Breton.

All the languages mentioned, and many others besides, belong to the Indo-European classification. However dissimilar they may appear today, all have a common ancestry and many common root-words, as well as a basically similar grammatical structure, which becomes more evident as we go back in time (the grammar of Anglo-Saxon, for instance, is much closer to that of Latin than is that of English to that of Italian). Each branch, each sub-branch, and each individual language is characterized by certain specific, distinctive features, which have arisen over the course of centuries by a natural process of diversification or dialectalization; still, the common origin, the common roots and the common original structure are unmistakable.

It is on the basis of the common roots that we are able to attempt some kind of reconstruction of the Indo-European parent language. The reconstruction is quite hypothetical, yet it gives us a glimpse of that mysterious early form of speech of which no written documents are in existence.

How is the reconstruction achieved? By laying side by side the earliest attested forms of each branch and, as we compare them, arriving at some conclusion as to what the form that gave rise to all of them must have been like. This very often involves a process similar to an election or a Gallup Poll. When we find, for example, that the common word appears with an initial *p* in Indo-Iranian, Balto-Slavic, Italic, Greek, but with *h* in Armenian, *f* in Germanic, and complete disappearance of the initial consonant sound in Celtic, we assume that the majority group has kept the original sound while the three minority groups have changed it (the fact that they show different forms, not the same form, is added proof); so we assume that in a word like that for "father", the original parent tongue had the *p* indicated by four out of seven of our descendants, rather than the *h*, *f*, or nothing indicated by the minorities. Where six of our branches show *t*, and only Armenian and Germanic show *th*, we assume that *t* shows the original state of affairs.

The sequence *p-p-p-p-p-h-f-zero*, or that of *t-t-t-t-t-t-th-th* must appear in a large number of words before we accept it as definitive. In works of a scientific nature, chance or stray resemblances or relationships do not suffice. But once the relationship is established, it permits us to prophesy with some degree of assurance what *ought to be* the form in a language in which we have not yet found it. In other words, it tells us what to look for or expect.

It is formulas of this kind that tell us that *capio*, not *habeo*, is the Latin word that comes from the same Indo-European root as English *have* or German *haben*; if Germanic has *h*, then Latin should have *c*, not *h*; if Germanic has *b* (English *have* was *habban* in Anglo-Saxon), then Latin should have *p*, not *b*. *Capio*, not *habeo*, is the Latin word that fits the pattern. But what about the meaning? Shifts in meaning are extremely common in Indo-European development; shifts in sound pattern are not. To accept *habeo* as stemming from the same Indo-European root as *have*, we would have to make one of two assumptions: either that Latin borrowed the word from Germanic (or vice versa), and this is not likely in the case of words in very general use; or that there was, in either Latin or Germanic, a special development in the case of this word, which would be so exceptional as to be little short of miraculous.

A similar formula tells us that if *day* came from the same root as Latin *dies*, Spanish *día*, French *-di*, it would have *t*, not *d*. Strange as it may seem, it is in the *Tues-* part of *Tuesday*, not in the *-day* part, that we get the Anglo-Saxon relative of both Latin *dies*, "day" and Latin *deus*, "god". *Day* comes directly from Old Norse *daga*, and more remotely from an Indo-European root *dhagh[1] or *dhegh, "warm period", which develops in Latin into the forms that ultimately come to English in *foment* and (possibly) *fever*.

The comparative method we have described serves to give a measure of predictability to our work as we pass from one branch to another and from one language to another. It also permits us to reconstruct, with some measure of plausibility, the original Indo-European word roots. In fact, it permits the more imaginative Indo-European specialists to determine, more or less correctly, how the primitive Indo-European

---

[1] The asterisk in front of an Indo-European form indicates that this form is hypothetical, and reconstructed from a comparison of all the others, which are attested. It is also used for any other hypothetical or unattested form.

speakers might have phrased a sentence like "God gave teeth; God will give bread". Placing side by side the translation of this statement in three of the most conservative Indo-European known languages, Sanskrit, Lithuanian and Latin, this is what we get:

Sanskrit: *Devas adadāt datas; Devas dadāt dhānās.*

Lithuanian: *Dievas dawe dantis; Dievas duos duonos.*

Latin: *Deus dedit dentes; Deus dabit panem.*

Indo-European: *Deivos ededōt dn̥tns;* [2] *Deivos dedōt dhōnās.*

Even in as simple and primitive a sentence as this, it is of interest to note that in its word for "bread" Latin has already strayed away from the original *dhōnās* evidenced by Sanskrit *dhānās* and Lithuanian *duonos*, and replaced it with another word.

But this is a mere curio, and a hypothetical one at that. Of greater importance is the fact that the reconstruction process shows us that as against the hundreds of thousands of words of the modern descendants, the parent tongue was far from rich. A very few thousand common roots are all that we have been able so far to establish. Out of those few thousand have developed, by infinite combinations and changes in both form and meaning, the numerous words of today. But poverty of words is, after all, what we should expect to find in a truly primeval language.

Our reconstruction process also indicates that the original roots were of a highly concrete nature. Abstract concepts are the aftermath of civilization, and the original speakers of Indo-European had not yet attained the cultural levels that were later reached by the speakers of Sanskrit, Greek and Latin, let alone the modern tongues.

Among the original Indo-European root words we find such concrete verbal ideas as *drive, burn, breathe, grow, bend, sleep, go, increase, see, live, die, join, sit, stand*; we do not find *refute, vindicate, dominate, endure, evade*, which are the later result of the blending of the earlier roots. Maximum concessions to abstraction are *praise, know, pledge, remember*. There are substantive forms denoting animals (*horse, dog, bear, bird, fish*); trees and plants (*oak, beech, barley*); parts of the body (*hand, foot, beard, heart*); materials and tools (*stone, metal, plow, cooking pot*); natural phenomena (*sun, moon, fire, water*); family relationships (*father, mother, brother, sister*). There are a few additional human relations, like *guest,*

[2] The symbol n̥ indicates a vowel value for the n sonant.

host, orphan, or *heir.* But we miss such later products as *phase, faith, hope, charity, efficiency,* though we find the means by which they were later put together. At the most, the abstract concept is represented in the earlier tongue by terms like *honor, sorrow, illness,* or by such superstition words as *magic* and *demon.* Among adjective forms, there are colors (*white, brown, red, green*); shapes (*sharp, flat, hooked*); words descriptive of what is visible or perceptible through the senses (*big, small, high, low, full, empty, bright, dark, sweet, bitter, hot, cold*); numerals (*one* to *ten*); at the most we get such abstractions as *good* and *bad, friendly* and *hostile.* We find pronouns (*I, you, this, that*) and various connecting words (*with, from, under*), along with a few adverbial forms (*now, here*).

Often the reconstructed roots appear in two or more variant forms, to account for the divergences of their later descendants, or for extensions produced by the addition of formative elements that serve to modify what appears to be the original meaning.

With the small number of root words appearing, we are sometimes astonished at what seems to be idle repetition of the same concrete concept: *flow, call, shine* (or *glimmer,* or *shimmer*), *grasp* (or *seize,* or *grip*), *twist* (or *wind*), *cut* and all its variants (*hew, split, saw*), *strike* (*hit, smite*); until we pause to realize that in the primitive Indo-European mind these near-synonyms represented different modes of action, as they still do today, since they are still with us.

Not all of the ascertained roots get into all the branches of the Indo-European family of languages. Often we find a root that appears in Sanskrit, but for some reason or other skips the kindred Avestan, then reappears in Greek, but not in Latin, and makes its westernmost bow in Germanic, but does not show up in Celtic. The root that appears in all eight living branches is very much the exception. Almost equally exceptional is the root that appears in only one branch. Roots appearing in three, four, and five branches are quite common.

It is at this point that our families of words come into play. The identical Indo-European root may get into Germanic, then pass on to Anglo-Saxon and thence to English; it may have another Germanic form that gets into Scandinavian and is then passed on to English by King Canute's Danes. It may also appear in Latin, in vastly different form, be passed by Latin on to French, become disguised by radical

French sound-changes, and eventually finds its way into English by reason of the Normans and 1066; but the same Latin word, picked up by Renaissance scholars, may likewise appear in almost straight Latin form in the English vocabulary. The original root may also appear in Greek, and give rise to some modern English scientific term. It may appear in Slavic or Celtic or one of the languages of India, and then be borrowed by English as a totally foreign word.

This sort of process accounts for the kinship of *full*, *plenty*, *plenary*, *plethoric*, the *-pur* of *jodhpurs*, the *-polis* of *metropolis*; or of *water*, *undulation*, *hydrant*, *whiskey*, and *vodka*; or of *royal*, *regal*, *right*, *ruler*, and *rajah*. The story has often been told of how an English word goes back to an Anglo-Saxon one, or a Latin one, or a Greek one, or how it has been borrowed from Sanskrit or Russian. We propose to carry the story a little farther back, to the Indo-European stage, and show how entire groups of words are the ultimate outcomes of one and the same root word.

English, in its original form, is Anglo-Saxon, a Low German dialect of the western sub-branch of the Germanic branch of Indo-European. Perhaps 25 per cent of our words (at least 50 per cent, however, of our words of most frequent occurrence) go back to Anglo-Saxon or to Middle English (when the dictionary describes a word as being of Middle English origin, it means that it cannot be traced all the way back to Anglo-Saxon, but also that there is no evidence that it was borrowed from any other source; this means that it is more likely to be of native, or Anglo-Saxon, origin than of any other).

Even Anglo-Saxon, however, borrowed from the Latin and Greek of the missionaries who came to Christianize the heathen Saxons, or of the earlier Roman merchants who traded with the Germanic tribes while they were still on the European mainland. Many English words, despite their deceptive native appearance, come from those early borrowings (*church*, *street*, *cheese*, *kitchen*, *mint*, *minster* are a few).

Then came the Danes, occupying half of England and bringing their Scandinavian North Germanic to mingle with the Low West Germanic of the Anglo-Saxons, thus producing a merger of two sub-branches of the same Indo-European branch. *They*, *them*, *take*, *cut*, *shall*, *knife* are samples of Scandinavian words that found their way into everyday Old English, often displacing the Anglo-Saxon form previously used (*take*, for instance, displaces a West Germanic,

Anglo-Saxon *nimman* that has as its close kinsman the modern German *nehmen*).

The Norman Conquest of 1066 brought French to England. French stems largely from Latin, but French also has other elements: Celtic words from the ancient Gauls, Germanic words from the Franks, Greek words that had previously been adopted by Latin. French words brought into English in the centuries that preceded Chaucer generally managed to adapt themselves very well to English speech-habits, and many of them look quite native: *very, pay, soldier, money, catch*. Special interest attaches to those words which were originally not Latin but Germanic, were brought into French by the Franks, then carried on to England, where they met, usually without recognition, their Germanic kinsmen that had peacefully developed on English soil from Anglo-Saxon. The Germanic root-word *wadio*, for instance, meaning "pledge", becomes Anglo-Saxon and modern English *wed*; the same *wadio*, carried into French by the Franks, then by the Normans to England, becomes *gage*; but in the Norman-Picard dialect of Old French this appears as *wage*. Not too many people would think of *wed, wedding, gage, engage* and *wage, wages* as all stemming originally from the same word.

After Chaucer's time, English, becoming a highly cultural language, went in for wholesale borrowing of Latin and Greek words in their Classical forms. Many of these learned borrowings duplicate words already brought into English by the French. Thus *fragile* duplicates *frail*, and *compute* duplicates *count*. Other learned borrowings duplicate old English words that Anglo-Saxon had already taken from Latin and Greek. Thus *presbytery* duplicates *priest*, and *casein* duplicates *cheese*. One interesting case of triplication is the Latin *moneta*, "coin" (so named because coins were minted in the old temple of Juno Moneta, the "Warner"; this surname had been bestowed after her sacred geese warned the Romans with their cackling that the Gauls were trying to scale the walls by surprise); the Anglo-Saxons had already borrowed *moneta* in the form of *mint*; the Normans brought the word to England again in the form of Old French *monneie*, and it became *money*; the learned Renaissance form, close to the original Latin, is *monetary*; since *moneta* comes from the root of *moneo*, "to warn", we also have *admonish* and *monitor* from the same source.

Becoming more cultural and widespread, English borrowed from every language under the sun, Indo-European and otherwise. Already having *beam* from Anglo-Saxon, it borrows *boom* (originally the same word) from Dutch. Already having *study* from Old French, which had taken it from Latin *studium*, English proceeds to take over the Italian *studio* and the modern French *étude*, from the same original Latin source. From French and Italian sources, it adapts *saloon* and *cartoon*, while at the same time it borrows and adopts *salon* and *carton*.

Of course, not all the borrowings of English are from Indo-European sources. *Sherbet* and *syrup* both come from the same Arabic (Semitic, non-Indo-European) source. *Tycoon* and *typhoon* both show the Chinese root *tai*, "big". The families of English words need not all be Indo-European, though the majority of them are.

This book sets forth a certain number of word-families within the English language, those which are more striking, and for which the evidence seems more assured. It is far from exhaustive.

There are perhaps 2,000 productive Indo-European roots that have been established with some degree of assurance. Of these, perhaps half have recognizable descendants in English. Only about 200 are discussed here.

As with all families, some are very large, others quite small. For what concerns English, there are some to which only one Indo-European branch has contributed, usually the Germanic, or the Latin, or the Greek. These will be presented first. Next come word-families where two of the great Indo-European branches have made contributions to the English vocabulary; these are more numerous and, as a rule, more extensive. The two-branch combinations are usually Greek-Latin, Greek-Germanic, or Latin-Germanic; but there are also cases where one of the "Big Three" joins forces with Celtic, Slavic, or Indo-Iranian. Then come families where three branches, usually Greek, Latin and Germanic, have collaborated in supplying English with descendants; these are also quite numerous. Beyond three, there is a sharp drop, since contributions to English from Slavic, Celtic and Indo-Iranian are only occasional, and contributions from Albanian and Armenian practically non-existent, save for a few place names and proper names. But four, five and six-branch families of words are as a rule quite large and cover a great deal of ground; they will therefore appear last.

In a good many cases, there is no agreement among authorities as to whether certain contributions to the English vocabulary belong together or not. These uncertainties are more likely to arise in the case of branches where the documentation is relatively scanty, such as the Germanic; but they appear even in the case of heavily attested languages, like Greek or Latin. Where an inclusion is doubtful, it will be described as such.

In the case of the Germanic branch, it must be borne in mind that while contributions to English may come from Anglo-Saxon, Scandinavian, Dutch or German, such contributions are still from a single branch, the Germanic. *Thorp*, *dorp*, and *dorf* reflect, respectively, Anglo-Saxon, Dutch, and German; but they are all Germanic. It is unfortunate that we do not have at our disposal the parent Germanic tongue, intermediate between Indo-European and the later attested languages, as Latin is intermediate between Indo-European and the Romance tongues. While Gothic was the first Germanic language to appear in fully recorded form, and is often presented as the Germanic representative, it is in no sense the parent language of Anglo-Saxon, Old High German, Old Norse, etc., but only an older brother; and even that not in the true sense of "older", but only in order of appearance. It is quite safe to assume that older versions of Anglo-Saxon, Old High German, Old Norse, were spoken contemporaneously with Gothic; but these older versions, like primitive Germanic and Indo-European itself, did not come down to us in written form.

Latin may make its contribution to English directly or indirectly, through one of the Romance languages (usually French). *Student* goes back directly to Latin, *studio* is Italian, *étude* is French, but they all have a common Latin origin.

The fact that a certain word enters English from a certain language is immaterial for purposes of basic classification if the word comes to that language from a different source. *Kirsch* comes to English from German, but German itself had taken it from Latin, which in turn had taken it from Greek; *Kirsch* therefore joins *cherry* and *cerise* under a Greek heading. *Dégagé* comes to us from French; but French formed it from a Germanic root, the same one that gives us *wed*; therefore, for purposes of ultimate word-origins, *dégagé* appears under its Germanic root. In the case of learned words that largely retain their Latin or Greek forms, it is immaterial for our present purpose whether they were adopted directly by English scholars, or adopted into the learned vocabulary of French by French scholars, then passed on to English in practically unchanged form. Hence, many of our entries will be labelled "directly, or through French".

In listing English descendants of the various Indo-European roots, we generally omit forms that are little known and little used, archaic, dialectal, or too highly specialized in a certain field. There exist in English forms like *lamellibranch* and *lamellirostral*, but they are known only to zoologists, and are therefore omitted from our list of descendants of Latin *lama*, "blade", while *omelet*, which everyone is familiar with, is given. We also often omit obvious derivatives, like *castigation, castigator*, from *castigate*.

On the other hand, there is no good reason to omit well-known place names and personal names derived from a certain root, like the *-bert* of *Albert, Robert*, etc., which comes from the same root as *bright*. Nor is there good reason to omit significant, well-known foreign forms, like the *pro tempore* (or its abbreviation *pro tem*) and the *tempus fugit* which, despite the fact that they are straight Latin, appear in all standard handy English dictionaries.

The family trees which we offer are simplified for reasons of space. They repeat, in schematic form, what is already set forth in our discussion of each root and its descendants. In doubtful cases, the doubts are expressed in the main discussion and not repeated in the trees, save for a possible question mark. Many learned forms, taken directly from Latin and Greek from the fifteenth century on, and easily identifiable by reason of their close resemblance to their Latin or Greek prototypes, appear first in French, then are passed on to English; others appear first in English; in the case of some, there is doubt as to whether English or French first created or adapted them. In our simplified family trees, they will often appear as stemming directly into English from Latin or Greek, since the intermediate French stage is unimportant.

For the convenience of those who are interested in the major sound-changes that occur within the Indo-European family, and also to satisfy the curiosity of those who wonder at some of the drastic differences appearing among words of the same word-family that come into English from different branches of Indo-European, a brief series of tables follows in Chapter 2. These tables present, in simplified form, the major consonant shifts that occur in the various Indo-European branches. Each word-family is accompanied by one or more references to one of these tables, describing the consonant shift exemplified in the discussion and in the family tree.

Chapter 3 contains a very limited and elementary description of some of the later changes from Anglo-Saxon or Scandinavian to modern English, and similar changes occurring in words of Greek, Latin and Romance origin.

CHAPTER 2

Indo-European Sound Correspondences

The following tables of sound correspondences are a simplification of those appearing in A. Meillet's *Introduction à l'étude comparative des langues indo-européennes* (Paris, Hachette, 1922). Only the major consonants, presenting the really striking features of change, are given here. Since very little that is worthy of note takes place in the liquid and nasal consonants *r*, *l*, *m*, *n*, we have omitted them (normally, they appear unchanged in all the branches of the family, save for a very occasional interchange of *l* and *r*). The vowels present, in some ways, greater complexities, while at the same time they do not lend themselves so well to the points we are trying to bring out, hence we do not discuss vowel changes save in a few specific instances. Vowel length is indicated by the appropriate mark (*ā*, *ē*, *ō*, etc.) for Sanskrit and Germanic (including Anglo-Saxon, Gothic, Old Norse and Old High German), but not, ordinarily, for Latin or Greek, where it can easily be checked in the ordinary school dictionary of those languages. The very rare occurrence of the symbol (*ĕ*) indicates that the vowel, in the parent language, could be long or short.

Of the eight living Indo-European branches, Albanian is omitted, by reason of its late appearance, the uncertainty of many of its forms, and its scanty interest from the standpoint of English (very few, if any, words from Albanian have found their way into English, save for occasional place and personal names). The Indo-Iranian branch is represented by its oldest member, Sanskrit. Balto-Slavic is represented by Old Church Slavic, which does not differ widely from such a modern Slavic tongue as Russian; Lithuanian could have been included as a representative of the Baltic sub-branch, but its divergences from Slavic are not at all striking, and very few words from the Baltic tongues appear in English. Armenian and Greek are given, the former by reason of its strong consonant-shifts which are often reminiscent of Germanic, the latter because of its vast contributions to our language. Italic appears in its Latin form; occasional references to the Oscan-Umbrian sub-branch, and copious references to Latin's Romance descendants, appear in the text. Celtic is represented by Old Irish, with references to Welsh (Brythonic) where the two diverge. For Germanic, the representative is Gothic, which was spoken in the region of the Crimea at the time it was first recorded in Bishop Wulfila's fourth-century A.D. translation of the Bible. The speakers of Gothic, Ostrogoths and Visigoths (eastern and western Goths) shortly there-after moved into the territory of the Roman Empire and were even-tually absorbed by Latin-speaking populations, so that their language ceased to be spoken. Gothic is a member of the extinct East Germanic sub-branch of the Germanic or Teutonic languages, but it offers the earliest complete set of attested forms. Its consonant system does not diverge too widely from that of Anglo-Saxon or Old Scandinavian, the two languages that join forces to produce the earliest English; modern German, on the other hand, diverges from all the other Germanic tongues by reason of a second, or High German, consonant-shift.

The first Germanic consonant-shift, whereby all the primitive Germanic tongues differentiated themselves from the general Indo-European pattern, occurred in preliterary times, and cannot be precisely dated. It applies equally to the eastern sub-branch (rep-resented by Gothic), the northern or Scandinavian (represented by Old Norse and modern Swedish, Danish, Norwegian, and Icelandic), and the western (represented by the ancestors of modern English, Dutch, and German). Its chief features appear in our tables under the Gothic heading.

In the course of the sixth century, the West Germanic sub-branch underwent a further cleavage. The Low West Germanic dialects (roughly, those closer to the seacoast, including Old Frisian, Old Saxon, and Anglo-Saxon, which are the immediate ancestors of Dutch, Flemish, and English) retained the same general consonant structure that appears in Gothic. The High West Germanic dialects (roughly, those of the mountain regions, particularly Austria, Bavaria, and Switzerland) went through a second transformation of the consonants, the major feature of which was that Gothic or Anglo-Saxon *p*, *t*, *k*, which already represented a shift from Indo-European or Latin or

Greek *b*, *d*, *g*, further shifted, respectively, to *pf*, *ff* or *f*; *zz* (later represented by *z* or *ss*); and *kh* (later represented by *ch*). The other consonants underwent similar changes, but not so universally. It is this second consonant-shift of High German that supplies the more striking differences between modern English and modern German where the two languages use the same word. *Water*, retaining a *t* which appears also in Gothic, Scandinavian, and Dutch, has as its German counterpart an older *wazzar* and a modern *Wasser*. English *hemp*, with a *p* that comes from an Indo-European *b* appearing in Greek *cannabis*, has as its German counterpart *Hanf*. The Latin and Greek *ego* of *alter ego* and *egotist* had as its Anglo-Saxon counterpart *ik*, which modern English has reduced to *I*; but German has *ich*. Other consonants involved in the second or High German shift which frequently appear in their shifted form in German, in their unshifted form in English, are Gothic and Anglo-Saxon *th* coming from an original Indo-European *t*, which in German appears as *d* (Latin *tu*, English *thou*, German *du*); and Gothic and Anglo-Saxon *d*, issuing from Indo-European *dh*, which in German appears as *t* (English *door*, German *Tor*).

Consonants which were shifted in Old High German, but where the shift has generally been rejected by modern German, so that the English and German forms coincide, are Gothic and Anglo-Saxon *h* from Indo-European *k* (English *heart*, German *Herz*, Latin *cord-*, Greek *kard-*); Gothic and Anglo-Saxon *b* from Indo-European *bh* (English *brother*, German *Bruder*, but Old High German *pruoder*); Gothic and Anglo-Saxon *g* from Indo-European *gh* (English *goose*, German *Gans*, but Old High German *kans*).

One consonant that remained unshifted by Old High German, and that consequently appears in the same form in English and German, is initial *f* from Indo-European *p* (English *feather*, German *Feder*, from an Indo-European root **peter* or **pter*). Further reference to the second consonant-shift will appear in the individual tables.

Vowel shifts among the Indo-European branches are complicated and, to a certain degree, still uncertain. The consonants are far more stable and easily traceable. Hence, in a book designed for the general public, we shall omit any discussion of the vowel transformations from group to group, and endeavor to explain only the consonant shifts, which at all events furnish the main basis for the classification and affiliation of words, even among the experts.

The Indo-European system of consonants is the product of comparison and reconstruction. It is supposed to have comprised the following set of consonant sounds:

	UNVOICED PLOSIVES	VOICED PLOSIVES	ASPIRATES
Labial	*p*	*b*	*bh*
Dental	*t*	*d*	*dh*
Velar (Guttural)	*k*	*g*	*gh*
Labialized Velar	*kw* (or *ku̯*)[1]	*gw* (or *gu̯*)[1]	*gwh* (or *gu̯h*)[1]

SEMI-VOWELS	NASALS	LIQUIDS	SIBILANTS
y, w (or *i̯, u̯*)[1]	*n, m*	*l, r*	*s*

[1] The symbols *u̯* and *i̯* are often used in linguistic works to indicate the sounds of *w* and *y*. A raised *u̯* indicates a reduced grade of the *w* sound.

There is some uncertainty concerning the precise nature of the aspirates (*bh, dh, gh, gwh*). The most widely accepted theory is that they represented the sounds of *b + h, d + h, g + h, gw + h*; for the first three, we could construct imaginary English place names like *Knobhill, Fordhill, Bighill*. *Kw* and *gw* represent, approximately, the sounds of *qu* in *quart* and of *gu* in *language*.

The absence of certain sounds from this hypothetical primitive scheme will be noted. The palatal sounds represented by English *ch* and *j*, *sh* and *s* of *pleasure*, the spirant or fricative sounds represented by English *f* and *v*, English voiced and unvoiced *th*, German *ch* (both in *ach* and *ich*), the voiced sound of English *z*, do not appear, though they develop later in the attested languages.

The detailed series of correspondences that follows is numbered with Roman numerals. The appearance of one or more of these Roman numerals in the text is intended to guide the reader to the proper set of correspondences among the various Indo-European groups. Thus, where an Indo-European root has an initial *p*, he may expect English words derived from Greek or Latin (or any of the Romance languages that stem from Latin) to have an initial *p*, which should also appear in English words borrowed from Slavic or from the languages of India; but for words from the same original root that English inherits from Anglo-Saxon or Scandinavian, he should expect an initial *f*, and for words that come from Celtic he should expect the disappearance of the initial consonant. There are many divergences from the regular scheme, for most of which there are explanations that are more or less satisfactory and involved. A summary of all the correspondences listed will appear at the end of the detailed discussion given in the tables.

For the reader's convenience, Sanskrit, Slavic, Armenian, Greek, Irish, and Gothic are given in Roman-alphabet transcriptions. In its original form, Sanskrit appears in an alphabet called *Devanagari* ("pertaining to the city of the gods"), which is still used by some of the modern languages of India, notably Hindi and Bengali. Slavic appears in Cyrillic, which is still used today by Russian, Ukrainian, Serbian, and Bulgarian, though in slightly divergent forms. Armenian has a special alphabet which is still in use. The ancient Greek alphabet is still used by modern Greek. The Irish alphabet, still used by modern Irish, is a modified form of the Roman. The Gothic alphabet, no longer is use, was an adaptation of the Greek. The Roman or Latin alphabet itself comes from the Greek, probably through the Etruscan.

TABLE I

Indo-European	Sanskrit	Slavic	Armenian	Greek	Latin	Irish	Gothic
*p[1]	p	p	h, w[2]	p	p	–[3]	f, b[4]

1. The asterisk in front of an Indo-European form indicates that this form is hypothetical, and reconstructed from a comparison of all the others, which are attested.

2. In Armenian, Indo-European *p appears as *h* initially, but as *w* between vowels (the Armenian word that corresponds to the Latin *pater* and the English *father*, for example, is *hayr*).

3. In Celtic, Indo-European *p disappears. The Irish word that corresponds to *pater* and *father* is *athair*.

4. In Germanic, Indo-European *p appears as *f* initially, as *b*, usually, between vowels when the original Indo-European accent did not fall on the preceding syllable. The *f* development is general, even though modern German often spells it with *v* (English *full*, German *voll*, corresponding to Latin *plenus*, Greek *pleres*, etc.). The *b* development between vowels generally appears as *b* in modern German, but changes to *v* in English. This means that Greek *hyper* and Latin *super*, which keep the original Indo-European *p*, have as their modern German correspondent *über*, while English has *over*. In an original *sp* group, Germanic does not shift the *p* to either *f* or *b*, but retains the *sp*.

TABLE II

Indo-European	Sanskrit	Slavic	Armenian	Greek	Latin	Irish	Gothic
*t	t	t	th	t	t	t	th, d[1]

1. In Germanic, Indo-European *t appears as *th* initially, as *d*, usually, between vowels or sonants where the original Indo-European accent did not fall on the preceding syllable. The *th* remains unchanged in English, while German usually shifts it to *d* (Latin *tu*, English *thou*, German *du*). In an original *st* or *kt* group, Germanic does not shift *t* to either *th* or *d*, but retains the *st*, *kt*.

TABLE III

Indo-European	Sanskrit	Slavic	Armenian	Greek	Latin	Irish	Gothic
*k	ç[1]	s[1]	s[1]	k	c[2]	c[2]	h, g[3]

1. Here we have an interesting divergence between the eastern and the western members of the Indo-European family. While the eastern members (Sanskrit, Slavic, Armenian) turn Indo-European *k into a sibilant sound (*s* in Slavic and Armenian, *ç*, pronounced more or less like English *sh*, in Sanskrit), the western members keep the original *k*-sound. Germanic shifts this to *h* (*g* between vowels or sonants when the Indo-European accent is not on the initial syllable). This means that where English and German have initial *h* in *heart*, *Herz*, the Latin and Greek corresponding words have hard *c* or *k* (*cordial*, *cardiac*), while the eastern members of the family have initial *s* (the Russian word for "heart", for example, is *serdtse*). Corresponding to the *hund-* of English *hundred* and German *hundert*, Latin, Greek and Irish have, respectively, *centum*, *hekaton* and *cet*, with a *k*-sound; Slavic has *sto*, with an *s*-sound; and Sanskrit has *çata*. The eastern members are accordingly often described collectively as the *satem*-languages, the western as the *centum*-languages. Occasionally, however, under circumstances not yet precisely determined, the *k*-development appears even in the *satem* languages. (One explanation is that there were two different points of articulation for Indo-European *k; that in the western languages these two sounds

merged; but in the eastern tongues they remained separate, giving rise respectively to a sibilant and a velar.)

2. Both in Latin and Irish, the pronunciation of *c* is invariably "hard" (velar), and represents the sound of *k*.

3. Between vowels or sonants, when the original accent did not fall on the preceding syllable, Germanic has not *h*, but *g*. Corresponding to the Latin *oculus* that gives us *oculist*, German has *Auge*, and Anglo-Saxon has *ēage*, which modern English has changed to *eye*. In an original *sk* group, Germanic does not change *k* to *h* or *g*, but keeps the Indo-European *sk*.

TABLE IV

INDO-EUROPEAN	SANSKRIT	SLAVIC	ARMENIAN	GREEK	LATIN	IRISH	GOTHIC
*kw	k or ch[1]	k, ch, ts[2]	kh	p, t[3]	qu[4]	c (p)[4]	hw, w[5]

The original **kw* of Indo-European appears intact only in Latin (*qu*). The only other branch that retains the *w*-element of **kw* is Germanic, but Germanic changes the *k*-element to *h*. In all the other branches, the *w*-element is lost, and further changes occur, as described below.

1. Before front vowels (*e, i*), Sanskrit palatalizes **kw* into the sound of *ch* in English *cheese.* (This sound, in the conventional transliteration of the Sanskrit alphabet, appears as *c*.) Elsewhere, it turns **kw* into *k*.

2. Before some front vowels, Slavic turns **kw* into the sound of *ch* in *cheese* (transcribed as *č*); before others, into *ts*; elsewhere, into *k*.

3. Greek usually turns **kw* into *p*; but in most old Greek dialects, **kw* becomes *t* before long or short *e*.

4. Irish and the other languages of the Goidelic sub-branch of Celtic turn **kw* into "hard" *c* (*k*). The languages of the Brythonic sub-branch (Welsh, Cornish, Breton), as well as ancient Gaulish, turn **kw* into *p*. The same occurs in Oscan-Umbrian, where *pid* corresponds to Latin *quid*.

5. Germanic turns **kw* into *hw*, which English retains in the spelling *wh*. German not only loses the *h*-element of *hw*, but also pronounces the *w* as *v*. English *what* appears in German as *was*, in Latin as *quod*.

TABLE V

INDO-EUROPEAN	SANSKRIT	SLAVIC	ARMENIAN	GREEK	LATIN	IRISH	GOTHIC
*b	b	b	p	b	b	b	p[1]

1. Germanic, which is with Armenian the only branch to diverge from the universal *b*, shifts it to *p*, which English retains. German, however, by its second consonant shift turns this *p* into *f*, *ff* or *pf* (*f* is usual in final position, *ff* between vowels, *pf* initially). Corresponding to Greek-Latin *cannabis*, English has *hemp*, German *Hanf*. Since *b* is of rare occurrence in Indo-European roots, many of the words in which English *p* corresponds to German *f*, *ff*, *pf* are borrowed from Latin or Greek, and represent not original Indo-European *b*, but *p*. The second consonant shift that separates High from Low German, however, appears even in most words of this description, since it occurred after the borrowings had taken place: Latin and Greek *piper*, borrowed by the Germanic languages, becomes *pepper* in English, *Pfeffer* in German; Latin *pondus* becomes English *pound*, German *Pfund*.

TABLE VI

INDO-IRANIAN	SANSKRIT	SLAVIC	ARMENIAN	GREEK	LATIN	IRISH	GOTHIC
*d	d	d	t	d	d	d	t[1]

1. Again, Armenian and Germanic are the only groups to shift *d* to *t*. In English, *t* remains. In German, by reason of the second consonant-shift, it is changed to *z*, *zz* (later becoming *z*, *ss*), according to its position in the word. The *t* of English *foot* appears as *ss* in German *Fuss*, but as *d* in words which English derives from Greek or Latin (*podium*, *pedal*). English *water*, with *t*, corresponds to German *Wasser* (*wazzar* in Old High German), and to Greek *hydor*, Latin *unda*, Slavic *voda*, which have *d*. English *heart*, with *t*, corresponds to German *Herz*, with *z*, and to the Greek and Latin-derived *cardiac* and *cordial*, with *d*. English *tooth*, with *t*, corresponds to German *Zahn* (formerly *zand*), with *z*, and to Latin-derived *dentist* and Greek *odont-*.

TABLE VII

Indo-European	Sanskrit	Slavic	Armenian	Greek	Latin	Irish	Gothic
*g	j[1]	z[1]	ts[1]	g	g	g	k[2]

1. Again we have the interesting cleavage between East and West that we saw in Table III. The eastern branches (Indo-Iranian, Slavic, Armenian) turn the original velar *g into a palatal j or a sibilant z or ts, while the western members retain the sound unchanged, and Germanic shifts it to k. But the velar g-development appears occasionally even in the eastern branch, as was the case with *k (q.v.).

2. Anglo-Saxon and English usually retain the k-sound derived from *g, but High German further shifts it to the sounds indicated by the German ch-spelling (ach, ich). In the initial position, however, standard German rejects this shift and retains the original Germanic k. As against Latin and Greek ego, Anglo-Saxon has ik (I in modern English), and German has ich. In the case of Greek and Latin gnosco, from which we get gnostic and ignorant, English has know. Old High German has chennan, pronounced with the ch of modern German ach; but modern literary German has kennen. The Russian word for "know", znat', shows the eastern sibilant z replacing the western velar g and the Germanic k. In the Indo-European period, *gt was changed to *kt by assimilation, and in Germanic *kt was later shifted to ht. This accounts for such forms as Latin rectus and Anglo-Saxon riht from *reg-tos.

TABLE VIII

Indo-European	Sanskrit	Slavic	Armenian	Greek	Latin	Irish	Gothic
*gw	g or j[1]	g, zh, dz[2]	k	b or d[3]	w or gu[4]	b	q[5]

As in the case of *kw, Latin alone retains the original *gw, but not in all cases. The Gothic spelling q represents a qu or kw sound, and may therefore be said to retain the w-element of *gw.

1. Sanskrit, in addition to losing the w-element, turns *gw into j before front vowels.

2. Slavic turns *gw into zh (the sound of s in pleasure) before some front vowels, into dz before others, into g elsewhere.

3. Greek normally has *b*; but before long or short *e*, most Greek dialects have *d*.

4. Latin usually has a *w*-sound, represented in Latin spelling by *v*.

5. The *kw* or *qu*-sound indicated by Gothic *q* is retained by both English and German. The German spelling *qu*, however, indicates a modern pronunciation closer to that of *kv* than to that of *kw* (English and German *qualm*; English *quail*, German *quälen*). English *quick* has for its correspondents Sanskrit *jivah*, Latin *vivus* (appearing in *vivacious*), and the Greek *bios* of *biology*, as well as the Russian *zhyt'*, "to live". In Anglo-Saxon spelling the sound is represented by *cw*, not by *qu* (*cwic*); the *qu* spelling was introduced by the Normans, who had taken it from Latin.

TABLE IX

Indo-European	Sanskrit	Slavic	Armenian	Greek	Latin	Irish	Gothic
*bh	bh[1]	b	b	ph[2]	f or b[3]	b	b[4]

1. Sanskrit *.bh* was pronounced as in *knobhill*. This is supposed to coincide with the original Indo-European pronunciation.

2. Greek *ph* was at first pronounced as in *uphill*. Later the sound shifted to that of *Philadelphia* (*f*).

3. Latin has *f* initially, *b* between vowels. Oscan, one of Latin's kindred languages of the Italic branch, has *f* in both positions. Latin words in which *f* appears between vowels (save in compounds like *deficio*, from *de* + *facio*) are therefore generally of Oscan origin, and were borrowed by Latin (Latin *bubalus*, Oscan-derived *bufalus*, from which English eventually gets *buffalo*).

4. The *b* of Gothic appears also in Anglo-Saxon. High German, in accordance with the second consonant-shift, turns *b* into *p*, and Old High German actually offers the form *pruoder* where modern German, using a Low German variant, has *Bruder*. The word for *brother*, appearing throughout Indo-European, takes the form *bhrāta* in Sanskrit, *brat* or *bratr* in Slavic, *phrater* in Greek, *frater* in Latin, *bráthair* in Irish. Between vowels, Anglo-Saxon turns *b* to *f*, which becomes *v* in modern English (*wifel* to *weavil*).

TABLE X

Indo-European	Sanskrit	Slavic	Armenian	Greek	Latin	Irish	Gothic
*dh	dh[1]	d	d	th[2]	f or d[3]	d	d[4]

1. Sanskrit *dh*, pronounced as in *madhouse*, is supposed to conserve the original Indo-European sound.

2. Greek *th* was pronounced as in *hothouse* at an earlier period, as in *thing* later.

3. Latin has *f* in the initial position, *d* between vowels; *b* occurs after *r*.

4. English has the same *d* as Gothic. High German shifts it by the second consonant-shift to *t*, and this shift is generally adopted by modern German. English *door* has *Tor* as its German counterpart, while *thyra* appears in Greek.

TABLE XI

Indo-European	Sanskrit	Slavic	Armenian	Greek	Latin	Irish	Gothic
*gh	h[1]	z	j or z	ch[2]	h[3]	g	g[4]

1. Sanskrit shifts *gh* to *h*, despite the presence of *gh* in the Sanskrit sound-scheme.

2. Greek *ch* was originally pronounced as in *blockhead*, later as in Scottish *loch* or German *ach*, while modern Greek has two sounds similar to those of German *ach* and *ich*, the former before back vowels (*a, o, u*) and most consonants, the latter before front vowels (*e, i*).

3. Latin, like Sanskrit, shifts *gh* to *h*, but often tends to lose the *h*, as in the word for "goose", *anser*, which was originally *hanser*.

4. Gothic *g* appears also in Anglo-Saxon, but in the transition to modern English *g* is turned to *y* before *e* or *i*. High German, by the second consonant-shift, changes *g* to *k*, but modern German usually prefers the Low German form with *g*. Corresponding to English *goose* we have German *Gans* (*kans* in Old High German), Sanskrit *hansa*, Greek *chen*, Latin (*h*)*anser*. Corresponding to English *yester-* (with *y* from *g* before *e*), we have German *gestern* (Old High German *kestern*), Sanskrit *hyes*, Greek *chthes*, Latin *heri*.

TABLE XII

INDO-EUROPEAN	SANSKRIT	SLAVIC	ARMENIAN	GREEK	LATIN	IRISH	GOTHIC
*gwh	gh or h[1]	g, zh, dz[2]	g, j[3]	ph, th[4]	f, w[5]	g	k, w[6]

1. Sanskrit has *h* before front vowels, *gh* elsewhere.

2. In Slavic, *zh* appears before some front vowels, *dz* before others, *g* elsewhere.

3. Armenian has *j* before front vowels, *g* elsewhere.

4. Greek has *th* before long or short *e*, *ph* elsewhere.

5. Latin has *f* initially, *v* (pronounced *w*) between vowels.

6. Gothic *k* is doubtful in the initial position. The *w* that appears between vowels is the favorite English and German outcome, in all positions. Corresponding to English and German *warm* (note that German pronounces the *w* as *v*), we have the Greek-derived *thermal* and the Latin-derived *furnace*. English *snow* (German *Schnee*, in which the *w* is lost) has for its correspondents Latin *nivem* and Greek *nipha*.

TABLE XIII

INDO-EUROPEAN	SANSKRIT	SLAVIC	ARMENIAN	GREEK	LATIN	IRISH	GOTHIC
*y (i)	y	y	y	h, z, −[1]	y[2]	−	y[3]

1. In Greek, the *h*-sound that stems from Indo-European **y* is represented initially by the rough breathing (‘), pronounced as *h*; occasionally, under circumstances not yet precisely determined, *z* appears in the initial position. Between vowels, *y* falls.

2. In Latin, the sound of *y* is represented by the written symbol *i*; but medieval and modern Latin writings often use *j* (*IAM, IVSTVS, jam, justus*).

3. In Gothic, the sound of *y* is represented by the written symbol *j*. Anglo-Saxon represents it by *g* before *e* and *i*. English prefers a *y*-spelling, German a *j*-spelling (English *young*, German *jung*, Latin *IVVENIS* or *juvenis*; English *yoke*, German *Joch*, Latin *IVGVM, jugum*).

TABLE XIV

Indo-European	Sanskrit	Slavic	Armenian	Greek	Latin	Irish	Gothic
*w (u̯)	v	v	g or v	—[1]	v[2]	f	w[3]

1. In archaic Greek there appears a letter called *digamma* which had the sound of *w*, but which later disappeared, so that *woida* becomes *oida*.

2. Latin *v* used as a semi-vowel had the sound of *w*, but in Vulgar Latin and the Romance languages this becomes the sound of English *v*, without change of spelling. The symbol *V* was used in Latin with three different phonetic values: that of the semi-vowel *w*, that of short *u*, and that of long *u* (*VILLA, PVER, MVRVS*, for what later appear as *villa, puer, mūrus*).

3. The *w* of Gothic appears also in English and in German; but German pronounces it *v*. Corresponding to English *wit, wot* are German *wissen*, Latin *video*, Sanskrit *Veda*, Slavic *videt'*, Greek *oida*, with interesting shifts of meaning (the root that means "to see" in Latin and Slavic means "to see" or "to hear" in Greek, and "to know" in Sanskrit and Germanic).

TABLE XV

Indo-European	Sanskrit	Slavic	Armenian	Greek	Latin	Irish	Gothic
*s (initial)	s	s	h[1]	h[1]	s	s (h)[1]	s

1. Armenian, Greek, and the Brythonic (Welsh, Cornish, Breton) sub-branch of Celtic turn initial *s* into *h* (Greek represents this by the rough breathing). Corresponding to English *six*, German *sechs*, Latin *sex*, Irish *sé*, Greek has the *hex* of *hexagon*, Welsh has *chwech* (Welsh *ch* represents a strongly aspirated *h*-sound).

TABLE XVI

INDO-EUROPEAN	SANSKRIT	SLAVIC	ARMENIAN	GREEK	LATIN	IRISH	GOTHIC
*s (between vowels)	s	s	–	–[1]	r[2]	s	s[3]

1. Greek drops *s* between vowels (as does Armenian). *Genos* has a genitive form *geneos* from **genesos*.

2. Latin turns *s* between vowels into the sound of English *z*, then further shifts it to *r*. *Genus* has a genitive form *generis* from **genesis*. This

SUMMARY OF TABLES

	INDO-EUROPEAN	SANSKRIT	SLAVIC	ARMENIAN
I	*p	p	p	h, w
II	*t	t	t	th
III	*k	ç (= sh)	s	s
IV	*kw	k, c (= ch)	k, č (= ch), ts	kh
V	*b	b	b	p
VI	*d	d	d	t
VII	*g	j	z	ts
VIII	*gw	g, j	g, zh, dz	k
IX	*bh	bh	b	b
X	*dh	dh	d	d
XI	*gh	h	z	j, z
XII	*gwh	gh, h	g, zh, dz	g, j
XIII	*y	y	y	y
XIV	*w	v	v	g, v
XV	*s (initial)	s	s	h
XVI	*s (between vowels)	s	s	–

shift to *r* does not appear in the Oscan-Umbrian sub-branch of Italic; Oscan *-azum* corresponds to the Latin *-arum* ending of the first declension genitive plural feminine. Latin words with single *s* between vowels are usually loan-words from Oscan.

3. In Germanic languages other than Gothic, including Anglo-Saxon, *s* between vowels generally turns to *z*, then to *r*, just as in Latin. Corresponding to Gothic *auso*, which conserves the original Indo-European *s* between vowels, Anglo-Saxon has *ēare* (modern English *ear*), Old High German has *ōra* (modern German *Ohr*), Old Norse has *eyra*, just as Latin has *auris* (of *aural*, *auricular*) from an original **ausis*.

GREEK	LATIN	IRISH	GOTHIC
p	p	–	f, b
t	t	t	th, d
k	c (= k)	c (= k)	h, g
p, t	qu	c (= k)	hw, w
	(Oscan and Brythonic p)		
b	b	b	p
d	d	d	t
g	g	g	k
b, d	v, gu	b	q
ph	f, b	b	b
th	f, d	d	d
ch (= kh)	h	g	g
ph, th	f, v	g	k, w
h, z, –	y	–	y
–	v	f	w
h	s	s	s
		(Brythonic h)	
–	r	s	s
	(Oscan z)		(others r)

CHAPTER 3

Later Changes in Anglo-Saxon, Greek, Latin, and Romance

A. GERMANIC

In addition to the general sound-shifts whereby the Germanic tongues differentiate themselves from the other Indo-European branches, there are some further considerations that concern English words of Germanic origin. Some apply to the Germanic group as a whole, others are specific to the development of Anglo-Saxon and, occasionally, Old Norse, into modern English.

The reader may be reminded of a few interesting exceptions, caused mostly by the position of the sound in the word, to the general consonant-shifts already presented:

1. While the Germanic group of languages shifts Indo-European *p, *t and *k to f, th and h, the original p, t, k are retained by Germanic in the combinations sp, st, sk. Thus in the *spek root, where Latin, reflecting original Indo-European conditions, has -spicio, which ultimately gives us aspect, suspicion, etc., Old High German has not *sfehōn, but spehōn, from which we ultimately get spy and espionage; in the *ghostis root, where Latin has hostis (host, hostile, etc.), Anglo-Saxon has not *giesth, but giest (guest); in the *peisk root, where Latin has the piscis of piscatorial, Anglo-Saxon has not *fis + h, but fisc (fish is the result of a later palatalization).

2. In the Indo-European *pt, *kt groups, p and k change in Germanic to f and h respectively, but t stays unchanged instead of shifting to th. In the *nepōt root, where Latin has neptis ("niece"), Anglo-Saxon has not *nifth, but nift (this word, which would have come down to us unchanged, was displaced by the French nièce); in the *oktō root, where Latin has octo ("eight"), Anglo-Saxon has eahta, not *eahtha.

3. Between vowels and in final position, when the preceding vowel did not bear the original Indo-European accent, *p, *t, *k, instead of producing Germanic f, th, h, produce spirant b, d, g sounds resembling those of modern Spanish *caballo*, *amado*, *pagar*; these, in the historical period of most of the Germanic languages, appear in writing as b, d, g. In Anglo-Saxon, however, the first often appears as f, which later, between vowels, generally becomes v. Corresponding to Greek *heptá*, Anglo-Saxon has *seofon*, later *seven*, compared with Gothic and Old High German *sibun*, modern German *sieben*.

4. An s between vowels was generally voiced to z and then turned to r in most Germanic languages, including Anglo-Saxon, but not in Gothic (see Table XVI, 3).

5. Indo-European *gwh and *kw, save before u, develop generally into w. In the *sneigᵘh root, where Greek has *nipha* and Latin *nivem*, Anglo-Saxon has *snāw*, later *snow*.

6. There are assorted phenomena of assimilation, in which a group of two different consonants changes into a double consonant: *-nd- becomes -nn- (Latin *spondeo*, Anglo-Saxon, Old High German *spannan*); *-nw- becomes -nn- (Latin *tenuis*, Anglo-Saxon *thynne*, English *thin*, Old High German *dunni*, modern German *dünn*); *-ln- becomes -ll- (Latin *plenus*, Slavic *polny*, Gothic *fulls*, Anglo-Saxon *full*, German *voll*); *-dhl- becomes -ll- (Latin *stabulum*, Anglo-Saxon *steall*, *stall*).

7. There is an occasional phenomenon of epenthesis (the insertion of a consonant between two other consonants to facilitate the transition from one to the other): in the *(s)roum root, where Sanskrit has *sravati* and Greek, dropping initial s, has *rheuma*, Anglo-Saxon has *strēam*, with t inserted between s and r.

A few consonant phenomena peculiar to Anglo-Saxon are the following:

1. Loss of n, with lengthening of the preceding vowel, before h: *thencean*, "think", but *thōhte* (instead of *thonhte*), "thought".

2. Loss of h between vowels: Gothic *saihwan*, Old High German *sehan*, modern German *sehen*, but Anglo-Saxon *sēon*, English *see*.

3. Loss of n before s (the same phenomenon that is so widespread in the development of Latin into Romance, where *mensis* becomes *mese*, *mes*, *mois*, and *mensa* becomes *mesa*): Old High German *uns*, but Anglo-Saxon *ūs*, English *us*.

Later phenomena that attend the transition from Anglo-Saxon and Old Norse to Middle and modern English are:

1. Loss of *h* before *l* and *r*: *hlōwan* to *low*, *hlēotan* to *lot*, *hlūt* to *loud*, *hlystan* to *listen*, *hrēaw* to *raw*, *hrēr* to *rare*.

2. Loss in pronunciation (but not in spelling) of *k* and *g* before *n* and of *w* before *r*: *cnyttan* to *knit*, *cniht* to *knight*, *cnedan* to *knead*, *cnēo* to *knee*, *gnagan* to *gnaw*, *gnæt* to *gnat*, *wrecan* to *wreak*, *wryhte* to *wright*.

3. Change of *cw* to *qu*, under Norman-French influence; but this affects merely the spelling: *cwēn* to *queen*.

4. A similar spelling change, without change of pronunciation, from *hw* to *wh*: *hwīl* to *while*.

5. The Indo-European **kt* or **gt* group, which had undergone general Germanic change to *ht*, undergoes a further spelling change in Middle English to *ght*; later, in modern English, the *gh* becomes silent and the preceding vowel, if short, is lengthened: *beorht* to *bright*, *gesiht* to *sight*, *neaht* to *night*, *feohtan* to *fight*, *flyht* to *flight*, *meahte* to *might*, *lēoht* to *light*. A final Anglo-Saxon *h* in modern English also becomes *gh* in spelling and silent in pronunciation: *heah* to *high*.

6. In some verbs, Anglo-Saxon *-bb-* between vowels becomes modern English *v* under the analogical influence of the third person singular, which has *f* (see page 33, for the change of *f* to *v*): *habban* (third person singular *hafath*) to *have*, *hebban* (third singular *hefeth*) to *heave*, *libban* (third singular *lifath*) to *live*.

7. There are widespread phenomena of palatalization, affecting Anglo-Saxon *cg*, *sc*, *c* and *g*:

Anglo-Saxon *cg* regularly palatalizes into a *j*-sound, generally represented by *dg* in modern English spelling: *brycg* to *bridge*, *secg* to *sedge*, *mycge* to *midge, midget*. In some verbs, however, the *cg* is affected by the analogical influence of the third person singular, which has *g* between vowels, and the result is the *y* or *i* development of *g* instead of the *dg* development of *cg*: *licgan* (third singular *ligeth*) to *lie*, *lecgan* (third singular *legeth*) to *lay*, *secgan* (third singular *segeth*) to *say*.

In the case of *sc*, palatalization to *sh* is regular in Anglo-Saxon words, and even in early borrowings from Greek or Latin: *wascan* to *wash*, *fisc* to *fish*, *biscop* (from Greek *episkopos*, Latin *episcopus*) to *bishop*. Words of Scandinavian origin do not show palatalization: as against *shell* from Anglo-Saxon *scell*, we have *skull* from Old Norse *skel* or *skalla*; Anglo-Saxon *scyrte* gives us *shirt*, but the kindred Old Norse *skyrta* becomes *skirt*.

In the case of *c*, palatalization to *ch* is widespread, though not universal, before the front vowels, *e* and *i*, but better resisted before back vowels, including *y*: *cinn* to *chin* (but *cynn* to *kin*), *cēosan* to *choose*, *ciele* to *chill* (but *ceald* to *cold*), *cealc* to *chalk* (but *cealf* to *calf*), *ceorl* to *churl* (but *cēne* to *keen*, *cēpan* to *keep*, *cennan* to *ken*). There is a possibility of dialectal or Scandinavian influence in the case of some of the words that do not show palatalization.

In the case of *g*, palatalization to *y* or *i* depends in part on position in the word, in part on preceding and following vowels (if these vowels are the front vowels, *e* or *i*, the usual change of *g* is to *y*, *i*; if there is a predominance of back vowels, *a*, *o*, *u*, a labial development to *w* is usual). Words of Scandinavian origin show the labial development to *w* if they are early borrowings, but leave the *g* unchanged if borrowed at a later period: Anglo-Saxon *drǣge* to *dray*, but *dragan* to *draw*, and Old Norse *draga* to *drag*. Old Norse *flaga* gives us both *flaw* and the *flag* of *flagstone*. Other examples of a *y* or *i* development are: (initially) *ge-* to *y-* to *i-* to complete fall in the prefix of the past participle (the archaic *yclept*, for instance, represents an earlier *geclipod*); *geoc* to *yoke*, *gieldan* to *yield*, *geard* to *yard* (but *gyrdan* to *gird*), *geostra* to *yester*; (medially) *regn* to *rain*, *fæger* to *fair*, *segel* to *sail*, *plegian* to *play*, *ēage* to *eye* (but Old Norse *vindauga* to *window*), *flēogan* to *fly*, *wægn* to *wain*, *blēgen* to (*chil*) *blain*; (in final position) *mǣg* to *may*, *dæg* to *day*, *weg* to *way*. Examples of the labial *w* development are: *fugol* to *fowl*, *sagu* to *saw*, *āgen* to *own* (adjective), *sorg* to *sorrow*, *morgen* to *morrow*, *galga* to *gallow(s)*, *bylgan* to *bellow*.

B. GREEK

The majority of Greek words in the English language are learned creations and compositions, made in relatively modern times for scientific and cultural purposes. Most of these words, though built on Greek roots, would have puzzled the ancient Greeks. Combinations like *telephone*, constructed out of the Greek words for "distance" and "sound", or *antibiotic* ("against life"), are used by us to betoken objects and activities unknown to the ancients.

This learned segment of Greek loan words follows quite closely the original Greek forms and spellings. In English, French, German, and many other modern western languages, Greek *theta*, *phi* and *chi* are faithfully represented by *th*, *ph* and *ch*, and *upsilon* and *zeta* are treated with equal respect as *y* and *z*. This is not the case in Italian, Spanish and Portuguese, but it is very seldom that modern scientific creations from Greek come to us through the latter languages.

The same holds true, in the main, for those Greek words which represent ancient cultural activities, and came to us through Latin, which had adopted them as cultural words. Whether they come into English directly from Latin or through the intermediary of French makes very little difference in their form and appearance. *Philosophy*, *history*, *geography* are typical samples.

There are, however, two other Greek streams to be considered. One consists of those words which came into Anglo-Saxon through the missionaries, and developed on English soil. The other includes those forms which, having entered Latin as fairly popular words, went on to a normal Romance (usually French) development, and were only later adopted by English. The first group assumes popular English form, while the second takes the familiar aspect of words that join the great stream of English from French, Italian or Spanish.

Typical of the first are *kyriakon* ("the house of the Lord") which enters Anglo-Saxon with the missionaries as *circe*, and goes on to become *church*; *episkopos*, which having been latinized into *episcopus*, becomes *biscop* and *bishop*; *pyxis*, which turns into Latin *buxus*, Anglo-Saxon *bocse* and English *box*; *schole*, which becomes the Latin *schola* and the Anglo-Saxon *scōl*, is joined by Norman-French *escole*, and ultimately results in *school*; *martyr*, which preserves its original form in Latin, Anglo-Saxon and English; *boutyron*, which gives Latin *butyrum* and Anglo-Saxon *butere* to go on to *butter*.

Typical of the second are *thesauros*, which enters Latin as a cultural word, *thesaurus*, but becomes popularized in French *trésor* and English *treasure*; *camera*, which becomes French *chambre* and English *chamber* (along with the more conservative *camera*); *hora*, which yields French *(h)oure*, *heure* and English *hour*; *mekhane*, which coming into Latin from a Greek dialectal form, becomes *machina* and later *machine*; *kathedra*, which as the learned Latin *cathedra* yields *cathedral*, but in popular French development goes on to *chaire*, *chaise*, and gives us both *chair* and *chaise longue*; *plateia*, which becomes Latin *platea*, French and English *place*, Italian and English *piazza*, Spanish and English *plaza*; *kybernan*, which becoming Latin *gubernare* and French *gouverner*, ultimately results in *govern* (*cybernetics* is a learned modern relative); *paidion*, which becomes Italian *paggio*, French and English *page* (boy). In these Greek words which receive popular treatment in Latin or Romance, the original spelling is generally changed and disguised. Greek *theia*, for instance, yields the Spanish *tía* of *Tía Juana*; *kolaphos*, the Latin *colaphus*, becomes French and English *coup*; *chrisma* gives the learned *chrism*, but also the popular French *crème* and English *cream*; *phainein*, "to appear", yields forms like *phenomenon*, but also popular and semi-popular forms like *fantastic*, *fancy* and *tiffany* (*theophania*, "the showing of God").

In this more popular sector of the Greek-derived vocabulary, it is common for Greek *th* to appear as *t*, *ph* as *p* or *f* (*p* is the earlier Latin popular treatment of Greek *phi*, *f* the later), *ch* as *c*, *y* as *u* or *i* (*u* is the earlier, *i*, the later treatment). Even in learned treatment, Greek *k* normally appears as *c* (*kathedra—cathedral*), *ai* as *æ* or *e* (*phaino—phænomenon* or *phenomenon*), *oi* as *æ* or *e* (*oikia—œcology* or *ecology*), by reason of the equivalence of the Latin sounds of *c*, *æ*, *œ* to those of Greek *k*, *ai*, *oi*, and the later Latin equivalence of *æ*, *œ* and *e*.

Also, where Classical endings are retained, these are more frequently the Latin substitutes than the Greek originals: *-us* for *-os*, *-um* for *-on*, etc. (*acanthus* for *akanthos*, *cranium* for *kranion*; but *logos*, *phenomenon*, etc.).

C. LATIN

Among important changes that differentiate Classical Latin from archaic Latin and earlier Indo-European (in addition to or repetition of those mentioned in Chapter 2), the following are of interest:

1. The change of *s* between vowels to a voiced *z*-sound and then to *r*, as in most Germanic languages. This is reflected in forms like the genitives *generis*, *floris*, as compared with the nominatives *genus*, *flos*, or in the genitive plural feminine *-arum* ending which in the kindred Oscan appears as *-azum*. Words which in Classical Latin appear with single *s* between vowels are generally borrowed, often from Oscan, sometimes from other sources: *asinus*, "ass", for instance, is claimed to have come from Sumerian *anshu*.

2. The change of earlier, attested *du* before vowels (*dw*) to *b*, as in *duonos* to *bonus* and *duellum* to *bellum*.

3. Widespread assimilation and simplification of troublesome

internal consonant clusters, as shown-by *stella* from **stelna, posco* from **porcsco, luna* from **leuksna* or **loukna, lumen* from **leuksmen.*

4. The fall of *n* before *s*, widely reflected in later Romance development, but appearing even in the Classical and pre-Classical periods: *sponsa* becomes Old French *espose* and English *spouse*; *mensa* gives Spanish *mesa*; **mansuetinus* becomes *mastinus* and ultimately *mastiff*.

5. The change in sound of semi-vowel *ṷ* (written as *v*) from *w* to dentolabial *v* (as pronounced in modern French or English), which probably occurred while the language was still basically Latin (this seems attested, among other things, by widespread *b*-spellings for *v* in Latin inscriptions: *biginti* for *viginti*, etc.). In Romance development, this phenomenon becomes practically universal: Latin *veracus*, derived from *verus* (pronounced *werus*) becomes Old French *verai* (modern French *vrai*), and enters English as *very*.

Many other changes are of doubtful chronology, and are variously described as Vulgar Latin, primitive Romance, etc. It will be best to discuss them under the Romance heading.

English forms which may be described as derived from Latin without Romance intervention are of three kinds:

1. Latin words that came into Anglo-Saxon through the missionaries and acquired early naturalization in English before the Norman Conquest. Typical of these are *street* (Latin *strata*), *cheese* (Latin *caseus*), *cheap* (Anglo-Saxon *ceapian*, derived from Latin *caupo*, "merchant"), *shrive* (Latin *scribo*). There are even words that came into Anglo-Saxon from Latin, but were later displaced by French words from identical sources brought in by the Normans: Greek-Latin *cerasia*, for instance, produced Anglo-Saxon *cirs*, which was displaced by Norman-Picard *cherise*, understood as a plural and turned into a singular *cherry*; *persica* (the "Persian fruit") gave Anglo-Saxon *persoc*, but this was displaced by the French-developed *pessica, pesca, pesche, pêche*, which became *peach*.

2. Ultra-learned Latin forms adopted by English without any change whatsoever in form, usually for legal or governmental use (*agenda, alibi, propaganda, quorum, veto*, etc.). Some of these are quite modern in their formation or use (*facsimile, quantum, gallium*).

3. Vast numbers of cultural Latin words adopted in the Renaissance and later with a minimum of change in form. Some of these were brought directly from Latin into English, others were first adopted by Italian or French, then passed on to English. It seldom makes any

difference which process occurred, so far as the English form is concerned. Whether a learned Latin form like *simulate, simplification, dedicatory*, is adopted directly by English writers and scholars from the Latin lexicon, or whether it is adopted by French scholars and later passed on to English is of importance only with reference to the history of that particular word. On the other hand, prefixes and suffixes in learned and semi-learned words are often quite revealing: the *-fy* of *simplify* is obviously the French *-fier*, while the *-ficate* of *pontificate* comes directly from the Latin *-ficare*, of which *-fier* is a development. The *pro-* of *provide* is obviously Latin (though it could also appear in words that come to English from French, such as *provenance*); but the *pur-* of *purvey* can only be the French *pour-*.

D. ROMANCE (FRENCH, ITALIAN, SPANISH, PORTUGUESE)

Among the numerous and complex changes that mark the development of Latin into French (Spanish, Portuguese, and particularly Italian, are far more conservative of Latin forms), and that are reflected in Romance words that pass into English, are the following:

1. Latin stressed *a* in the free position (i.e., coming at the end of the Latin syllable) becomes *e* in French: Latin *mare*, "sea" becomes *mer* (*mal de mer*); Latin *fratrem* becomes *frère* (*confrere*).

2. Latin stressed short *e* in the free position becomes French *ie*: Latin *pedem* to *pied* (*Piedmont*); Vulgar Latin *pettia* or *petia*, of Gaulish origin, to *pièce* (*piece*). The same development appears in words of Spanish origin, save that in Spanish the change occurs in any position: *festa* to *fiesta*, *sexta* to *siesta*.

3. Latin stressed long *e* and short *i* in the free position become in French first *ei*, then *oi*; these changes are reflected in English spelling, or pronunciation, or both, according to the time when the word was borrowed: Latin *fidem* becomes Old French *feidh* (modern French *foi*), which English borrows as *faith*; Latin *tres* becomes Old French *treis*, later *trois*, and English, borrowing it at the earlier stage, has *trey*; Latin *flebilem* becomes French *feible*, then *foible*, ultimately *faible*, and English borrows it at the first stage as *feeble*, then again at the second as *foible*. Similar alternations of *ei* and *oi* in French endings are reflected in *convey, purvey*, vs. *convoy, envoy, invoice*.

4. Latin stressed short *o* becomes French *eu* and Italian *uo* in the free position, Spanish *ue* in all positions: *novum* to French *neuf* (*Neufchâtel*), Italian *nuovo* (*dolce stil nuovo*), Spanish *nuevo* (*Nuevo Laredo*). Latin *domina*, *dom'na* to Spanish *duenna*, later *dueña*.

5. Latin stressed long *o* and short *u* in the free position are in French changed to *ou*, later *eu*. The *ou* spelling is reflected in the British spellings *honour*, *labour* (Latin *honorem*, *laborem*, modern French *honneur*, *labeur*); both spelling and pronunciation are reflected in *flour*, *flower* (Latin *florem*, Old French *flour*, modern French *fleur* of *fleur de lys*).

6. Latin stressed *au*, whether original or arising as the result of other sound changes, becomes *o*: Latin *aurum*, "gold", becomes French *or*, which English uses in heraldry; *parabola* becomes *paraola, paraula, parole*; *avunculum* becomes *aunclum, oncle*, and this is reflected in English *uncle*.

7. Latin *l* preceded by a vowel and followed by a consonant in French becomes *u*: *talpa*, "mole", to *taupe*; *altum* to *haut*, which appears in English *haughty*.

8. In Italian, *l* preceded by a consonant and followed by a vowel turns into *i*, while in Spanish it absorbs the preceding consonant and produces *ll*: Latin *planum* becomes Italian *piano* and Spanish *llano*; Latin *clarum* becomes Italian *chiaro* in *chiaroscuro*.

9. Plosive consonants between vowels, even when followed by *r*, tend to pass from unvoiced to voiced, from voiced to fricative, and ultimately to disappear, in accordance with the following scheme: *p* to *b* to *v* to –; *k* to *g* to semi-vowel *i̯* (*y*) to –; *t* to *d* to the sound of *th* in *this* to –. In this type of change, French is most drastic, Italian most conservative, Spanish, Portuguese, Provençal in between: Latin *capra*, "goat" (*capricorn*) to Italian *capra*, Spanish and Provençal *cabra* (*cabriolet, cab*), French *chèvre* (*chevron, Chevrolet*); Latin and Italian *opera*, Spanish *obra*, French *oeuvre* (*hors d'oeuvre*); Latin *superanum*, Italian *soprano* (but also *sovrano*), French *souverain*, English *sovereign*; Latin *pacare*, "appease, pay off", to Italian *pagare*, Spanish *pagar*, French *payer*, English *pay*; Latin *spatha*, Italian *spada*, Spanish *espada*, French *épée*; Latin *patrem*, Italian and Spanish *padre*, French *père*; Latin *cauda* (*caudal*), Italian *coda* (used in English as a musical term), French *queue* (English *to queue up* and *cue*). Spanish and Portuguese examples of the process include *lobo* from Latin *lupum*, *Madeira* from *materiem*, *peón* from *pedonem*, *Ladino* from *latinum*.

11. Latin groups of initial *s* plus consonant receive in French and

Spanish a prefixed *e-*; French then goes on to drop the *s*, in fully popular words, as illustrated by *épée*, above, or *écu* from *scutum*, or *état* from *statum*; but in semi-learned words the *s* is retained (Latin *spiritum* to French *esprit*, as in *esprit de corps*). The fall of *s* before consonants appears also within words in French (Latin *testa*, French *tête-à-tête*).

12. The suffix *-aticum* in French yields *-age*, widely reflected in English (Latin *viaticum*, *missaticum* to French and English *voyage*, *message*). The suffix *-arium* gives *-ier* in French, *-ero* in Spanish, and these are also reflected in English (Latin *caballarium*, French *chevalier*, Spanish *caballero*). In English, the *-ier* suffix often appears as *-eer* (*volunteer*, *cannoneer*, etc.). Italian, adopting the French *-ier*, turns it into *-iere*, *-iero*, then passes it back to French and on to English in *cashier*, *cavalier*, *gondolier* etc.

13. Widespread phenomena of palatalization appear in all the Romance languages, but most of all in French. Latin *c* (= *k*) before *e* or *i* acquires the sound of *ch* in Italian and in the Norman-Picard dialect of French, of *ts*, later *s* and *th* respectively, in standard French and Spanish. The Norman-Picard *ch* development is reflected in *cherise*, from Latin *cerasia*, which becomes *cherry*, for the regular French *cerise* which also comes into English, but at a later date. Standard French words that have *c* before *e* or *i* come into English with the same *s*-sound they have in modern French (*cell* from Old French *celle*, Latin *cella*; *circle* from French *cercle*, Latin *circulum*).

14. Standard French, based on the Francien dialect of the Paris region, palatalizes Latin *c* before *a* into *ch*; Spanish, Italian, Provençal, and the Norman-Picard dialect of French do not make this change. English, taking words both from standard French and from Norman-Picard (less frequently from the other Romance sources), often shows both forms: *cant* vs. *chant*; *cavalry* vs. *chivalry*; *cape* vs. *chief*; *cattle* vs. *chattel*; *candle* vs. *chandle*; *carry* vs. *charge*; from an original Latin *captiare* English derives *chase* from standard Old French *chacier* (modern *chasser*) and *catch* from Norman-Picard *cachier*. Other samples of standard French palatalization of *c* before *a* that come into English are *chemise* from *camisia*, *chasten* from *castigare*, *change* from *cambiare*. Samples of unpalatalized *c* before *a* in words that enter English from Norman-Picard, Provençal, and Italian are *cat*, *car*, *caitiff*, *camp*, *castle* (standard French *chat*, *char*, *chétif*, *champ*, *château*).

15. Latin *g* before *e* and *i* and, in French, also before *a*, shifts its

value from the *g* of *good* to the *g* of *general* (English *j*). Accordingly, we have *gelid, jelly* from original Latin *gelidum, gelata*, and *jardinière*, which is standard French, vs. *garden* from Norman-Picard, which does not palatalize *g* before *a*; cf. French *jardin*.

16.   Latin semi-vowel *i̯* (spelled *j* in modern Latin works, but not by the Romans themselves) generally changes its value from that of English *y* to that of English *j*: Latin *judicem* becomes French *juge* and English *judge*; *justum* becomes French *juste* and English *just*. This change is made even in words that English takes directly from Latin (*jocare* to *joke*, *junior* to English *junior*).

17.   Other palatalization phenomena include the change of *vi* and *bi* plus vowel to palatal *g*: *rabiem* to French and English *rage*, *cavea* to *cage*, *servientem* to *sergeant*; as well as the change by which a French *-ss-*, becoming final in English, is turned to *-sh* (*push* from *pousser*, *finish* from *finiss-*, *nourish* from *nouriss-*).

18.   Germanic words beginning with *w*, coming into Vulgar Latin or preliterary French, receive a *g*-sound which is prefixed to the *w*; the latter then frequently disappears, leaving only the *g-*. In this fashion, *wadio* becomes *gage*, *warnjan* becomes *garnir*, *wardôn* becomes *garder*, *wīsa* becomes *guise* (in modern French, as in English, the *u* is silent). However, the extreme northern French dialect, Walloon, which frequently affects Norman-Picard, leaves the original Germanic *w* unchanged. The *w* also remains unchanged in words which are not brought in by the Normans, but form part of the original Anglo-Saxon Germanic stock of English. A single Germanic root, consequently, gives us Anglo-Saxon *wed*, standard French *gage*, and Walloon *wage*. *Ward* is Anglo-Saxon; *guard* is the same root with standard French treatment, and so is *guardian*; but *warden* is the Walloon treatment of the standard French *gardien*. *Watch* is Anglo-Saxon *wacian*; *wait* is the same root, treated in Walloon fashion (*waitier*); while standard Old French has a *guaitier* which ultimately becomes *guetter*, "to lurk, lie in wait", in modern French. Taking two examples where only Anglo-Saxon and standard French treatments appear, *warn* is Anglo-Saxon, while *garnish* is the French development of the same original Germanic root; the *wise* of "in wondrous wise" is Anglo-Saxon, and has *guise* as its French counterpart.

19.   A special Anglo-Norman development is the *-oon* of *boon*, corresponding to the French *-on* of *bon* (in Anglo-Norman manuscripts,

spellings like *raisun* for standard French *raison* are frequent). An occasional variant is *-oom*, as in *mushroom* from *moucheron*. The *-oon* treatment is later applied to Italian words ending in *-one* and other French words in *-on* (*saloon, poltroon, buffoon, macaroon, cartoon, pontoon*). Many of these *-oon* forms have *-on* variants (*salon, carton*).

20. As a general rule, French and other Romance words borrowed at an early date tend to shift their stress to the initial syllable to conform with the Anglo-Saxon and general Germanic law of initial accentuation, as shown by *very, dinner, supper, venison, mutton, jelly, butler, dandelion, laundry*, from French *verai* (later *vrai*), *dîner, souper, venaison, mouton, gelée, boutelier, dent de lion*, Italian *lavanderia*. Later borrowings are more likely to keep the Romance accent on the final or non-initial syllable (*brunette, ballet, patrol, garage, dessert, canteen, cartoon*, from French *brunette, ballet, patrouille, garage, dessert*, Italian *cantina, cartone*).

21. The distinction between learned words, which tend to keep their Latin or Greek form and spelling, and popular words, showing the sound changes normal to the development of the language, is very pronounced in both French and English, and leads to numerous doublets (pairs of words coming from the same original source, of which one receives learned, the other popular treatment). There may even be triplets, quadruplets, quintuplets, according to the degree of learned, semi-learned or popular treatment, or to the factor of derivation through different dialects. *Hotel, hostel* and *hospital* all come from Latin *hospitalem*; *Gentile, genteel, gentle* and *jaunty* all have their roots in Latin *gentilem*; *discus, disc, disk, desk, dish*, and *dais* are all derived from Latin *discus*, as is also the German *Tisch*, "table". *Parabola, parable*, and *parole* all go back to Greek *parabole*. Other examples are *frail* and *fragile* (French *frêle, fragile*, Latin *fragilem*); *forge* and *fabricate* (French *forge, fabrique*, Latin *fabrica*); *coy* and *quiet* (French *coi, quiet*, Latin *quietum*); *caitiff* and *captive* (French *chétif* with Norman-Picard treatment, and *captif*, Latin *captivum*); *count* and *compute* (French *conter, compter, computer*, Latin *computare*); *treason* and *tradition* (French *trahison, tradition*, Latin *traditionem*); *allow* and *allocate* (French *alouer, allocation*, Latin *allocare*); *priest* and *Presbyterian* (Greek *presbyter*, "elder"); *triumph* and *trump* (Greek *thriambos*, "dance of rejoicing"); *robe* and *rob* (French *robe* and Old French *rober*, from Germanic *rauba*, "booty", Old High German *roub*; here the Anglo-Saxon cognate is the *-reave* of *bereave*).

CHAPTER 4

One-Branch Families

Families of English words showing derivation from a single Indo-European branch (Germanic, Greek, or Latin) are not so numerous as those that combine two or three of these branches, and some of them are sufficiently simple to give the impression of resembling the man who is all alone in the world. This simplicity should not deceive us, because, while they may appear singly in English, they almost invariably have wide connections in other languages. Two illustrations are supplied by words of family relationship, *son* and *daughter*, which appear in English only in Germanic and Anglo-Saxon guise. This is because Latin, instead of using the two roots involved, rejects them, and prefers an altogether different root, which appears in *filius* and *filia* (the root preferred by Latin, **dhē(i)*, has the original meaning of "suckle", and will be discussed later). Since Latin does not choose to give admission to the Greek words for *son* and *daughter*, which are related to the Germanic, and since these Greek words do not give rise to any modern learned borrowing, Germanic *son* and *daughter*, despite their vast extensions in other branches of Indo-European, find themselves isolated in English.

In discussing one-branch word-families, we shall begin with those issuing from Germanic, which is basic to English, then pass on to Greek and Latin. In families of two or more branches, we shall arrange the branches and our own discussion of them in order of historical precedence (Indo-Iranian, Greek, Latin, Germanic, Celtic, Slavic).

A. GERMANIC

The Indo-European root **sŭ*, **seu*, "to bear, bring forth", with its derivative *sūnus*, has ramifications in Greek *hyios*, "son", in Indo-Iranian, in Celtic, and in Slavic (the form represented by Russian *syn*). In Anglo-Saxon, it produces *sunu*, which becomes *son* (with *sonship*, *son-in-law*, *sonny*, etc.). Close cognates of *son* are in evidence throughout the Germanic branch (German *Sohn*, Scandinavian *son*, *sen*, etc.).

The family tree for the English word is extremely simple:

IE *sū, seu, sūnu ("to bear, bring forth; son")
|
AS sunu
|
Eng. son, etc. (TABLE XV, 1)

Another root with extensive outside connections, but a single line of English descent, is that of **dhug(h)ǝter*, "daughter". The root appears in Indo-Iranian (Sanskrit *duhitā*, Persian *duhitar*); in Armenian; in Oscan (but not in Latin); in Slavic (Russian *doč'*, with root *doč̌er-*); in Greek (*thygater*). Anglo-Saxon *dohtor*, which gives us *daughter*, *daughter-in-law*, *daughterly*, etc., has cognates in all the Germanic languages (German *Tochter*, Icelandic *dōttir*, etc.). Again, the English family tree is extremely simple:

IE *dhug(h)ǝter ("daughter")
|
AS dohtor
|
Eng. daughter, etc. (TABLE X, 2, 4)

One Indo-European root, **bhel*, "sound, roar, bellow", has an extremely simple Germanic development that leads to Anglo-Saxon and English forms. From AS *belle* comes *bell* (*bell buoy*, *bellwether*, *bellboy* or *bellhop* are compound forms), while the verb form, *bellan* or *bylgan* in Anglo-Saxon, goes on to English *bellow*. The only thing *bell* and *bellow* have in common semantically is that both refer to sounds. The tree:

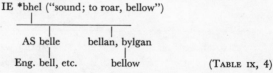

IE *bhel ("sound; to roar, bellow")

AS belle   bellan, bylgan

Eng. bell, etc.   bellow   (TABLE IX, 4)

There is a Germanic root derived from IE **del*, "to reckon, count", which, appearing in Anglo-Saxon as *tǣl* (noun) and *tellan* (verb), gives rise to English *tell* and its derivatives, such as *teller* and *telltale*. From the same root comes Anglo-Saxon *talu*, which becomes English *tale*. Two other variants of the root are Middle English *talken*, leading to *talk*, with its derivatives *talkative*, *talkie*, etc., and Middle English *tal* (modern English *tall*), which seems to go back to Anglo-Saxon *getæl*, "quick". The semantic link is between the idea of reckoning, counting, telling and that of docile or quick to learn (to reckon or count). The meaning of *tall* at its earliest appearance is "comely, fine, excellent, brave", which is linked to "quick to learn". The tree:

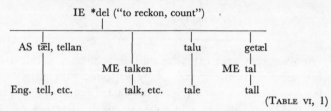

IE *del ("to reckon, count")

AS tæl, tellan | talu | getæl
ME talken | ME tal
Eng. tell, etc. | talk, etc. | tale | tall

(TABLE VI, 1)

A Germanic root meaning "pledge", derived from IE *wadh*, first appears in Gothic *wadi*. With a slight change of form, it appears in Anglo-Saxon *wedd* (noun) and *weddian* (verb), which eventually turn into English *wed*, with such derivatives as *wedding* and *wedlock*. The same Germanic root, carried by the Franks into the Vulgar Latin of northern Gaul after the fall of the Roman Empire, appears in Vulgar Latin documents as *wadjo*, later giving rise to French *gage* and its derivatives (*engager*, *engagement*, etc.). In the northern French dialects (Walloon, Picard, Norman) the original *w* of the Germanic form is kept instead of being turned to *gu* and *g*, so that these dialects show *wage*, *wagier*, etc. Both variants get into English, giving rise on the one hand to *gage* or *gauge*, *engage*, *engagement*, on the other to *wage*, *wages*, *wager*. Much later English borrows from standard French the term *dégagé*, "unpledged, free from pledges", therefore "free and easy, unconstrained". Here the progression is:

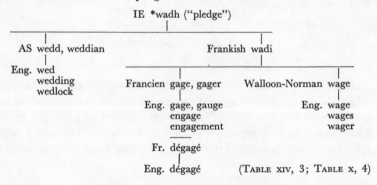

IE *wadh ("pledge")

AS wedd, weddian | Frankish wadi
Eng. wed
wedding
wedlock

Francien gage, gager | Walloon-Norman wage
Eng. gage, gauge | Eng. wage
engage | wages
engagement | wager

Fr. dégagé

Eng. dégagé   (TABLE XIV, 3; TABLE X, 4)

Another Germanic root whose original form seems to have been an IE *dheub, "deep", or *dhumb, "hole", appears first in Gothic as *diups*, "deep", with a verb *daupjan*, "to deepen" or "to dip". In Anglo-Saxon we have *dēop*, "deep", *dīepan*, "to deepen", and *dyppan*, "to dip". There is also a variant of *dīepan* which is *dīefan*, "to dive" (i.e., "to make yourself deep"). Modern English forms derived from these are *deep*, with *deepen* and *depth*; *dip*, with *dipper*; *dive*, with *diver*; and, very possibly, *dimple*, which is a "deepening" of some part of your anatomy. Two other forms that come in from kindred Germanic tongues are *dump*, from the Scandinavian (either "to drop with a thud" or "a deep, water-filled hole"), and *dope*, from Dutch (something that is prepared by a process of dipping). Not to be overlooked are special uses of these words in certain combinations (*deep freeze*, *depth charge*, *dive bomber*, *big dipper*). Here our line of progression is:

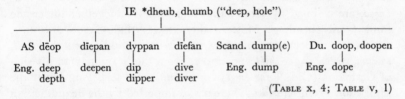

IE *dheub, dhumb ("deep, hole")						
AS dēop	dīepan	dyppan	dīefan	Scand. dump(e)		Du. doop, doopen
Eng. deep	deepen	dip	dive	Eng. dump		Eng. dope
depth		dipper	diver			

(TABLE X, 4; TABLE V, 1)

Another Germanic root that has wide ramifications in English is the IE *bherəg or *bhrēg, "to gleam, white". This first appears in Gothic as *bairhts*, later in Anglo-Saxon as *beorht*, and ultimately becomes the English *bright*, with its derivatives *brighten*, *brightness*, *brightly*, etc. The Germanic tribes also used it as a proper name (*Bert*, *Bertha*), and it forms the second part of a veritable army of first and family names (*Robert*, *Albert*, *Herbert*, *Lambert*, etc.). These, however, are carried by the Germanic-speaking Franks into French, then taken by the Normans to England. As a common noun, the *lambert* is the unit of brightness, after the name of its inventor. *Bright's disease* shows the Anglo-Saxon form used as a family name, while the name of *Bertillon*, the discoverer of the finger-print method of identification, contains the Frankish form of the root. *Big Bertha*, the nickname given a German siege-gun in World War I, shows another special use. German variants of the form used in names are *-brecht* and *-precht* (*Albrecht*, *Rupprecht*), and Scandinavian names containing *Bjerk* or *Björk* display the same root. Another form of the IE root is shown by *birch*, "the white tree", with its derivative *birchen*, which appears in Anglo-Saxon as *bierce*, a form used also as an English family name. The family tree:

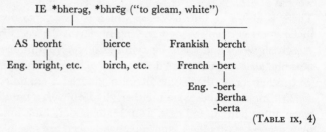

IE *bherəg, *bhrēg ("to gleam, white")

AS beorht	bierce	Frankish bercht
Eng. bright, etc.	birch, etc.	French -bert
		Eng. -bert
		Bertha
		-berta

(TABLE IX, 4)

One Germanic root which combines several ideas is the one derived from IE *gen*, "to press together". Here the semantic connections are doubtful, and the sound similarities paramount. *Knap* (mountain top), *knit, knob, knoll, knock, knot*, possibly also *knave* and *knight*, as well as *knead*, are claimed by some authorities to belong together under the same family heading. Most of them have Anglo-Saxon ancestors, which are, respectively, *cnæpp, cnyttan, knobbe* (Middle English), *cnoll, cnocian, cnotta, cnafa, cniht* and *cnedan*. From the Scandinavian division of Germanic (Old Norse *knifr*) comes *knife*, said to belong under the same root. From Russian, where it was imported by the Scandinavian Varangians, comes *knout*, and from Dutch *knobhout*, "knotted stick", comes the South African *knobkerrie*, where the Germanic *knob* is combined with the Hottentot *kirri*, "club". Derivatives of the words listed above are numerous (*knapweed, knitting, knobby, knockout, knock-knee, knothole, knavery, knighthood*, to mention some). Granting that the original link is correct, the family tree would be:

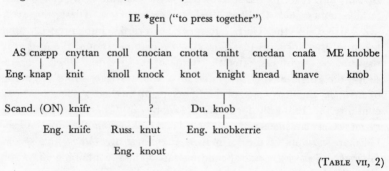

IE *gen ("to press together")

AS cnæpp	cnyttan	cnoll	cnocian	cnotta	cniht	cnedan	cnafa	ME knobbe
Eng. knap	knit	knoll	knock	knot	knight	knead	knave	knob

Scand. (ON) knīfr	?	Du. knob
Eng. knife	Russ. knut	Eng. knobkerrie
	Eng. knout	

(TABLE VII, 2)

It must, however, be stressed that there is considerable uncertainty about the derivation of all these semantically dissimilar forms from a single root. Doubt attaches particularly to *knave*, *knight* and *knead*.

B. GREEK

A one-branch family with dubious connections elsewhere appears in Indo-European *yek̯u̯rt*, "liver". This, in Latin, produces *iecur*, which disappears from the Romance languages because it is replaced by an accompanying adjective, *ficatum* ("stuffed with figs"; the Romans were apparently fond of combining liver and figs into a single dish; *ficatum* eventually turns into Italian *fegato*, Spanish *hígado*, French *foie*, etc.). In Slavic, the root appears in Russian *ikra*, "caviar". The doubtful Germanic descendant is represented by Anglo-Saxon *lifer*, English *liver*, which would call for a prefix with *l*; but many authorities prefer to derive *liver* from the root of *life* and *live*. Greek *hepar* definitely gives us *hepatic* and *hepatitis*. All we can surely claim for the English tree is:

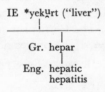

IE *yek̯u̯rt ("liver")

Gr. hepar

Eng. hepatic
hepatitis

(TABLE XIII, 1, 3)

An Indo-European root *gwadh*, "to plunge, sink", comes into Greek with an initial *b* replacing *gw* and *th* replacing *dh* of the original. *Bathos* and the *bathy-* of *bathysphere* and similar words are the English descendants, as well as the *abyss* and *abysmal* that issue directly from the Greek *abyssos*. There is a very remote possibility that the slangy Latin *bassus*, whose immediate ancestor is either Oscan or Celtic, may be from the same root, in which case our family would expand to include such words as *base* (in the sense of "low"), *basso*, *bassoon*, *basset*, *basement*, *debase*, *abase*, *bas relief* and *bas bleu*. Picturing our family tree with only that portion of the family of whose relation-ships we are sure, we have:

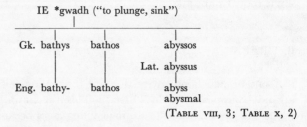

IE *gwadh ("to plunge, sink")

Gk. bathys	bathos	abyssos
Eng. bathy-	bathos	Lat. abyssus
		abyss
		abysmal

(TABLE VIII, 3; TABLE X, 2)

From the IE root *ker, "cherry", the earliest Greek form is kerasos, "cherry tree". This, coming into Latin in the form cerasus, cerasia, gives rise to the French cerise, which in the northern French dialects (Picard-Norman, which contribute heavily to early borrowings from French in the centuries immediately following the Norman Conquest) appears as cherise. English speakers misunderstood this to be a plural, turned it into cherries, and built a singular cherry. Centuries later, the regular French form cerise was appropriated by English to denote a color. The brandy made by a distillation of cherries is named Kirsch-wasser, "cherry water", German having borrowed cerasus from Latin and turned it into Kirsch. The German term gets into English in the form of Kirsch or Kirschwasser. The progression here is:

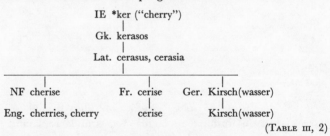

IE *ker ("cherry")

Gk. kerasos

Lat. cerasus, cerasia

| NF cherise | Fr. cerise | Ger. Kirsch(wasser) |
| Eng. cherries, cherry | cerise | Kirsch(wasser) |

(TABLE III, 2)

An IE root that appears in Greek and Germanic is that of *segh, "to hold fast, victory". We include it in one-branch discussions because in English the Germanic derivatives appear only in proper names (Sigmund, Siegfried, Siegfried Line, etc.; German has Sieg, "victory"). In Greek, the major exemplification of the *segh root is the verb ekho, "to have, hold", from which comes the English epoch (ep-ekho, "to have a hold upon, check a course, check the course of a star", eventually the period of the course itself), and *eunuch* (*eune ekho*, "to hold the couch", the person who guards the couch or harem).

There are two other Greek variants of the root. One is represented in English by *Hector, hector, hectic* (with initial IE *s* appearing as *h*; *Hector* is "one who holds firm"; *to hector* is to behave as Hector did on the battlefield in the absence of Achilles; *hectic* is "holding, habitual, behaving like one suffering from consumption"; cf. Italian *etico*, "consumptive"). The other is represented by forms pertaining to *scheme* and *school* (some also claim *schedule*, but this is disputed), in which the verb *ekho* appears in tense-forms beginning with *eskh-* or *skh-*. *Schema* produces, in addition to *scheme* and its derivatives (*schematic, schematize,* etc.), also such forms as *sketch, esquisse* and *schizzo*, the first through Italian and Dutch, the second through French, the third representing the Italian original of *sketch*. *School* (the original Greek *schole* indicated a "holding period" of leisure, then that for which leisure is profitably employed, schooling or instruction or intellectual development), goes on to Latin *schola* and Anglo-Saxon *scōl*, which, blending with Norman-French *escole*, from the same Latin source, gives us *school* and *scholar*. *Scholiast, scholastic, scholasticism* and *Schola Cantorum* are later and more learned borrowings. *School* forms such compounds as *schoolboy* and *schoolhouse*, while *scholar* gives rise to *scholarly, scholarship,* etc. With the elimination of Germanic forms and of *schedule*, this is the tree:

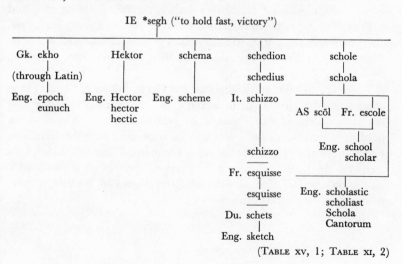

IE *segh ("to hold fast, victory")

(TABLE XV, 1; TABLE XI, 2)

The IE root *$g^u el$, "to throw", produces in Greek the verb *ballo* and the noun *bole*. The former leads directly to such English forms as *ballista* and *ballistics*, the latter to learned compounds of the type of *embolism, hyperbole, metabolism, bolograph, bolometer*, with their adjectives in -*ic*, as well as to older, more disguised words like *emblem, problem* and *symbol*, with their derivatives (*emblematic, problematical, symbolic*, etc.). Two extremely productive compounds of *ballo* and *bole* are the ones formed with the prepositional prefixes *para-* and *dia-*. The former gives us, as a learned word, *parabola* and *parabolic*, but in Christian parlance *parabola* becomes *parable*, a "throwing around, talking around, circumlocution". This word goes on to replace, in Vulgar Latin and early Romance, such Classical words as *verbum, locutio* and *sermo*, and to become the regular form for "word" (*parola, parole, palabra*); it also gives rise to a new verb "to speak", *parabolare*, which eventually becomes Italian *parlare* and French *parler*. The French forms eventually give rise to English *parole, parley, parlance*, and *parlor*, the Portuguese *palavra* becomes *palaver*, and Italian directly contributes the musical term *parlando*. The diplomatic *pourparler* is a more recent borrowing from French. In addition, French *parlement* gives rise to English *parliament* and *parliamentary*.

Diaballo, "to throw through", also means "to slander", and *diabolos* becomes in Christian parlance the "slanderer" of mankind. Turning into the Latin *diabolus*, it enters Anglo-Saxon in the form *dēofol*, which becomes *devil*, with its derivatives *deviltry, devilish, devilment*, etc., and with such picturesque combination forms as *devil's advocate, devil's-food*, etc. Later and more learned borrowings give us *diabolic* and *diabolism*, while modern French contributes *diablerie* and the title of a film, "*Diabolique*".

There is a remote possibility that the Greek *balaneion*, "bath", may come from the same root, in which event the learned *balneology* and the Italian-derived *bagnio* would be related forms. There is also a possibility that Greek *ballo, bole* may be connected with the Germanic *qualm* (originally "black smoke", as in German). These two connections seem too uncertain to warrant inclusion of the root in a two-branch discussion, or inclusion of *balneology* and *bagnio* in the family tree, which accordingly takes this form:

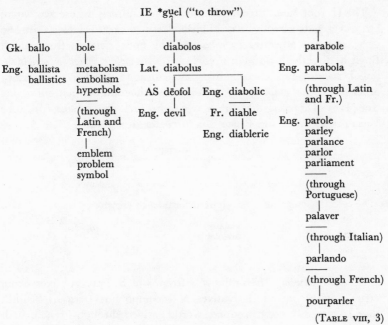

(TABLE VIII, 3)

C. LATIN

Indo-European had two roots that conveyed the idea of "fire".
One, inanimate and neuter, appears in Greek *pyr*, English *fire*, German
Feuer, etc. The other, personified and masculine, is *egnis*, *ognis*,
which produces, among other things, the Sanskrit *agnis*, "the fire-god,
fire", and the Slavic word for "fire" represented by Russian *ogon'*.
In Latin, *ignis* gives us *ignite*, *ignition*, *igneous* and similar words. The
tree:

IE *egnis, *ognis ("fire")

Lat. ignis

Eng. ignite
ignition
Eng. igneous, etc.

(TABLE VII, 1: note that
the changes for *g do not
occur in the *gn* group)

The IE root *wei, "strength", appears in Latin vis, whose accusative form, vim, gets directly into English. Latin derivatives of vis are the verb violo, the adjective violentus and the noun violentia, from which English, directly or through French, acquires violate, violation, inviolable, violent, violence, etc. There is disagreement as to whether the same or other roots yield via, vie, envy, and invite, so they are best left out of our tree. It is of interest that the Slavic word for "war", voina (Tolstoi's Voina i Mir, "War and Peace") is from the same root.

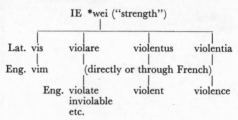

(TABLE XIV, 2)

IE *wer, *werə, "friendliness", from which Latin derives verus, "true", with various derivatives and compounds (veritas, "truth", severus, "severe", etc.) produces words derived through French, such as very, verity, verdict, verify, veritable, verily, aver, and such direct appropriations as veracious, veracity, verisimilitude. Latin severus seems to be compounded of se, "without", and the original meaning of the IE root, "friendliness"; from it we inherit severe, severity, persevere, perseverance, asseverate. It is of interest that while Germanic descendants of the IE root appear in other Germanic languages (German wahr, Wirt), none appear in English.

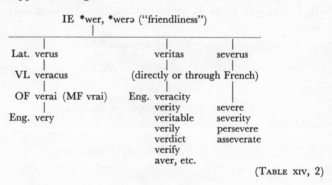

(TABLE XIV, 2)

An IE root *al, "to wander, roam about aimlessly, go astray, be mentally wrong", gives rise to Latin ambulo, from which English derives, directly or indirectly, amble, preamble, ambulance, ambulant, ramble, perambulator (shortened to pram), somnambulism, funambulism. If it is true that the same root gives rise to French aller, "to go", then English alley and possible even allure belong in this group.

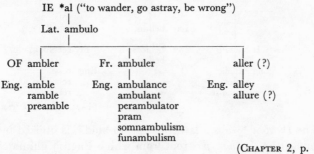

IE *al ("to wander, go astray, be wrong")
|
Lat. ambulo
|

OF ambler	Fr. ambuler	aller (?)
Eng. amble	Eng. ambulance	Eng. alley
ramble	ambulant	allure (?)
preamble	perambulator	
	pram	
	somnambulism	
	funambulism	

(CHAPTER 2, p. 17)

The IE root *bhlag, "to strike", gives rise to Latin flagellum, "little whip", from which we get directly flagellant, flagellation, flagellate, and, through French, flail. English flog, which begins to appear only in the seventeenth century, is claimed to be a schoolboy abbreviation of flagellate. If it is true that this root is also at the bottom of Latin flagro, "to burn brightly", then we would have as part of this family flagrant, conflagration, effulgence, fulminate, etc., but the connection is not definitely established.

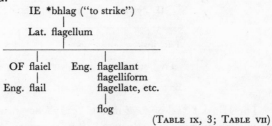

IE *bhlag ("to strike")
|
Lat. flagellum
|

OF flaiel	Eng. flagellant
Eng. flail	flagelliform
	flagellate, etc.
	flog

(TABLE IX, 3; TABLE VII)

There is a root which is simple if accepted in one interpretation, but would have numerous links in other branches if differently interpreted. Latin bellum, "war", coming from an earlier duellum, is by some linked to the root of duo, "two", which would give it numerous Germanic and Greek relatives; by others it is connected with an IE root *dāu, *dəu, *dū, "to burn, hurt, annihilate". In this acceptance, it yields in English, from the older variant and through Italian, *duel*, *duellist*, *duello*; from the Classical *bellum* come *bellicose*, *belligerent*, along with a series of compound forms represented by *rebel*, *rebellion*, *rebellious*.

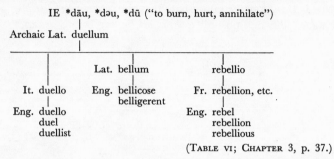

IE *dāu, *dəu, *dū ("to burn, hurt, annihilate")

Archaic Lat. duellum

	Lat. bellum	rebellio
It. duello	Eng. bellicose	Fr. rebellion, etc.
	belligerent	
Eng. duello		Eng. rebel
duel		rebellion
duellist		rebellious

(TABLE VI; CHAPTER 3, p. 37.)

The IE root *yewos*, "law, precept, to bind", is utilized by Latin to manufacture the *jus-*, *jur-* root from which English ultimately derives on the one hand *just* and all its compounds (*justice*, *unjust*, *injustice*, *justify*, *adjust*, *adjustment*, etc.); on the other, its various *jur-*, *jure-*, *-jury* forms (*juror*, *jury*, *jurist*, *jurisprudence*, *jurisdiction*, *abjure*, *adjure*, *conjure*, *perjury*, *injure*, *injury*, etc.). In addition, the *jus-* root combines another widespread root, that of Lat. *dico*, "to say", to produce *judge*, *judicial*, *prejudice*, etc. There are also proper names such as *Justin*, *Justine*, *Justinian*, and foreign expressions accepted into the English vocabulary, such as *jus gentium* and *juste milieu*.

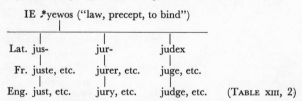

IE *yewos ("law, precept, to bind")

Lat. jus-	jur-	judex	
Fr. juste, etc.	jurer, etc.	juge, etc.	
Eng. just, etc.	jury, etc.	judge, etc.	(TABLE XIII, 2)

The IE root *kel* or *kāl* means "gray" or "brown", but acquires a secondary meaning of "warm". The primary meaning appears in Latin *columba*, "dove", which goes on to English *columbarium*, *columbine*, *columbium*, and the proper name *Columbus* with its derivatives (*Columbia*, *Columbian*, *Colón*, *Colombia*, etc.). The secondary meaning of "warm" appears in Latin *caleo*, "to be warm", *calidus*, "warm", *caligo*, "mist", *calefacio*, "to make warm". Some of these appear directly in English (*calefaction, caliginous, calorie, calorimeter*, etc.). But an even greater number of English words comes from the French descendants of the Latin words (*chaud, échauder, chauffer*, etc.). Here we have *chafe, chafing dish, chauffeur, nonchalant, nonchalance*, even *chowder* (from *chaudière*, which goes back to Latin *caldaria*, "stew-pot"); while *cauldron, caudle, scald* go back to Norman-Picard forms.

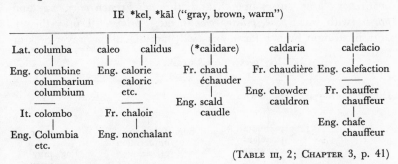

IE **kel, *kāl* ("gray, brown, warm")

Lat. columba	caleo	calidus	(*calidare)	caldaria	calefacio
Eng. columbine columbarium columbium	Eng. calorie caloric etc.	Fr. chaud échauder	Fr. chaudière Eng. scald caudle	Eng. chowder cauldron	Eng. calefaction Fr. chauffer chauffeur
It. colombo	Fr. chaloir				Eng. chafe chauffeur
Eng. Columbia etc.	Eng. nonchalant				

(TABLE III, 2; CHAPTER 3, p. 41)

The IE root **mā*, "good, opportune", produces in Latin *Manes*, "ancestor spirits"; *mane*, "in the morning, tomorrow" (which the Romance languages generally use in compound form: French *demain*, Italian *domani*, Spanish *mañana*, which finds its way into English dictionaries); *Matuta*, "dawn goddess", who gives us *matutinal, matins*, and *matinee; maturus*, "ripe", leading to *mature, maturity, immature, premature* and possibly, through French, *demure*; and the negative *immanis*, leading to *immane*. There is a possibility that Greek *mania* may be connected, but for semantic reasons it seems best to link it with the root of *mind* and *mental*.

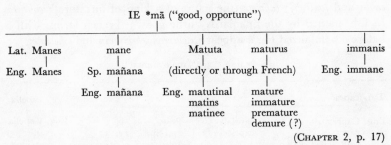

IE **mā* ("good, opportune")

Lat. Manes	mane	Matuta	maturus	immanis
Eng. Manes	Sp. mañana	(directly or through French)		Eng. immane
	Eng. mañana	Eng. matutinal matins matinee	mature immature premature demure (?)	

(CHAPTER 2, p. 17)

The root **perk, *prek* "to ask, ask for" produces in Germanic the verb that appears in modern German as *fragen* and in Anglo-Saxon as *fricgan*, but the latter does not survive in modern English. On the Latin side, we have *posco* (originally **porcsco*), "to ask, demand", with a derivative *postulo* from which we get *postulant, postulate, expostulate, expostulation*. Another derivative is Latin *precor*, "to pray", from which, directly or through French, we obtain *precarious* (that for which you pray, but are not sure of obtaining), *deprecate* "pray off, ward off", *imprecation* "pray curses upon", and, through French *prier, pray* and *prayer* (with *prayer book, praying mantis*, etc.), *prithee* ("I pray thee"), and, in straight French form, *prie-dieu* ("pray-God", a prayer desk or seat).

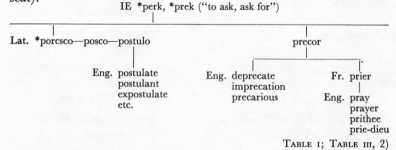

IE **perk, *prek* ("to ask, ask for")

Lat. **porcsco—posco—postulo*   *precor*

Eng. postulate   Eng. deprecate   Fr. prier
      postulant   imprecation
      expostulate   precarious   Eng. pray
      etc.   prayer
                                           prithee
                                           prie-dieu

TABLE I; TABLE III, 2)

The IE root **kapro* means "goat, male animal". Here we have Latin *capra*, "goat", which appears directly in *caper, capriole, Capricorn, caprifoliaceous*, possibly *caprice* and *capriccio* (these come through French from Italian *capriccio*, but they may go back to *caput*, "head", rather than to *capra*). The diminutive *capella*, "little goat", appears in the name of a constellation. Provençal and Spanish forms, in which *p* is voiced to *b*, appear in *cabriolet* (shortened to *cab*, with its derivatives *cabby* and *taxicab*); *cabriole* (the name of a kind of furniture); *cabrilla* (a fish, named by the Spaniards "little goat"). French forms, with *c* before *a* palatalized to *ch*, appear in *chevron, chevrotain* and *Chevrolet*.

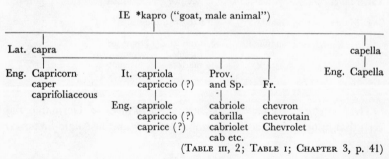

IE **kapro* ("goat, male animal")

Lat. capra   capella

Eng. Capricorn   It. capriola   Prov.   Eng. Capella
      caper   capriccio (?)   and Sp.   Fr.
      caprifoliaceous
                     Eng. capriole   cabriole   chevron
                          capriccio (?)   cabrilla   chevrotain
                          caprice (?)   cabriolet   Chevrolet
                                     cab etc.

(TABLE III, 2; TABLE I; CHAPTER 3, p. 41)

A slightly doubtful, yet very extensive family is that of IE *pōi, *pī, "to drink". Although this has extensive ramifications in Greek (*pino*) and in Slavic (*pit'*, "to drink", *pivo*, "beer"), its English members all come from Latin *bibo* and *poto*, "to drink". *Bibo* is described as a case of assimilation of the first *b* in a hypothetical *pibo* to the second *b*, and this hypothesis is supported by the form *pipafo*, "I shall drink", in a Faliscan inscription (Faliscan was a dialect of the Latinian branch of Italic). *Bibo* gives us, directly or through Old French *beivre* (modern French *boire*), *bib*, *bibulous*, *imbibe*, *wine-bibber*, *beverage*, *bevy* (from Old French *bevée*, "hunting party at which one drinks"), possibly *buffet* (from an alternative French form *buvette*). *Poto* gives *potable*, *potation*, and, through *potio*, a noun formation, *potion*, and *poison* (with *poisoner*, *poisonous*, *poison ivy*, etc.). In addition, there is an Anglo-Saxon *pott* which seems borrowed from the root of Latin *poto*; this merges with French *pot*, from the same source, and becomes *pot*, with *potter*, *potter's field*, *pottery*, *poteen*, *pottage*, or *potage*, *potboiler*, *pothook*, *pothouse*, *pot luck*, *potsherd*, *pot shot*, *pot roast*, *potpie*, *pot liquor*, *pot walloper*, *pot belly*, *potash* and *potassium*, the half-disguised *porridge* and *porringer*, *putty*, *hotchpotch* or *hodgepodge*, and the French *potpourri* and *potiche*.

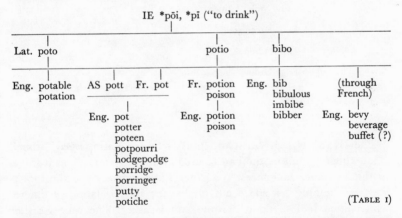

IE *pōi, *pī ("to drink")

Lat.	poto			potio	bibo	
Eng.	potable potation	AS pott	Fr. pot	Fr. potion poison	Eng. bib bibulous imbibe bibber	(through French)
		Eng. pot potter poteen potpourri hodgepodge porridge porringer putty potiche		Eng. potion poison		Eng. bevy beverage buffet (?)

(TABLE I)

The IE root *stel, "to broaden, broad", gives rise to Latin *lātus*, (earlier *stlātus*, arising by metathesis, or transposition, of *l*), an adjective meaning "wide, broad"; as well as to the noun *latus*, with short *a*, meaning "side". The first gives us *latitude*, "broadness", and, by an extension to the meaning of "broad fields", *Latium*, which in turn gives us *Latin, Latinity*, and such compound forms as *Latin cross, Latin Quarter* and *Latin America*. *Latinus*, "Latin", also gives us *lateen* sails, *Ladino*, the Romance tongue of the Sephardic Jews, and *Ladin*, the Rheto-Romansh dialects of Switzerland and northeastern Italy. It is possible that *Lateran* also belongs here (the Lateran Palace was originally the residence of the Laterna family). By a further extension, *lātus* produces *lama*, "blade", which gives us *laminate, lamellate, lame* (in the sense of "thin plate"), and *omelet* (the last is Latin *lamella*, a diminutive meaning "small blade", which gets another diminutive ending in French at the same time that it loses its initial *l*, and so turns into *ómelette*, a "small, thin blade" of egg). The noun *latus*, meaning "side", gives us *lateral, bilateral, collateral, unilateral, equilateral, quadrilateral*, etc., as well as *dilate, dilatation, elate, elation*.

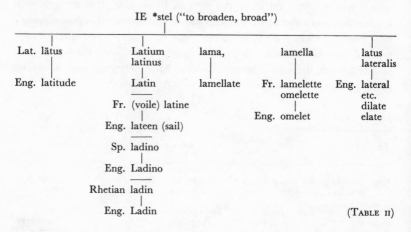

IE *stel ("to broaden, broad")

Lat. lātus	Latium latinus	lama,	lamella	latus lateralis
Eng. latitude	Latin	lamellate	Fr. lamelette omelette	Eng. lateral etc.
	Fr. (voile) latine		Eng. omelet	dilate elate
	Eng. lateen (sail)			
	Sp. ladino			
	Eng. Ladino			
	Rhetian ladin			
	Eng. Ladin			(TABLE II)

The IE root *temp*, "to span, spin", leads to Latin *tempus*, "time" (that which is spun by the Fates), used also for "weather", as it still is in the Romance languages. A further Latin extension of the root is *templum*, "temple", a space cut off for the interpretation of omens, which often had to do with time and weather. The time–weather combination ultimately results in English *temper, temperate, temperament, temperance, temperature, distemper, tempest, temporal, temporize, extemporaneous, contemporary*, as well as *tamper* (a variant of *temper*), *tense* (in a grammatical sense, the time denoted by the verb), the Italian *tempo* and *tempera* (paint), the French *contretemps*, the Latin *tempus fugit*, and *pro tempore* (or *pro tem*). One curious extension is Japanese *tempura*, "shrimp fried in batter", from the *Quattuor Tempora*, "four times of the year", "Ember days", of the Portuguese navigators, who called for seafood on those days. *Templum* gives us *temple*, *Templar* and *contemplate* (with *contemplative*, *contemplation*, etc.). Two additional possibilities arise: one is *antenna*, the other is *tempt* (with *temptation*, *attempt*, *contempt*, *tentacle*, *tentative*, even *tent* and *taunt*). Leaving these two out of the reckoning by reason of the uncertainty of the connection, we have:

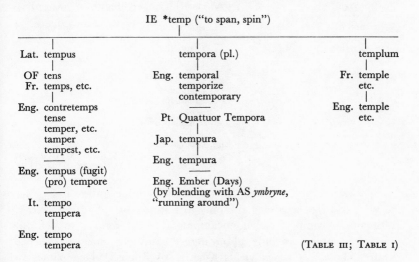

IE *temp ("to span, spin")

Lat. tempus	tempora (pl.)	templum
OF tens	Eng. temporal	Fr. temple
Fr. temps, etc.	temporize	etc.
	contemporary	
Eng. contretemps	————	Eng. temple
tense	Pt. Quattuor Tempora	etc.
temper, etc.		
tamper	Jap. tempura	
tempest, etc.		
————	Eng. tempura	
Eng. tempus (fugit)	————	
(pro) tempore	Eng. Ember (Days)	
————	(by blending with AS *ymbryne*,	
It. tempo	"running around")	
tempera		
Eng. tempo		
tempera		(TABLE III; TABLE I)

The IE root *(s)kand* means "to shine, glow, bright". In Latin, this produces the verb *candeo*, "to glow, gleam white", with such derivatives as *candor*, *candela*, *candidatus* (the one who wears the clean white robe when he runs for political office), and compounds like *candesco*, *incendo*, *accendo* (the last does not get into English, but note the Italian *accendere*, "to light up"). Directly or through French, we get *candid* (with *Candid Camera*), *candidate* and *candidacy*, *candor* (also the French proper name *Candide*, immortalized by Voltaire); also *incense* and *incendiary*, along with *incandescent*. *Candle* was borrowed directly from Latin *candela* by Anglo-Saxon, where it appears as *candel* (note also *candle light*, *candle power*, *Candlemas*). *Candelabrum* and *candelabra* come directly from Latin ("candle lip" is the original meaning). French forms in which *c* before *a* turns to *ch* are responsible for *chandelier*, *chandler*, and aviation's *chandelle*. There is a possible inter-branch relative in the *sandal* of *sandalwood*, which comes from a Greek *sandalon* or *santalon* said to go back to Sanskrit *chandala*, but this relationship is uncertain.

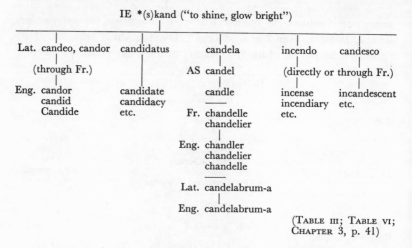

IE *(s)kand ("to shine, glow bright")

Lat. candeo, candor	candidatus		candela	incendo	candesco
(through Fr.)		AS	candel	(directly or through Fr.)	
Eng. candor	candidate		candle	incense	incandescent
candid	candidacy		——	incendiary	etc.
Candide	etc.	Fr.	chandelle	etc.	
			chandelier		
		Eng.	chandler		
			chandelier		
			chandelle		
			——		
		Lat.	candelabrum-a		
		Eng.	candelabrum-a		

(TABLE III; TABLE VI; CHAPTER 3, p. 41)

The IE root **kes* means "to cut, knife". Some authorities prefer to view this root as giving rise only to Latin *castrum*, "cut-off place", ultimately "camp, fortified encampment", and *castro*, "to cut off, castrate"; others include also *castus*, "castrated, purified", hence "pure, chaste". *Castrum* yields a series of English place names in *-caster*, *-cester*, *-chester*, as well as Spanish *alcázar*, which is Latin *castrum* borrowed by the Moors, who prefixed the Arabic article *al-*, turned the word into *al-qasr*, from which the Spaniards made *alcázar* (it is of interest that a seafront drive in Palermo, Sicily, bears the name of *Cassaro*, which is the Arabic *qasr* without the article). A diminutive of *castrum*, *castellum*, becomes *castle* (through Norman-Picard *castel*), *château* (this is from the standard Old French *chastel*), and, through Spanish, *castillo*, whence *Castilla*, "land of castles", and *Castile* (*soap*). Derivatives of the French forms are *castellan*, *châtelain* and *châtelaine*. It is worth noting that the Swiss *chalet* (not *châlet*) is not a diminutive form derived from *chastelet* and *castellittum*, but comes either from an ancient Mediterranean (non-Indo-European) language, or possibly from the root of *casa*, "house" *Castro* gives us *castrate* and *castration*, while *castus*, if it is correct to include it under this root, give rise to *chaste*, *chastity*, *chastisement* and *chastise*, *castigate* and *caste* (the last through Portuguese *casta*, a "pure race or breed"). A derivative is *incest*, with *incestuous*, "that which is impure, unchaste".

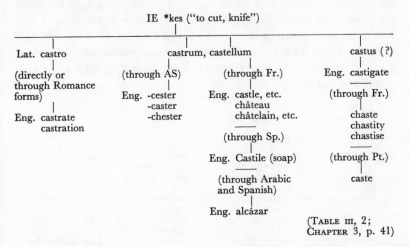

IE **kes* ("to cut, knife")

Lat. castro

(directly or through Romance forms)

Eng. castrate
castration

(through AS)

Eng. -cester
-caster
-chester

castrum, castellum

(through Fr.)

Eng. castle, etc.
château
châtelain, etc.

(through Sp.)

Eng. Castile (soap)

(through Arabic and Spanish)

Eng. alcázar

castus (?)

Eng. castigate

(through Fr.)

chaste
chastity
chastise

(through Pt.)

caste

(Table iii, 2;
Chapter 3, p. 41)

An IE root **kamp*, "bend, edge", gives rise to Latin *campus*, which appears in English as *campus*, *camp* (with numerous compounds, like *camp fire* and *camp follower*), and derivatives of the type of *campaign* and *camping*, as well as *encamp*, *decamp*, and even *scamp* and *scamper*. (The last is variously described as issuing from the Italian *scampare* or the Old French *eschamper*, while *scamp* is a back-formation from *scamper*, "one who runs away from a fight"). There are Italian forms which enter English directly, like *campagna* (the Roman *campagna*), *campo*, and *campo santo* (Italian graveyard, literally "holy field"). The French *champ* goes on to *champagne* (the older form was *champaign*) and *champignon*, "mushroom". Place names abound (*Champagne*, *Campania*, *Champs Elysées*, etc.). It seems likely that German borrowed the Latin word to form *Kampf* and *kämpfen* (*Kulturkampf*, the struggle waged by Bismarck against the Catholic Church). If the assumption of Germanic borrowing from Latin is correct, then the Germanic borrowed *kampjo* gives rise to the French and English *champion* (with *championship*, etc.), and to the Spanish (*Cid*) *Campeador*. A more doubtful connection appears with Celtic *cam*, *camb*, "bent, crooked", which gives rise to

Latin *cambio*, "to change". This goes on to French *change, changer*, and English *change* (*exchange, interchange, changeless*, etc.), while the Italian form *cambio* appears in the antiquated financial terms *cambial, cambist*; the scientific *cambium* is best taken as coming directly from Latin; and *gambit* (the exchange of a pawn for a positional advantage in chess) may also come from this root, though there is also a possibility that it represents the Italian *sgambetto*, the act of tripping someone. At any rate, the Celtic root is best left out of consideration for family tree purposes, while it seems reasonably safe to include the Germanic *Kampf* and *kampjo*.

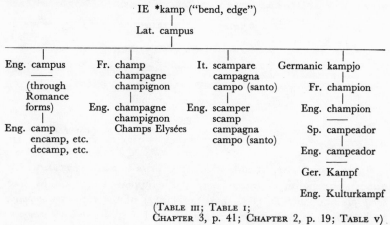

IE **kamp* ("bend, edge")

Lat. campus

Eng. campus	Fr. champ	It. scampare	Germanic kampjo
(through Romance forms)	champagne champignon	campagna campo (santo)	Fr. champion
Eng. camp	Eng. champagne champignon	Eng. scamper	Eng. champion
encamp, etc.	Champs Elysées	scamp	Sp. campeador
decamp, etc.		campagna campo (santo)	Eng. campeador
			Ger. Kampf
			Eng. Kulturkampf

(TABLE III; TABLE I;
CHAPTER 3, p. 41; CHAPTER 2, p. 19; TABLE V)

The IE root **dhē(i)* means "to suck, suckle". In Latin, it gives rise to *femina, fecundus, fetus, felix*, and *filius*, all of which become extremely productive in the Romance languages and English. Inter-branch connections appear in Slavic (Russian) *dyeti*, "children", and *dyeva, dyevitsa, dyevushka*, "girl", and in the doubtful Illyrian or Albanian place name *Dalmatia*, from which we get *Dalmatian* (dog) and *dalmatic*. *Femina* yields, directly or through French, *female* (Fr. *femelle*), *feminine, feminist, effeminate*, etc.; in modern French form we have *femme fatale* and *femme de chambre*, along with the archaic legal *feme covert* and *feme sole*, used to refer to a woman who is married (covered) or unmarried (alone). *Fecundus* becomes *fecund, fecundate*. *Fetus*, "offspring", gives *fetus* and also *effete*, "no longer bearing fruit". *Felix* gives us, in addition to the proper name and to *Arabia Felix* ("fruitful,

ONE-BRANCH FAMILIES

fertile", therefore "happy"), *felicity, felicitate, felicitation, felicitous,* and some opposites prefixed by *in-*. *Filius* and its feminine form *filia* go on to English *filial, affiliate, affiliation,* the Norman-French family name prefix *Fitz-* (*Fitzgerald, Fitzpatrick,* etc., "son of"), such modern literary French forms as *Dumas Fils* (where English would normally use *Junior* or *Younger*), other French forms like *fille de joie* and *fille de chambre,* and the Spanish-derived *hidalgo* (originally *fidalgo, fijo de algo,* "son of something", "nobleman", as opposed to a peasant whose ancestry mattered little).[1]

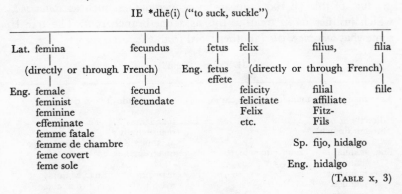

IE *dhē(i) ("to suck, suckle")

Lat.	femina	fecundus		fetus	felix		filius,	filia
	(directly or through French)		Eng.	fetus effete	(directly or through French)			
Eng.	female feminist feminine effeminate femme fatale femme de chambre feme covert feme sole	fecund fecundate			felicity felicitate Felix etc.		filial affiliate Fitz- Fils	fille
						Sp.	fijo, hidalgo	
						Eng.	hidalgo	

(TABLE X, 3)

A very productive one-branch root is IE *mən*, "hand". This, becoming Latin *manus* and later French *main,* gives us a host of words: *manual, manacle, manage, manager* (with *managerial, management*), *emancipate* (with *emancipation, emancipator*), *manicure, manifest, manifesto, maniple, manipulate, manipulation, manipulator, manufacture, manuscript, manumit*. *Manus* plus *do,* "to give", produces *mandate* (that which is given by hand, or into your hands), *mandamus, mandatory,* and *Maundy Thursday* (the Thursday on which the disciples were commanded; Fr. *mandé*). In compounds, *mando* gives rise to *command, commander, commandment,* the Portuguese *commando,* the Afrikaans *commandeer,* as well as to *commend;* also to *demand, amend, remand*. There is *manure,* "that which is spread by hand"; *mansuetude,* from *manu suesco,* "to soothe by hand or stroking", which goes on to *mansuetinus,* which becomes *mastinus* and ultimately *mastiff*. There is *maneuver,* which is

[1] *Filly,* however, comes from a separate Scandinavian source, connected with *foal* and, more remotely, with *pullet, puerile* and the *-putra* of *Brahmaputra*.

French *manoeuvre* from Latin *manu opera*, "works by hand". From *main*, the French descendant of Latin *manus*, we get *maintain* and *maintenance*. There is a learned *amanuensis*, "one who copies manuscripts by hand", and a scientific *quadrumane*, "four-handed animal", such as an ape. There is even the French name of the English Channel, *La Manche*, which is "the Sleeve" (Latin *manica*, "that which comes down to the hand", which also gives rise to the Italian *manicotti*, large, hollow tubes of dough stuffed with cottage cheese, literally "muffs"). As against all these Latin derivatives, the only Germanic product of this IE root appears in proper names, such as *Rosamond*, which justifies us in treating this as a one-branch root. The tree is somewhat *unmanageable* (another word from the same root):

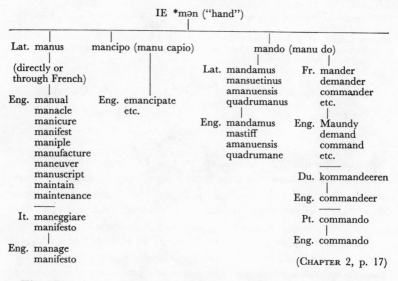

IE *mən ("hand")

Lat. manus	mancipo (manu capio)		mando (manu do)
(directly or through French)		Lat. mandamus mansuetinus amanuensis quadrumanus	Fr. mander demander commander etc.
Eng. manual manacle manicure manifest maniple manufacture maneuver manuscript maintain maintenance	Eng. emancipate etc.	Eng. mandamus mastiff amanuensis quadrumane	Eng. Maundy demand command etc.
			Du. kommandeeren
			Eng. commandeer
It. maneggiare manifesto			Pt. commando
Eng. manage manifesto			Eng. commando

(Chapter 2, p. 17)

The IE root **op*, "work", produces Latin *opus*, with a plural form *opera*, and also Latin *ops*, "might, wealth", with derivatives like *officium* (from *opi-ficium*, "work-doing place"), *opulentus*, *optimus*, *copia* (*cum-ops* or *co-opia*). There are possible, but not assured, links with *Osci*, the name of the Oscans, an Italic group related to the Romans, inhabiting southern and central Italy, and even to *omnis* (if the latter connection is correct, then English descendants of the root would also include *omnipotent*, *omniscient*, *omnipresent*, *omnivorous*, and *omnibus* or bus, whose original meaning is "for everybody"). *Opus* and its plural *opera* give us, in addition to the Latin words themselves, also the diminutive *opuscule*, *operate*, and *operation*, with their derivatives *cooperate*, *operational*, *inoperable*, etc.; the Italian *operetta*; and the Italian-French *opera bouffe*. *Officium* yields *office*, *officer*, *official*, *officialdom*, *officious*, *officiate*, etc. *Opulentus* gives *opulent*, *opulence*. *Optimus* gives us *optimate*, *optimist*, *optimism*, *optimistic*, even *soroptimist*. From *copia* we get *copy*, *copyist*, *copyright*, *copious*. A straight French form that gets into English is *hors d'œuvre*, "out of the main works", something eaten in advance of the main meal; another is *chef d'œuvre*, "masterpiece". *Maneuver* and *manure* represent the French combination of the root of "hand" with that of "work". *Lucubration* may be derived from *luce opero*, "to work in the light", but this is doubtful.

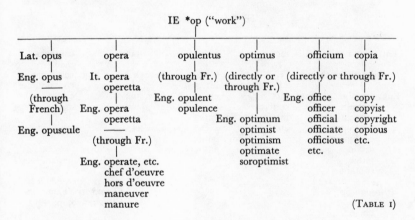

(TABLE I)

An IE root *tag*, "to seize", comes into Latin in the form of the verb *tango*, "to touch". This, with its past participle *tactus*, gives rise to many English forms (note that the shift from *g* to *c* in *ta(n)go*, *tactus* is merely a phenomenon of assimilation due to a desire to avoid the difficult pronunciation of *gt*; *ct* is easier to pronounce). From the *tang-* variant of the Latin root we get *tangible*, *tangent*, *tangential*, and the name of the dance *tango*, which comes from the Spanish verb *tangir*. The participial root *tact-* produces *tact* and its derivatives (*tactile*, *tactual*, *tactless*, *tactful*, *intact*, *contact*, etc.). The Latin *integer*, formed on the root of *tango*, gives on the one hand *integer*, *integrity*, *integral, integrate, integration,* on the other, through its French development, *entire* and *entirety* (see Chapter 3, p. 40). Other formations produce *contiguous* and *contiguity, contingence* and *contingent, contagion* and *contagious.* Another French development comes into English in the form of *attain, attainment, attainder, attaint, contain, retain, detain,* and all their derivatives. *Contaminate* and *contamination* also belong here, while a derivative verb of *tango, taxo* or *taxito,* produces *tax, surtax, taxable, taxation* and even *taxpayer,* as well as *task* and *taskmaster,* in addition to *taste* and all its derivatives (*tasty, tasteful, tasteless, distaste,* etc.). It may be noted in passing that *tact, tax,* and their compounds and derivatives are to be distinguished from words in which the idea of "arrangement" predominates (*syntax, tactics,* etc.); these come from a different root through Greek.

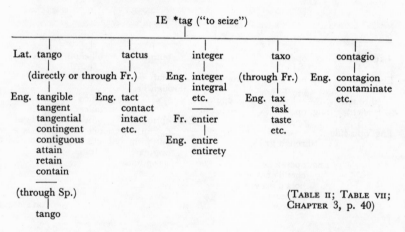

IE *tag ("to seize")

Lat. tango	tactus	Eng. integer	taxo	Eng. contagio
(directly or through Fr.)		integer	(through Fr.)	contagion
Eng. tangible	Eng. tact	integral	Eng. tax	contaminate
tangent	contact	etc.	task	etc.
tangential	intact	Fr. entier	taste	
contingent	etc.		etc.	
contiguous		Eng. entire		
attain		entirety		
retain				
contain				
——				
(through Sp.)				
tango				

(TABLE II; TABLE VII;
CHAPTER 3, p. 40)

The IE root *men* has the general meaning of "to project", later extended to "mountain" (a projection on the landscape). The "projecting" idea leads to that of something that overhangs, impends, threatens. Latin takes this root in two forms, that of the verb *minor,* "to threaten", later extended to include the sense of "to drive along by threats", as of a flock or herd of animals, and that of the noun *mons,* "mountain". From *minor,* generally through French, stem forms like *minatory* and *commination, menace, promenade* (and *prom*), *amenable, demean, demeanor, misdemeanor, eminent, prominent, pre-eminent, imminent,* with their respective nouns and adverbs (note also the legal compound *eminent domain*). Latin *mons,* "mountain", eventually gives rise to *mount* (both noun and verb), *amount, dismount, paramount, tantamount, catamount, surmount, mountain, mountaineer, mountainous, mountebank* (this comes through Italian *montimbanco*), *Mounties* (Royal Northwest Mounted Police), *promontory,* and all those place names in which the idea of "mountain" appears (*Montana; Vermont,* which is Green Mountain", *Montenegro,* which is Italian for "Black Mountain", a translation of the Serbo-Croatian *Crna Gora*; the Spanish *Monterey* and the French *Montréal,* which both mean "King's Mountain"; *Montevideo,* or "mountain saw I" in Magellan's Portuguese; and others too numerous to count). Other tempting connections present themselves for this root, but they are uncertain: the Latin *mentum,* "chin", which gives rise to an English adjective *mental* (not "pertaining to the mind", but "pertaining to the chin"; if this is accepted, we may have links with the Germanic branch, since *mouth* is linked with Latin *mentum*); *mine,* with its derivatives *mineral, miner,* and the German *Minenwerfer,* "mine-thrower"; but *mine* seems more likely to come from a separate Celtic root; lastly, there is *marmot,* which many authorities derive from *mus montanus,* "mountain mouse".

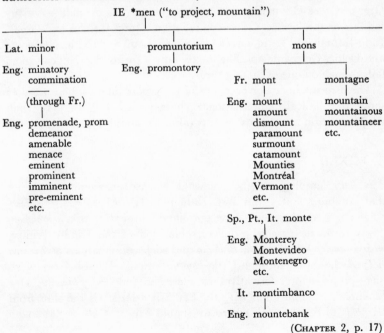

IE *men ("to project, mountain")

Lat. minor
Eng. minatory
   commination

   (through Fr.)

Eng. promenade, prom
   demeanor
   amenable
   menace
   eminent
   prominent
   imminent
   pre-eminent
   etc.

promuntorium
Eng. promontory

mons

Fr. mont
Eng. mount
   amount
   dismount
   paramount
   surmount
   catamount
   Mounties
   Montréal
   Vermont
   etc.

montagne
mountain
mountainous
mountaineer
etc.

Sp., Pt., It. monte
Eng. Monterey
   Montevideo
   Montenegro
   etc.

It. montimbanco
Eng. mountebank

(CHAPTER 2, p. 17)

CHAPTER 5

Two-Branch Families

English vocabulary being mainly compounded of Germanic, Greek, and Latin, it is natural that the most numerous word-families should be combinations of two of these, or all three. Two and three-branch families constitute the majority of our material.

In considering two-branch families, we discover an interesting division that gives a clue to the nature of the English vocabulary, if any were needed. Well over half of such families consist of the Latin-Germanic combination. Of the remainder, about half are Latin-Greek. Greek-Germanic groups account for about half as many families as the former. Other combinations (Indo-Iranian and Greek, Indo-Iranian and Latin, Greek and Slavic, Latin and Celtic, Germanic and Celtic, Germanic and Slavic) are only a sprinkling. None of them fails to include one of the big three.

These sprinklings, however, are of particular interest, because they show the basically international character of English. We shall therefore begin our discussion of two-branch families with them.

A. MIXED

A very simple, though somewhat learned, example of a root that combines Latin and Indo-Iranian is IE *bhlagh(men)*, "priest-magician", which gives on the one hand, through Sanskrit *brahman*, "prayer, divine essence", *Brahma*, chief god of the Hindu Trinity, with *Brahman, Brahmanism, Brahmin* and such combinations as *Brahma bull*; on the other, through Latin *flamen*, "priest", English *flamen*, with such proper-name derivatives as *Flaminius* and *Via Flaminia*. Unexplained, in connection with the Sanskrit *brahman*, is the shift from IE *bhl-* to Sanskrit *br-*, where we should expect **bhl-* or **bhr-* (the

70

interchange of *l* and *r* is common in Sanskrit). The same shift, however, appears in the only other *bhl-* root that is of frequent occurrence in Sanskrit (IE *bhlendh* to Sanskrit *bradhnah*, the root which in Germanic leads to English *blind, blend, blunder, blond*, etc.).

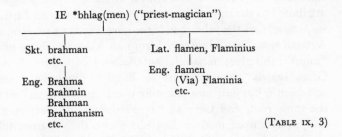

IE *bhlag(men) ("priest-magician")

| Skt. brahman etc. | Lat. flamen, Flaminius |
| Eng. Brahma Brahmin Brahman Brahmanism etc. | Eng. flamen (Via) Flaminia etc. |

(TABLE IX, 3)

The IE root *bhag*, "to divide, cut up, allot", appears in Greek *phagein*, "to eat", from which English derives several combining forms (*-phage, -phagous, -phagy* or *-phagia, phago-*), which appear in words like *anthropophagous, sarcophagus* (originating in *sarkophagos lithos*, "body-eating stone"), *œsophagus* or *esophagus* (combining the Greek roots of "to carry" and "to eat": "that which carries what you eat"), *ichthyophagous, phagocyte*, etc. From the same root, Indo-Iranian Persian derives *baksheesh*, from the Persian verb meaning "to give", and this is passed on to English. It is of interest to note that the same root produces in Slavic the word for "rich" (Russian *bogaty*), the word for "God" (*Bog*), and the Russian "thank you", *spasibo* (*spasi Bog*, "God save (you)". The English two-branch tree is:

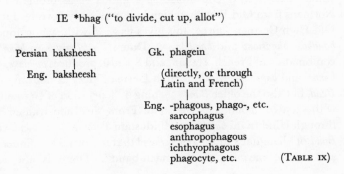

IE *bhag ("to divide, cut up, allot")

Persian baksheesh	Gk. phagein
Eng. baksheesh	(directly, or through Latin and French)
	Eng. -phagous, phago-, etc. sarcophagus esophagus anthropophagous ichthyophagous phagocyte, etc.

(TABLE IX)

Another IE root producing a Persian (Indo-Iranian) word which is borrowed by English is *nebh*, "cloud". Here we have on the one hand Latin *nebula*, with *nebulose, nebulous, nebular*, etc.; *nimbus*; *nubilous* (from *nubes*, a variant of *nebula*); possibly also *imbue* and *Neptune*, with *neptunium*, the name of a chemical element (though *Neptune* is also attributed to the root of *nepos*, "nephew", or given an Etruscan origin in *Nethuns*); on the other hand, we have Persian *naft*, with the earlier Avestan *napta*, possibly derived from an Akkadian form, but meaning "moist"; this gives us *naphtha, naphthalene, naphthol*, etc. There is also a Greek *nephele* which appears in English, along with *nephelite* and *nephelometer*, but only as a scientific word. Anglo-Saxon had *nifol*, from the same root, and German has *Nebel*, but the Germanic form has disappeared from modern English. Slavic derives from this root its word for "sky, heaven" (Russian *nebo*).

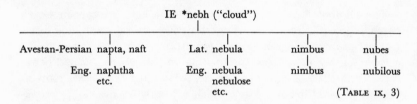

IE *nebh ("cloud")

| Avestan-Persian napta, naft | Lat. nebula | nimbus | nubes |
| Eng. naphtha etc. | Eng. nebula nebulose etc. | nimbus | nubilous |

(TABLE IX, 3)

A combination of which only the Indo-Iranian and Germanic members are beyond question is that of IE *bhendh*, "to bind". Here Anglo-Saxon offers *bindan*, with English *bind, bindery, binder*; *bendan*, which gives *bend* and *bends*; *bonda*, which is crossed with a kindred Old Norse *bōndi* to produce *bond, bondage, bondsman*, etc.; and *bend*, which merges with Old Norse *band* and a *bande* brought in by the Normans from Old French, which had previously borrowed it from an Old High German source; this gives us *band*, with such compounds as *bandbox, bandstand* and *bandwagon*. Dutch *bundel* gives us *bundle*, and a combination of French, Italian, and Spanish produces *bandage, bandolier, banner* and *banderole*. Modern High German gives us not only the Nazi *Bund*, but also the older *Bund* meaning a "federation of German states", with such compounds as *Bundesrat*. From the Indo-Iranian division, through Hindustani *band* and Hindustani-Persian *kamarband*, come the *Bund* of Shanghai and the *cummerbund* that is worn with dinner jackets, and whose meaning is "stomach-band". There is also *bandanna*, representing Hindustani *bāndhnū*, a form of dye. The very doubtful Latin and Greek cognates are on the one hand the *-fendo* of *fend, fence, fender, defend, defensive, offend, offensive,* which most authorities prefer to derive from IE *$g^u hen$*; and the *path-* of *pathos, pathetic, homeopath, allopath, osteopath, sympathy, antipathy, empathy, apathy, pathological,* etc., which is phonologically unsatisfactory, since Greek *p* should come from IE *p*, and IE *bh* should give *ph* in Greek; in addition, there are semantic difficulties.

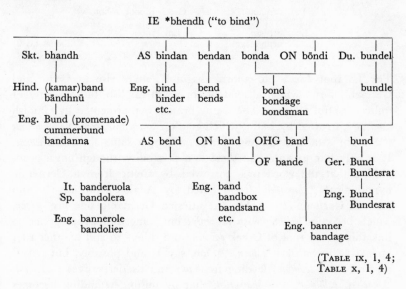

(TABLE IX, 1, 4;
TABLE X, 1, 4)

A Greek-Slavic combination appears in the IE root *orbho*, "orphan, heir". Here, through Greek *orphanos*, we get *orphan* and *orphanage*. In Slavic, the root has numerous developments (Russian *rebyonok, rebyata,* "child", "children"; *rab,* "slave" and *rabota,* "work"). On the basis of the "work" root, a Czech writer, Karol Čapek, formed the word *robot,* a "mechanical man" who works for his more fortunate human counterpart. Since the play was produced in English-speaking countries under the title "R.U.R.", the word *robot* has become part of the English vocabulary. There is also a Latin cognate *orbus,* "deprived of, bereaved", which gives rise to a specialized architectural term, *orb.* It is interesting that although the root appears in Anglo-Saxon and has vast ramifications in modern German (*Arbeit, arbeiten, arm, Erbe*), the Germanic forms disappeared from English. Leaving out of account the highly specialized *orb*, the present-day English picture is therefore:

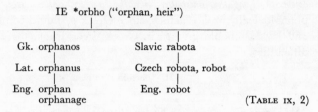

(TABLE IX, 2)

The IE root *kem*, "to adorn, disguise", gives rise to Celtic and Germanic forms which ultimately appear in English, but also present quite doubtful features. The Celtic branch is represented by Gaulish *camisia*, borrowed by Latin, which goes on to *chemise, camisole, camisade* ("a night attack in disguise") and *shimmy*, a slang form of *chemise*. It is only fair to state that there is a possibility, though not a probability, that the word was borrowed by Celtic from a Germanic hypothetical *khamithja* (represented by Anglo-Saxon *hemethe* and modern German *Hemd*). On the attested Germanic side are *heofon*, which becomes *heaven* (with *heavenly*; but some authorities prefer to link this to the root of Greek *camera*, and others to still another root appearing in Sanskrit *aśman*, "stone, sky"); and possibly, but not at all probably, *scamian*, leading to *shame* and its derivatives (*shameful, shameless, ashamed*, and *shamefast*, that by misunderstanding becomes *shamefaced*).

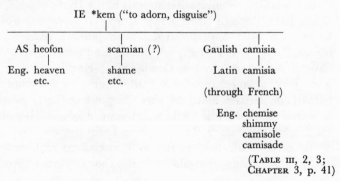

(TABLE III, 2, 3;
CHAPTER 3, p. 41)

The IE root *reidh, "to go, be in motion", produces on the Celtic side the Gaulish (ve)rēdus (possibly from an earlier *(wo)rēdos), which comes into Latin in the form veredus, and, being given a Greek prefix para-, turns into paraveredus, developed by French into palefroi and transferred to English as palfrey (through the fall of unstressed syllables, paraveredus, borrowed by German, turns into Pferd). On the Germanic side, Anglo-Saxon has rād, rīdan and (ge)rǣde, which in English become road (with its many compounds: roadbed, roadblock, roadhouse, etc.), ride (with rider), and ready (with readiness, readily, already, etc.). Raid, with raider, is a Scottish development of road, perhaps with some Scandinavian influence.

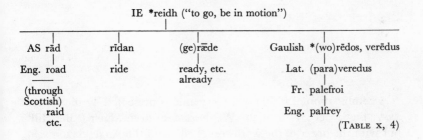

IE *reidh ("to go, be in motion")

AS rād	rīdan	(ge)rǣde	Gaulish *(wo)rēdos, verēdus
Eng. road	ride	ready, etc.	Lat. (para)veredus
		already	Fr. palefroi
(through Scottish)			Eng. palfrey
raid			
etc.			(TABLE X, 4)

In the case of the IE root *gᵘ̯er, "to raise one's voice, praise", we have on the one hand the Celtic word for "poet" (Irish bard, Welsh bardd, Gaulish bardo-), adopted by English as bard; on the other, an entire series of words coming from the Latin gratia, gratus and their derivatives. These, entering English directly or through French, give us grace, gracious, graceful, graceless, grateful, gratitude, ingrate, ingratitude; disgrace and disgraceful; ingratiate and ingratiating; gratify and gratification; gratis, gratuity, gratuitous; congratulate and congratulation, with other derivatives. Through Spanish we receive gracias and gracioso.

The French *bon gré, mal gré,* "willingly or unwillingly", is occasionally used in an English context, though in italics.

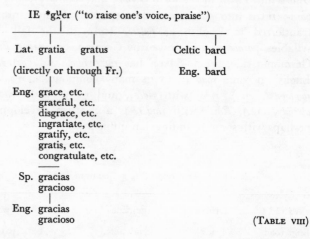

IE *$g\underset{.}{u}er$ ("to raise one's voice, praise")

Lat. gratia gratus	Celtic bard
(directly or through Fr.)	Eng. bard
Eng. grace, etc.	
grateful, etc.	
disgrace, etc.	
ingratiate, etc.	
gratify, etc.	
gratis, etc.	
congratulate, etc.	

Sp. gracias
gracioso

Eng. gracias
gracioso

(TABLE VIII)

A combination of Celtic and Germanic is presented by the IE root *$m\bar{e}$, "big". Here we have the Welsh *mawr* of Bryn Mawr ("Big Hill", but with the order of the words reversed), and the Anglo-Saxon *māra, mǣsst,* that turn into English *more* (with *moreover*) and *most* (with such derivatives as *mostly* and *foremost*); it may be mentioned in passing that the *r* of the Welsh *mawr* and that of Anglo-Saxon *māra* do not stem from the same source, and do not form part of the root. Other Celtic connections provide French with *maint*, German with *Märchen* (in addition to *mehr* and *meist*), along with proper names ending in *-mar* (*Volkmar, Waldemar*), and Slavic with the *-mir* of *Vladimir*. There is a possible, perhaps probable, connection with the root of Latin *magis, magnus,* Indo-Iranian *maha-* of *maharajah,* Greek *megas,* which supply us with *master, mister, megacycle,* and numerous other words (see pp. 225-227).

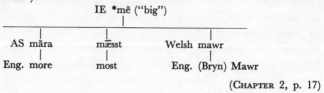

IE *$m\bar{e}$ ("big")

AS māra	mǣsst	Welsh mawr
Eng. more	most	Eng. (Bryn) Mawr

(CHAPTER 2, p. 17)

The root *kleu, "to hear", produces *clueo, inclitus* and *inclutus* in Latin, but none of these pass on into English. Nor does the Greek *klyo.* The Germanic forms appear in Anglo-Saxon *hlūd,* leading to *loud, loudness, loud-mouthed, loudspeaker,* etc.; and *hlyst, hlystan,* which become *list* and *listen.* In addition, the Germanic root with initial *hl-* (*hlūtha*) appears in Old High German personal names of the type of *Hlothwīg,* later *Ludwig* and *Louis* (with *louis d'or, Louise, Lulu, Louisiana, Heloise, St. Louis,* etc., and variants like *Lewis*); and *Hlothachar* or *Lothaire,* from which we get the name of the French *Lorraine* (*Lotharingia,* the land of Lothaire), and proper names such as *Lothario, Luther* (with *Lutheran, Lutheranism,* etc.). The Slavic branch, which turns initial *k* of IE into *s* under certain circumstances, gives us *slovo,* "word", from which come *Slovak, Slovene*; and *slava,* "glory", which gives not only *Slavic, Slavonic, Yugoslavia, Jaroslav, Vyacheslav,* etc., but also, owing to the medieval Frankish and Venetian practice of conducting slave raids on the Slavic lands and impressing into servitude people who called themselves by the name of "glorious", the Italian *schiavo* and the French *esclave,* which in English become *slave,* with *slavery, slavish, slavey, slave-driver,* etc. It is of interest that the same root in Slavic also produces a word that means "to hear" or "to listen" (Russian *slyshat', slushat'*).

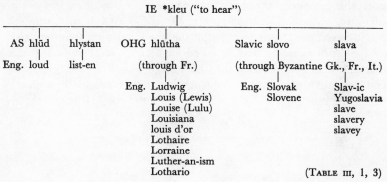

IE *kleu ("to hear")

AS hlūd	hlystan	OHG hlūtha	Slavic slovo	slava
Eng. loud	list-en	(through Fr.)	(through Byzantine Gk., Fr., It.)	
		Eng. Ludwig	Eng. Slovak	Slav-ic
		Louis (Lewis)	Slovene	Yugoslavia
		Louise (Lulu)		slave
		Louisiana		slavery
		louis d'or		slavey
		Lothaire		
		Lorraine		
		Luther-an-ism		
		Lothario	(TABLE III, 1, 3)	

B. GREEK-GERMANIC

Combinations of Germanic and Greek are the least numerous of the two-branch groups in which the big three alone appear. One that presents some doubtful features is the IE root *dhē,* described as "a child word for an older family member". This is said to have given us the native *dad, daddy*, with such compounds as *daddy longlegs* and the very modern *daddy-o* (the first recorded appearance of *dad* in English is 1500). According to some, but not all, authorities, the same root produces Greek *Thetis* (from an earlier *Tethis*), and *theios*, which eventually gives us the Spanish *tío, tía* (*Tía Juana*) and the Italian *zio, zia* (Greek *theios*, however, could also come from the root of *theos*, "god", and mean "god-given"). Slavic words for "grandfather" and "uncle" (Russian *dyadya, dyed*) are also claimed to come from this root, along with Gothic *atta* and Sanskrit *attas*, "father". To the extent that we can claim the Spanish and Italian forms on the ground of literary and place-name appearances, we have:

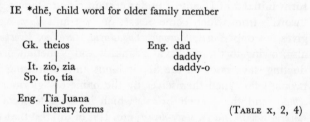

IE *dhē, child word for older family member

Gk. theios	Eng. dad
	daddy
It. zio, zia	daddy-o
Sp. tío, tía	
Eng. Tía Juana	
literary forms	

(TABLE X, 2, 4)

Another Greek-Germanic combination, concerning which there is no doubt, is supplied by the IE root *gwĕna*, "woman". On the Greek side, this produces the *gyne* that appears in *gynecology, gynecaeum, misogynist, philogynist, androgynous*, etc. On the Germanic side, through Anglo-Saxon *cwēn, cwēne*, we get on the one hand *queen* (with *queenly*), on the other *quean*, an archaic word for "harlot, slut, wench" (these semantic changes whereby the same word acquires both glorifying and pejorative meanings in the same language occasionally appear). The same root produces the Slavic word for "wife" (Russian *zhena*).

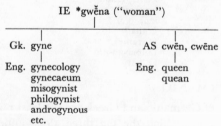

IE *gwĕna ("woman")

Gk. gyne	AS cwēn, cwēne
Eng. gynecology	Eng. queen
gynecaeum	quean
misogynist	
philogynist	
androgynous	
etc.	

(TABLE VIII, 3, 5: The Greek root should have *b* instead of *g*. The form *bana* appears in some Greek dialects. The shift from *b* to *g* is attributed to a crossing with the root of *gignomai*, "to be born".)

An IE root *sek^{u}, "to notice, see", gives on the one hand Greek *thespesios, "divinity-proclaimed, seer, soothsayer", which appears in the Greek proper name of *Thespis*, father of the Greek drama, from which comes the English *Thespian*. On the Germanic side, the root gives rise to the forms of both *see* and *say*. The Anglo-Saxon ancestor of *say* (with formations like *saying* and *say-so*) is *secgan*, which has as its hypothetical ancestor a Germanic form *sagja* or *sagwja* (see Chapter 3, p. 35). Connected with it are *sagu*, which Anglo-Saxon appears to have borrowed from Old Norse, and which becomes *saw* (in the sense of "proverb, saying"); and *saga*, taken directly from Scandinavian by modern English. For *see* (with *seer, unforeseen*, etc.) there is a Gothic prototype *saihwan* (see Chapter 3, p. 34); the Anglo-Saxon form is *sēon*, with a derivative *gesiht*, which becomes *sight* (with *sightless, unsightly, sight unseen*, etc.; German *Gesicht* is closer to the original Anglo-Saxon than modern English *sight*). There is also the German form *auf Wiedersehen*, which appears in English dictionaries.

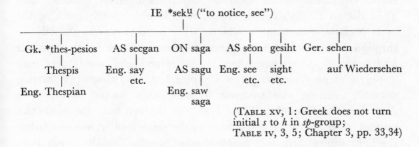

IE *sek^{u} ("to notice, see")

Gk. *thes-pesios	AS secgan	ON saga	AS sēon	gesiht	Ger. sehen
Thespis	Eng. say etc.	AS sagu	Eng. see etc.	sight etc.	auf Wiedersehen
Eng. Thespian		Eng. saw saga			

(TABLE XV, 1: Greek does not turn initial *s* to *h* in *sp*-group; TABLE IV, 3, 5; Chapter 3, pp. 33,34)

The IE root *sreu*, "to flow", in Greek changes its initial *s* to a rough breathing which is the equivalent of *h* (although the transcription of Greek *r* with rough breathing is *rh*, the value is *hr*), and gives rise to *rhein*, "to flow", which is at the bottom of such forms as *rheumatism, rheumatoid, rheumatic, rhythm* (which leads to *rhyme* or *rime*), *rhythmic, catarrh, diarrhea, hemorrhoid, logorrhea*, etc., as well as the *rheo-* of *rheostat* and other scientific and technological words. On the Germanic side, we have *stream* with its various compounds (*streamer, streamline*, etc.), stemming from Anglo-Saxon *strēam*, along with the Dutch-derived *maelstrom* (for the Germanic insertion of *t* between *s* and *r* to facilitate the pronunciation, see Chapter 3, p. 33). There are also interesting Slavic forms, such as the Struma River of Bulgaria and the word for "island", appearing in Rubinstein's "*Kamennoi Ostrov*" ("Stony Island").

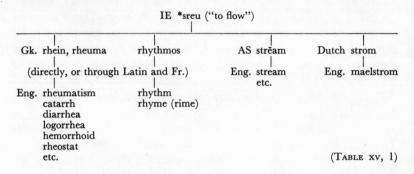

IE *sreu ("to flow")

Gk. rhein, rheuma	rhythmos	AS strēam	Dutch strom
(directly, or through Latin and Fr.)		Eng. stream	Eng. maelstrom
Eng. rheumatism	rhythm	etc.	
catarrh	rhyme (rime)		
diarrhea			
logorrhea			
hemorrhoid			
rheostat			
etc.			(TABLE XV, 1)

One of the several IE roots that mean "to shine, gleam", *bhā, enters Germanic in the form of Anglo-Saxon *bēacen, bēacnian*, and gives rise to English *beacon, beckon, beck*. It also enters Greek as the verb *phainein*, "to shine", which, with its derivatives, directly or through Latin and French, gives us *phase, emphasis* (with *emphasize* and *emphatic*), *phenomenon*, then an entire series of words that may appear with *ph, f*, or even *p* (see Chapter 3, p. 37): *phantasy* or *fantasia, fantastic, fantasque, phantasmagoria, phantom, fancy, fanciful, fancier* (with *fancy dress* and *fancy-free*). There is *phaeton*, derived from the name of a mythological character going back to the same root; *diaphanous* (what the light shines through); *Epiphany* (the "display" of the newly born Christ; also the *theophany*, "God-showing", that becomes *tiffany*, a light gauze, and the Italian *Befana*, the old woman whose name comes from *Epiphania* and who brings presents to the Italian children after the fashion of the Nordic Santa Claus). *Hierophant* and *sycophant* both contain this root ("showing what is sacred" and "showing figs", or "flattering"). *Pharos*, the name of the ancient Alexandrian lighthouse which was one of the seven wonders of the world, comes from this root. So does the verb *pant*, from Old French *panteier* which is derived from a Vulgar Latin modification of the Greek root, borrowed, seemingly, at an early period. There is *photo-*, "light", with all its derivatives (*photograph, photographer, photographic, photogenic, photofilm, photo-engraving, photo-offset*, the *photon* which is the unit of light, *photostat*, *photosynthesis*, etc.). There are *phosphate*, *phosphorus*, *phosphorescent*, *phosgene*, as well as *phenol*, *phenyl*, *pheno-barbitol*, *phenacetin*, and many other scientific terms.

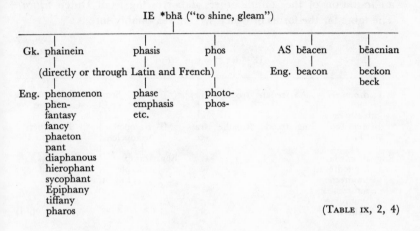

IE *bhā ("to shine, gleam")

Gk. phainein	phasis	phos	AS bēacen	bēacnian
(directly or through Latin and French)			Eng. beacon	beckon
				beck
Eng. phenomenon	phase	photo-		
phen-	emphasis	phos-		
fantasy	etc.			
fancy				
phaeton				
pant				
diaphanous				
hierophant				
sycophant				
Epiphany				
tiffany				
pharos				

(TABLE IX, 2, 4)

The IE root *der*, "to run, tread", produces on the one hand Greek *dromos*, "road", from which we derive *dromedary* (a "running" camel; the term is applied to the one-humped North African variety), as well as *prodrome*, *syndrome*, *palindrome*, *hippodrome*, *airdrome*. It also seems to be at the root of the name of the Drave River of Yugoslavia, through an Illyrian (Albanian) development, but since this is a place name and has doubtful features, it is best to exclude it from our count of branches. On the Germanic side, there is an entire series of words beginning with *tr-*, which come into English from numerous Germanic sources. Anglo-Saxon has *tredan*, *tredel*, from which come *tread* and *treadle*, along with *træppe* and *træppan* from which we get *trap* (with *trap-door*, *trap-shooting*, etc.). *Tramp* and *trample* have as their immediate ancestor a Middle English *trampen*, *trampelen*, with no known Anglo-Saxon progenitor; but one must have existed, as indicated by the corroborating evidence of the Gothic *trumpan*. *Trade*, with *trader*, *tradesman*, *trade-mark* and *trade name*, *trade union* and *trade wind*, are variously described as coming from Low German or from Norse. *Trip*, with *trippet* and *triphammer*, comes from Old French *triper* which in turn goes back to a Germanic source. *Trot* comes from French, which borrows it from Old High German *trottōn*. There is some doubt concerning *troll*, in the sense of "dwarf" (if it belongs here, it would come from Norse), and *trill* (from Italian *trillo*, which some claim is an imitation of the sound, others a borrowing from Dutch *trillen*). The table for the forms of which we are reasonably sure is:

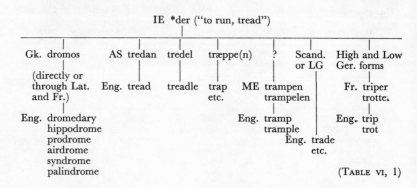

IE *der ("to run, tread")

Gk. dromos	AS tredan	tredel	træppe(n)	?	Scand. or LG	High and Low Ger. forms
(directly or through Lat. and Fr.)	Eng. tread	treadle	trap etc.	ME trampen trampelen		Fr. triper trotte.
Eng. dromedary hippodrome prodrome airdrome syndrome palindrome				Eng. tramp trample Eng. trade etc.		Eng. trip trot

(TABLE VI, 1)

The IE root *gerebh*, "to scratch", produces on the Germanic side a verb which appears in Anglo-Saxon as *ceorfan*, ultimately giving us *carve* and *carving*; and also a noun *crabba*, which turns into *crab* (with *crab apple*, *crab grass*, etc., as well as *craps*, the dice game, formerly *crabs*). This same Germanic noun, assuming in Old High German the form *chrebiz*, passes into French, which turns it into *écrevisse*, "shrimp", which then comes into English and becomes *crayfish* through a misunderstanding of the last part of the word (this is known as popular etymology). On the Greek side, the root produces *graphein*, "to write", and *gramma*, "a writing". The former gives us a long series of words: *graph*, *graphic*, *graphite*, *epigraph*, *telegraph*, *photograph*, *graphology*, etc.; while *gramma* goes on to *gram*, *epigram*, *anagram*, *telegram*, *program* or *programme*, *gramophone*, and many other words of the same type. It also becomes *grammar* ("the art of writing"), *grammatical*, *grammarian*, and, through a special Scottish development of the archaic *gramarye*, which meant "magic" (to the medieval mind, anyone who knew how to write was a magician, and most incantations came in written form), it becomes *glamor*, "that which casts a spell over you", with its modern derivatives *glamorous* and *glamorize*. Lastly, a derivative of the *graph* root, *graphion*, "a stylus for writing", then "a grafting-knife", turns into *graft*, both in its horticultural sense and in its modern semi-slang connotation of "money illegally obtained".

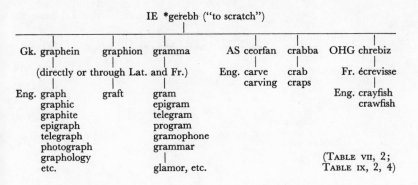

IE *gerebh ("to scratch")

Gk. graphein	graphion	gramma		AS ceorfan	crabba	OHG chrebiz
(directly or through Lat. and Fr.)				Eng. carve	crab	Fr. écrevisse
				carving	craps	
Eng. graph	graft	gram				Eng. crayfish
graphic		epigram				crawfish
graphite		telegram				
epigraph		program				
telegraph		gramophone				
photograph		grammar				
graphology						(TABLE VII, 2;
etc.		glamor, etc.				TABLE IX, 2, 4)

There is an IE root *werg*, with a variant *wreg*, which means "to work, do". On the Germanic side, this gives rise to Anglo-Saxon *wyrcan* and *weorc*, which turn into *work*, both noun and verb (with compounds and derivatives such as *handiwork, worker, workless, workshop, workday, workmanship*); also to *wrecan*, which becomes *wreak*; to the *wrohte* which is the past tense of *wyrcan*, and becomes *wrought*; and to the *wryhta* that gives us *wright* and its derivatives (*shipwright, cartwright, playwright, wheelwright, wainwright*, etc.). From Low German *bolwerk*, English imports *bulwark*; French, taking the same Low German word, converts it into *boulevard* (the original Paris boulevards were built along the lines of ancient fortifications which were demolished as the city expanded), and this is also imported into English. On the Greek side, the root produces the *erg-, org-* root which is at the bottom of *erg, ergon, energy, energetic*, etc., and of *organ* with its numerous derivatives (*organic, organism, organist, organize, disorganize, reorganize, organization, organizer*, etc.). There are also *orgy* and *orgiastic*. *Orgasm*, however, is best taken as coming from another root meaning "to swell". Through the French *chirurgien* ("hand-worker"), English derives an archaic *chirurgeon* and a modern *surgeon, surgery, surgical,* etc.

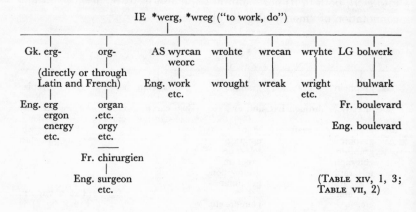

IE *werg, *wreg ("to work, do")

Gk. erg-	org-	AS wyrcan weorc	wrohte	wrecan	wryhte	LG bolwerk
(directly or through Latin and French)		Eng. work etc.	wrought	wreak	wright etc.	bulwark
Eng. erg ergon energy etc.	organ .etc. orgy etc.					Fr. boulevard
						Eng. boulevard

Fr. chirurgien

Eng. surgeon
etc.

(TABLE XIV, 1, 3;
TABLE VII, 2)

The IE *$g^u elbh$ root means "womb", and, by later extensions, "cub". In Germanic, this produces Anglo-Saxon *cealf* and *cealfian,* which become English *calf* and the verb *calve* (the irregularities in AS *cealf,* where we should expect *cwealb,* seem due to a crossing with another related root, *gelbh,* meaning "to bunch up"; ·the *f* and *v* of *cealf* and *cealve* are special Anglo-Saxon developments from an earlier *b* in certain positions; see Chapter 3, p. 33). On the Greek side, there is *adelphos,* "from the same womb, brother", which gives us such place names as *Adelphi* and *Philadelphia* (with *Philadelphia lawyer*), and by a series of somewhat far-fetched imageries, the *delphis* that gives rise on the one hand to *delphinium,* on the other to *dolphin* and *Dauphin* (there is a linguistic-historical mystery in the fact that the name of the dolphin should have been selected to denote the heir to the French throne in the fourteenth century; the best guess is that this usage started as a nickname, based not so much on the dolphin as on the fact that Latin *delphinus, delfinus,* had been in use for perhaps as long as ten centuries as a proper name for individuals; with the two French phonetic tendencies to change *el* to *al* and to turn *l* after a vowel and before a consonant to *u,* (see Chapter 3, p. 40), *Delphinus* became *Dalphinus,* then *Daulphin,* finally *Dauphin*; English, receiving the word at the *Daulphin* stage, when *au* was beginning to be pronounced *o,* turned it into *dolphin*). The name of the Greek city of *Delphoi* (Delphi), seat of the worship of Apollo and the most famous oracle of antiquity, also belongs to this root, and from it we get *Delphic* and *Delphian*. The name of the constellation *Delphinus* seems to go back to the *dolphin*. A Celtic connection appears possible in the personal name *Galba*, "fat man", but this appears in English only as a proper name.

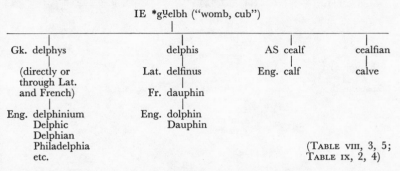

IE *gʷelbh ("womb, cub")

Gk. delphys	delphis	AS cealf	cealfian
(directly or through Lat. and French)	Lat. delfinus	Eng. calf	calve
	Fr. dauphin		
Eng. delphinium Delphic Delphian Philadelphia etc.	Eng. dolphin Dauphin	(TABLE VIII, 3, 5; TABLE IX, 2, 4)	

The *ghrēi* root means "to smear, spread, rub". Here Germanic produces Anglo-Saxon *grindan*, *grīst*, which become English *grind* (*grindstone*) and *grist*. There is a possibility of connection with *grīma*, "spectre", and *grislic*, which go on to *grim*, *grime*, *grisly*; also, through Old High German and French (*grommeler*), with *grumble* and *grumpy*; through another French connection, with *chagrin*; and through Spanish *grimazo*, with *grimace*; but these are all uncertain. Greek *chrisma*, "ointment", produces a series of derivatives, many of which find their way into Anglo-Saxon with the early Christian missionaries: *crisma*, *Crist*, *Cristmas*, *cristnian*, *cristen*, *cristendōm*, which give rise respectively to *chrism*, *Christ* ("the anointed One", "the Messiah"), *Christmas* ("Christ's Mass"), *christen*, *Christian*, *Christendom*. Later English additions include *Christianity*, *Christianize*, *Antichrist*, *Christian Science*, and, through the use of the root in a Norwegian personal and place name, the *Christiania turn* of skiing. There is also *criss-cross*, which was originally *Christ's Cross*. Most authorities hold that *cretin* and *cretinism*, terms first arising in the French Alps, are deformations of the word *Christian*, used in the sense of "human being"; a minority opinion is that *cretin* comes from *creta*, "chalk", and refers to the chalky complexion of people affected by cretinism. Through a possible crossing with Gaulish *crama*, *chrisma* also gives rise to French *crème* and English *cream*, with such derivatives as *creamy* and *creamery*. The tree, with only sure forms, is:

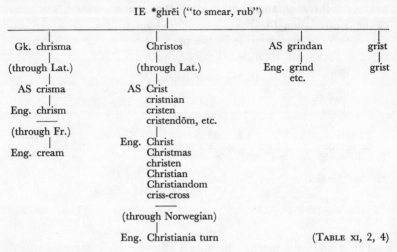

IE *ghrēi ("to smear, rub")

Gk. chrisma	Christos	AS grindan	grist
(through Lat.)	(through Lat.)	Eng. grind	grist
AS crisma	AS Crist	etc.	
Eng. chrism	cristnian		
	cristen		
(through Fr.)	cristendōm, etc.		
Eng. cream	Eng. Christ		
	Christmas		
	christen		
	Christian		
	Christiandom		
	criss-cross		

(through Norwegian)

Eng. Christiania turn   (TABLE XI, 2, 4)

C. GREEK-LATIN

Greek-Latin combinations, while not nearly so numerous as the Latin-Germanic, are nevertheless the second largest assortment of two-branch families. To begin with an extremely simple one, the IE root *serp*, "to creep", goes on in Greek to *herpein*, from which we get the zoological *herpetology*, "the study of snakes", while in Latin it becomes *serpo*, leading to *serpent* and *serpentine*. If the Latin root can be resolved into *se* + *repo* (another verb that means "to creep, crawl") then we would also have from *repo* such forms as *reptile*, *reptilian*. Since the Latin root appears in practically identical form in Indo-Iranian, it was one of the observations made by Sassetti in the fifteenth century that Italian *serpe* and Sanskrit *sarpas* seemed to point to a relationship between the two languages.

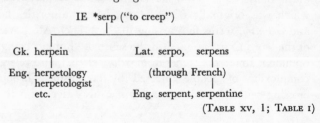

IE *serp ("to creep")

Gk. herpein	Lat. serpo, serpens
Eng. herpetology	(through French)
herpetologist	
etc.	Eng. serpent, serpentine

(TABLE XV, 1; TABLE I)

The IE root *wem, "to vomit, spit", produces on the Greek side *emein*, "to vomit", which eventually reaches us in the form *emetic*, "a preparation that induces vomiting". In Latin, it produces *vomo*, "to vomit", which we inherit in the forms *vomit, vomitive, vomitory*, and in the Latin *vomitorium*, "the passageway in circuses through which the audience could be spewed out into the open when the performance was over", as well as in medical terms such as *nux vomica*.

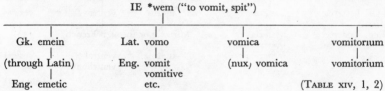

IE *wem ("to vomit, spit")

Gk. emein	Lat. vomo	vomica	vomitorium
(through Latin)	Eng. vomit vomitive	(nux) vomica	vomitorium
Eng. emetic	etc.		(TABLE XIV, 1, 2)

An IE root *swep "to sleep", produces in Greek the *hyp-nos* that later gives us *hypnotism, hypnosis, hypnotize*, etc. On the Latin side, it produces *sopor*, which gives us *soporific* and *soporiferous*, and, through an extension *sompn-, somn-*, the *somnus* which eventually appears in English *somnolent, somnolence, somnambulist, somniferous, insomnia, insomniac*. The root appears also in Germanic, and produces in Anglo-Saxon a form *swefen*, "to sleep, dream", which later becomes English *sweven*; but since this is archaic, we shall exclude it from our tree.

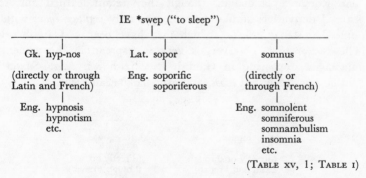

IE *swep ("to sleep")

Gk. hyp-nos	Lat. sopor	somnus
(directly or through Latin and French)	Eng. soporific soporiferous	(directly or through French)
Eng. hypnosis hypnotism etc.		Eng. somnolent somniferous somnambulism insomnia etc.
		(TABLE XV, 1; TABLE I)

One Greek-Latin combination which presents some phonological difficulties is the hypothetical *udero* or *udtero*, "belly", which, with various supposed insertions, produces the Greek *hysteros*, "hindmost", from which comes the expression *hysteron proteron*, "hindmost first, the cart before the horse", and also the noun *hystera*, "womb", from which are derived, by scientific formation, *hysteria, hysterical, hysterectomy* and similar words. In Latin, the root yields *uterus*, "womb", which, with *uterine*, passes into English; also, through what seems to be a derivative form **wendri*, with nasal infix, *venter*, "belly", which gives us *ventral* and *ventriloquist*. *Vesica*, the Latin word for "bladder", is also claimed for this root, and it gives us *vesical* and other scientific formations.

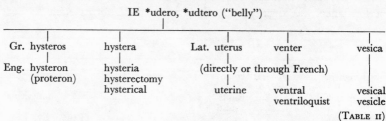

IE **udero, *udtero* ("belly")

Gr. hysteros	hystera	Lat. uterus	venter	vesica
Eng. hysteron (proteron)	hysteria hysterectomy hysterical	(directly or through French) uterine	ventral ventriloquist	vesical vesicle

(TABLE II)

The IE root **ekwos*, "horse", produces in Greek *hippos*, which appears in *hippopotamus* ("river horse"), *hippodrome, hipparch, hippogryph*, and in proper names (*Philip*, "horse-lover"; *Hippocrates*, from which we get the *Hippocratic oath* of the physicians; *Hippolytus, Hippomenes*, etc.). There is also *eohippus*, "dawn horse", the tiny ancestor of the modern horse. The Latin form is *equus*, which appears in *equestrian*, the French feminine *equestrienne, equine, equitation, Equites* (the Roman social class of people able to supply their own horses for war service). The Romance languages, though they retain learned and semi-learned derivatives similar to ours, generally replace *equus* with the somewhat slangy *caballus*, which may have been of Gaulish origin. The **ekwos* root, however, is very widespread in the ancient IE languages, appearing in Gaulish *epos*, Irish *ech*, Anglo-Saxon *eoh*, Gothic *aihwa*, Sanskrit *aśvas*, and even Tokharian *yakwe*.

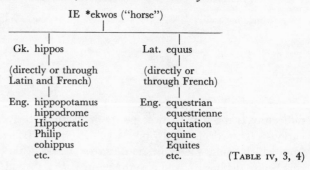

IE **ekwos* ("horse")

Gk. hippos	Lat. equus
(directly or through Latin and French)	(directly or through French)
Eng. hippopotamus hippodrome Hippocratic Philip eohippus etc.	Eng. equestrian equestrienne equitation equine Equites etc.

(TABLE IV, 3, 4)

The IE root *del, "to split", produces in Greek the proper name *Daedalus* ("worked with art") and probably *deltos*, "writing tablet", from which we get *deltiology*, "the collection and study of post-cards". On the Latin side, it produces *dolor*, "grief", which gives us *dolorous*, *dole* (in the sense of "sorrow", not of "city relief"), *doleful*, *condole*, *condolence*, the proper name *Dolores* (through Spanish: *los Dolores de Nuestra Señora*, "the sorrows of Our Lady"); and the scientific *dol*, the unit of pain.

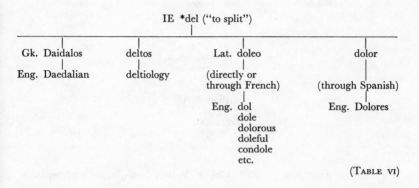

IE *del ("to split")

Gk. Daidalos	deltos	Lat. doleo	dolor
Eng. Daedalian	deltiology	(directly or through French)	(through Spanish)
		Eng. dol dole dolorous doleful condole etc.	Eng. Dolores

(TABLE VI)

The IE root *aw or *awēi, "to become aware, notice", gives rise to the Greek verb *aio*, "to hear", which forms the initial part of *aisthanesthai*, "to perceive", and *aisthetes*, "a person of keen perception", from which we ultimately get *esthete*, *esthetic*, *esthetics*, *anesthesia*, *anesthetic*, *anesthetist*, etc. In Latin, the root produces *audio*, "to hear", from which we derive the TV term *audio*, along with such compounds as *audience*, *audit*, *auditor*, *audition*, *audible*, *auditorium*, and negative forms like *inaudible*, coming either directly or through French. In Anglo-French form are the legal *oyez* and *court of oyer and terminer*, from the Anglo-French *oyer* (modern French *ouir*), which is a popular French development of Latin *audire*. A Latin compound of *audio*, *oboedio*, gives rise to *obey*, *obedient*, *obedience*, with negatives in *dis-*, as well as to *obeisance*, with definitely French form. A possible Indo-Iranian relative may be *Avesta*, the sacred book of the Persians

(*Avistāk* from *āvišya*, "public, well-known, evident"), but since it is both doubtful and a proper name, we shall omit it from our tree.

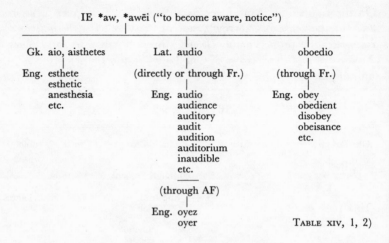

IE *aw, *awēi ("to become aware, notice")

Gk. aio, aisthetes	Lat. audio	oboedio
Eng. esthete esthetic anesthesia etc.	(directly or through Fr.) Eng. audio audience auditory audit audition auditorium inaudible etc.	(through Fr.) Eng. obey obedient disobey obeisance etc.

(through AF)

Eng. oyez
oyer

TABLE XIV, 1, 2)

From the IE *sēmi*, "half", Greek derives *hemi-*, which appears in numerous English compounds, largely of a scientific nature (*hemiplegia, hemistich*), but also *hemisphere* and *hemicrania*, which in French becomes *migraine*, and passes on to English in both forms, adding the quaint and archaic *megrim* (the *-crania* part of *hemicrania* represents Greek *kranion*, Latin *cranium*, "skull"; the literal meaning is "a headache on one side of the head"). The Latin development is *semi-*, which appears in English in very numerous compounds (*semiautomatic, semi-centennial, semicolon, semi-circular, semi-quaver, semivowel, semitone*, etc.); note, however, that *semester* is from the root of *sex*, "six"; "a six-month period". It is disguised in *sesqui-* (elliptical for *unus semisque*, "one and a half"), which appears in *sesquicentennial, sesquipedalian* ("a foot and a half long"); and in Latin *sestertius* ("two and a half" *asses*; literally, "half-third", or half-way between two and three), which appears in English either in Latin form or as *sesterce*, and its derivative *sestertium*, originally *sestertiorum* (*milia*), "thousands of *sestertii*". If the same root appears in *simplex*, which seems contradicted by the semantics, then *simple, simplify, simplicity*, etc., would also belong to this family.

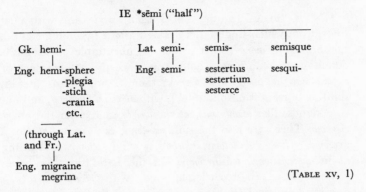

IE *sēmi ("half")

Gk. hemi-	Lat. semi-	semis-	semisque
Eng. hemi-sphere	Eng. semi-	sestertius	sesqui-
-plegia		sestertium	
-stich		sesterce	
-crania			
etc.			

(through Lat.
and Fr.)

Eng. migraine
megrim

(TABLE XV, 1)

The IE root *nek*, "death", produces in Greek a *nekro-* root that gives us *necromancy, necropolis, necrosis, necrology, necrophilia,* etc., as well as *nektar* (*nectar,* "a death-dispelling drink", to be used only by the immortal gods, with its modern derivative *nectarine*). On the Latin side, we have *neco,* "to kill", with such English descendants as *pernicious, internecine,* and with a French term *noyade,* a "collective drowning" that took place at Nantes during the French Revolution, from the French verb *noyer,* "to drown, to kill by drowning", which is the direct descendant of *necare.* We also have *noceo,* "to harm", giving us negative forms like *innocent, innocence, innocuous,* and even *ninny* (from an *innocent,* '*ninnocent*). *Nuisance* is a French development formed on the root of the French verb *nuire,* the direct descendant of Latin *nocere.* There is doubt as to whether *obnoxious* represents the root of *noceo* or that of *nancior, nanciscor,* "to find, run across", but *noxious* is clearly from *noxa,* "harm", a derivative of *noceo.*

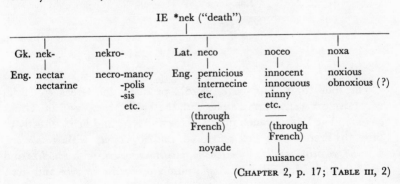

IE *nek ("death")

Gk. nek-	nekro-	Lat. neco	noceo	noxa
Eng. nectar	necro-mancy	Eng. pernicious	innocent	noxious
nectarine	-polis	internecine	innocuous	obnoxious (?)
	-sis	etc.	ninny	
	etc.		etc.	
		(through French)	(through French)	
		noyade	nuisance	

(CHAPTER 2, p. 17; TABLE III, 2)

IE *tem, "to cut", produces in Greek a verb *temnein*, with a participle *tomos*, from which English derives *tmesis*, *tome* (a "volume cut off from the others"), *atom* ("that which is uncuttable", "indivisible"; a definition that no longer holds true since the achievement of *atomic fission*, which, using first Greek, then Latin, means literally "the splitting of what is unsplittable"), with *atomize, atomizer,* and numerous compounds, like *atomic pile, atomic weight,* and even the abbreviated *A-bomb.* There are also the suffixes *-tomy,* or *-tome* a "cutting", as in *anatomy, epitome, dichotomy, phlebotomy;* and *-ectomy,* a "cutting out", as in *appendectomy, tonsillectomy.* On the Latin side, we have *tondeo,* "to cut, shear" (past participle *tonsus*), with *tonsure* and *tonsorial,* and possibly *tonsil* (in Latin, the original meaning of *tonsilla* is "a seabird" or "a mooring-spike"). More probable are *esteem* (*aes-timare,* "to cut off or evaluate or price brass"), with *estimate, estimation,* the modern and somewhat slangy *guesstimate,* and even the proper name *Esme,* occasionally used in British aristocratic circles (Old French *esmé,* "esteemed", from Latin *aestimatus*); also *contempt, contemptuous* and *contemptible* (from the Latin compound *contemno; contumacious* and *contumely* are more doubtful).

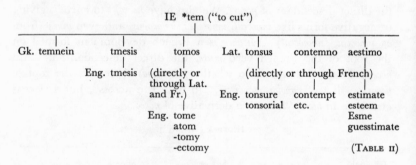

IE *tem ("to cut")

Gk. temnein	tmesis	tomos	Lat. tonsus	contemno	aestimo
	Eng. tmesis	(directly or through Lat. and Fr.)	(directly or through French)		
			Eng. tonsure tonsorial	contempt etc.	estimate
		Eng. tome atom -tomy -ectomy			esteem Esme guesstimate

(TABLE II)

The root *wekʷ,* "to speak, word", produces the Greek *epos* from which we get *epos* and *epic,* along with the French *épopée* and the Greek *epopoiia.* The Latin branch produces *vox* and *voco,* and here, directly or through French, we get *voice* and *voiceless, vocal,* with *vocabulary, vocalism, vocalist, vocalize, vocalization, vociferous; vowel,* with *vowelize* and *vowel point; vouch, voucher, vouchsafe;* numerous forms in *-voke* and *-voc-,* like *convoke, revoke, evoke, provoke, invocation, provocation, equivocation, equivocal, advocate, avocation, vocation, irrevocable,* and the French *agent provocateur*; also *avow* and *avowal,* and the Latin *vox populi.* Not belonging to this family despite its appearance is *invoice,* which comes from Old French *envois,* "sendings", from *envoyer,* "to send", which goes back to the root of Latin *via (inviare,* "to put on its way").

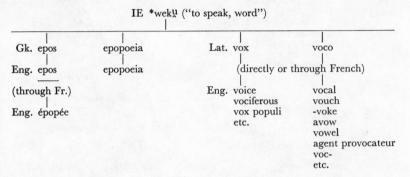

IE *wekụ ("to speak, word")

Gk. epos	epopoeia	Lat. vox	voco
Eng. epos	epopoeia	(directly or through French)	
(through Fr.)		Eng. voice	vocal
Eng. épopée		vociferous	vouch
		vox populi	-voke
		etc.	avow
			vowel
			agent provocateur
			voc-
			etc.

(TABLE XIV, 1, 2; TABLE IV, 3)

The IE root *weik,* "house", is a borderline case in this division, since in addition to Greek and Latin developments there is also a Germanic one, which appears in a place-name suffix and possibly, but not surely, in a noun of nationality. In Greek, the form is *oikia,* "house", from which we get *economy* and its group (*economist, economic, economize, economics*), as well as *ecology.* In compound form, we have *ecumenical, diocese, diocesan, parochial* and *parochialism, parish* and *parishioner* (through French *paroisse*). The Latin *vicus,* "village", and *villa,* "country estate", produce on the one hand *vicinage* and *vicinity,* on the other *villa, villain,* and *villein, villeinage, village, villager, ville, villainous, villainy,* and the Italian *villanella,* which we also have in French form, *villanelle.* It is interesting to note the semantic shift in *villein,* "serf", which in French becomes *vilain,* "ugly", and in English *villain,* "bad man". On the Germanic side, we have the Gothic *weihs,* "village", and the Anglo-Saxon *wic,* which leads to many place names ending in *-wick* or *-wich* (*Warwick, Greenwich*). The doubtful element comes in the Old Norse *vīkingr*, properly "inlet dweller", which produces *Viking*. The tree, for the assured Greek and Latin members, is:

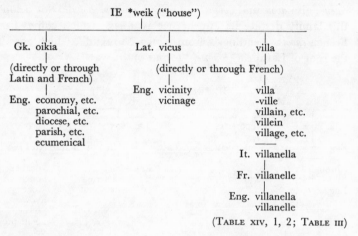

IE *weik ("house")

Gk. oikia	Lat. vicus	villa
(directly or through Latin and French)	(directly or through French)	
Eng. economy, etc. parochial, etc. diocese, etc. parish, etc. ecumenical	Eng. vicinity vicinage	villa -ville villain, etc. villein village, etc.

It. villanella

Fr. villanelle

Eng. villanella villanelle

(TABLE XIV, 1, 2; TABLE III)

A root *tel*, "to raise, carry", produces in Greek the verb *tlenai*, "to uphold, bear", with ramifications that appear in *Atlas* (the mythological character who bore the world on his shoulders), from which we get *atlas*, *Atlantic*, *Atlantis*; *Tantalus*, who gives us *tantalize* and *tantalum* (a chemical element); probably also *Atalanta* and *Anatolia* ("the rising of the stars"); the *talanton* from which we get *talent*, both as a coin and as "native genius"; and the *telonion* or *tolonion*, "tax", which becomes *toloneum* in Vulgar Latin, passes into Anglo-Saxon as *toll* (with *toll road*, *toll gate*, etc.), and into German as *Zoll*, with *Zollverein*, or "customs union", that finds its way into English dictionaries. In Latin the root takes two forms, that of *tollo*, "to raise" (*extol*, *tolerate*, *tolerance*, *toleration*, *tolerant*, *tolerable*, with negatives in *in-*), and, with metathesis (interchange of position of two consonants in one word), that of the past participle, *latus*, of the verb *fero*, "to bear". Forms from *latus* appear in numerous English compounds and derivatives (*superlative*, *translation*, *collation*, *ablative*, *dilatory*, *elation*, *legislation*, *oblation*, *prelate*, *prelacy*, *relate*, and even *delay*, which is the Old French outcome, *delaier*, of Latin *de-lat-are*. The same IE root passes from Sanskrit *tulā* into some of the Far Eastern, non-Indo-European tongues, and probably, but not surely, gives rise to *tael*. Germanic forms appear in Anglo-Saxon *tholian* and *tholl*, English *thole* of *tholepin*, but the verb is obsolete and the noun appears only in specialized nautical parlance, which permits us to exclude it from our tree.

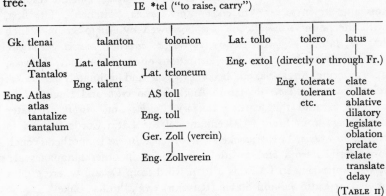

IE *tel ("to raise, carry")

Gk. tlenai	talanton	tolonion	Lat. tollo	tolero	latus
Atlas	Lat. talentum	,Lat. teloneum	Eng. extol (directly or through Fr.)		
Tantalos	Eng. talent	AS toll		Eng. tolerate	elate
Eng. Atlas		Eng. toll		tolerant	collate
atlas		Ger. Zoll (verein)		etc.	ablative
tantalize		Eng. Zollverein			dilatory
tantalum					legislate
					oblation
					prelate
					relate
					translate
					delay

(TABLE II)

The IE root *ost(h)*, "bone", produces on the Greek side the *osteo-* from which English gets *osteon, osteopath, osteomyelitis* and other scientific terms. A derivative of *osteon, ostrakon*, originally "shell, bony substance", later "tablet, tile" used in voting, gives us *ostracism, ostracize*, but is also borrowed by Latin in the form *ostrea*, which becomes Old French *oistre* (modern French *huître*) and English *oyster* (with *oyster bed oysterettes*, etc.). There is also *astragalus*, used in the sense of "die, gaming device", which passes into English as a physiological term. On the Latin side, we have, with loss of the final *-t* of the root, *os* (genitive *ossis*), "bone", leading to *ossature, osselet, osseous, ossification, ossify, ossuary, ossein*, etc. *Ossifraga*, "bone-breaker", the name of a type of hawk, comes into English in double form, *ossifrage*, and, through French *orfraie*, *osprey*.

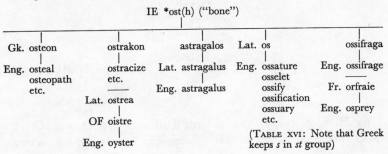

IE *ost(h) ("bone")

Gk. osteon	ostrakon	astragalos	Lat. os	ossifraga
Eng. osteal	ostracize	Lat. astragalus	Eng. ossature	Eng. ossifrage
osteopath	etc.		osselet	————
etc.	————	Eng. astragalus	ossify	Fr. orfraie
	Lat. ostrea		ossification	
	OF oistre		ossuary	Eng. osprey
	Eng. oyster		etc.	

(TABLE XVI: Note that Greek keeps *s* in *st* group)

IE *pek$\underset{\sim}{u}$, "to cook". appears in Greek forms that give us *pepo*, *pepto-* and *pepsin*, with formations like *peptone* and *Pepsi-Cola*. On the Latin side, there is an assimilation of *pek$\underset{\sim}{u}$ to *k$\underset{\sim}{u}$ek$\underset{\sim}{u}$, and the result of this appears in *coqueo*, "to cook" and *coquina*, "kitchen". The first, with the noun *coquus*, "cook", is borrowed by Anglo-Saxon, which has *cōc*, later *cook* (with *cookery*, *cook-book*; *decoction*, *concoct*, *precocious*, "before it is cooked", are later formations on the Latin root). *Coquina*, also entering Anglo-Saxon, becomes *cycene* and ultimately *kitchen*. A related word, *culina*, turns into Anglo-Saxon *cylen* and English *kiln*, as well as into the learned *culinary*. *Cuisine* and *biscuit* are later borrowings from French descendants of the Latin words (*coquina* to *cuisine*, *bis-coctum*, "twice cooked", to *biscuit*). *Bisque* is another French form derived from *biscuit*. Interesting forms in other languages are *popina*, appearing in Latin as a loan word from Oscan, where *p* does service for Latin *qu*, and Slavic (Russian) *pech'*, "to fry, bake".

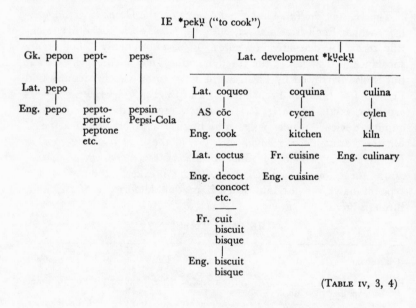

IE *pek$\underset{\sim}{u}$ ("to cook")

Gk. pepon	pept-	peps-	Lat. development *k$\underset{\sim}{u}$ek$\underset{\sim}{u}$		
Lat. pepo			Lat. coqueo	coquina	culina
Eng. pepo	pepto- peptic peptone etc.	pepsin Pepsi-Cola	AS cōc	cycen	cylen
			Eng. cook	kitchen	kiln
			Lat. coctus	Fr. cuisine	Eng. culinary
			Eng. decoct concoct etc.	Eng. cuisine	
			Fr. cuit biscuit bisque		
			Eng. biscuit bisque		

(TABLE IV, 3, 4)

The IE root *poti-s*, "house-lord, husband", appears in Greek *despotes* (analyzed as *dams-potis*, "house-lord"), from which we get *despot, despotism, despotic*, etc. In Latin, the adjective *potis* is compounded with the verb *esse*, "to be", to produce *posse*, "to be able, have power over". The two Latin root-forms, *poss-* and *pot-*, appear in the *posse (comitatus)* of Western stories, *possible, impossible, possibility,* etc.; in the French-derived *puissant* and *puissance*; in *potent, potency, impotent, omnipotent, potential, potentiality, plenipotentiary*; in *power, powerful, powerless* (the last are immediately derived from French *pouvoir*). *Possideo*, a compound of *pot-* and *sedeo*, "to sit in power", gives us *possess, possession, dispossess, possessive*, etc. The compound *compos (cum + pot-)* gives us the legal *compos mentis*, "in possession of one's mental powers". The Latin *potestas*, "power", appears in the Italian *podestà*, "mayor". The *pot-* root also appears in *hospes* (genitive *hospitis*), where it combines with the "guest"-root into **ghosti-pots*, and this comes out in *hospital, hospitality, hospitable, hotel*, etc. The only Germanic possibility, and it is a very doubtful one, is *fad*, which most authorities derive from other sources (Gothic, however, had *bruthfaths*, "the one who has power over the bride, the bridegroom").

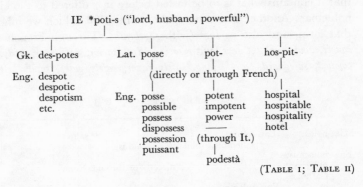

IE *poti-s ("lord, husband, powerful")

Gk. des-potes	Lat. posse	pot-	hos-pit-
Eng. despot despotic despotism etc.	Eng. posse possible possess dispossess possession puissant	(directly or through French) potent impotent power —— (through It.) podestà	hospital hospitable hospitality hotel

(Table i; Table ii)

An IE root **solo*, "whole, complete", assumes in Greek the form *holo-* which we have in numerous compounds (*holocaust, holograph, Catholic* and its derivatives *Catholicism, Catholicity*, etc., in which *holo-* is preceded by the preposition *kata*, "down, along"; "down-whole, down the line, universal"). In Latin, the main formations stem from two forms, *sollus* and *salus*. From the former, Latin forms *sollemnis* ("for the whole year", therefore "solemn"), with *solemn, solemnity, solemnize*, etc.; possibly, but not surely, *sollers*, leading to *solertious;*

sollicitus, "wholly or violently moved", with *solicit, solicitation, solicitous, solicitor, solicitude*, and, through French development, *souci, sans souci, insouciant, insouciance*; with an extension, *solidus*, from which we derive *solid, solidity, solidify, solidarity, console, consolidate*, and even the British *consols (consolidated annuities)*, a type of government bond. But *solidus* was used in Roman times as the name of a coin, which has come down into the Romance languages as *soldo, sueldo, sou*. The man hired to fight in the army was a *soldatus (soldato, soldado, soldat)* or a *soldarius* (Old French *soldier*, appearing in English as *soldier*, with *soldierly, soldiery*, etc.). The verb *solidare*, "to make solid", leads to *solder*. *Salus*, "health, safety, salvation", leads to *salubrious, salutary, salute, salutation, salutatory*, and, in Latin form, *salus populi suprema lex esto*, ("let the safety of the people be the supreme law"). It is probable that the name of Sallust also comes from this root. The adjective *salvus*, from *salus*, leads to *salvation, salvable, salvage, salve, salvo* (this through Italian *salva*, a firing of guns in greeting), with such side formations as *Salvation Army*. A *salver* is originally a *saver*, in the sense that it contains what is to be tasted before it is offered to the king or nobleman. Another derivative is the plant *salvia*, which we inherit in that form, and also as *sage* (with *sagebrush*). Through French *salver, sauver, sauf*, we get *save*, with *savings* and *savior, safe* and *safety, safe-conduct, safeguard, safe-keeping, safety razor, safety valve, safety belt*, etc.

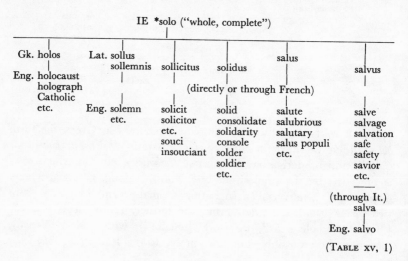

IE *solo ("whole, complete")

Gk. holos	Lat. sollus			salus	
Eng. holocaust	sollemnis	sollicitus	solidus		salvus
holograph			(directly or through French)		
Catholic					
etc.	Eng. solemn	solicit	solid	salute	salve
	etc.	solicitor	consolidate	salubrious	salvage
		etc.	solidarity	salutary	salvation
		souci	console	salus populi	safe
		insouciant	solder	etc.	safety
			soldier		savior
			etc.		etc.

(through It.)
salva

Eng. salvo

(TABLE XV, 1)

The IE root *dek* means "to take up, honor, fit, be convenient". It assumes several distinct forms both in Greek (*doxa*, "opinion, glory, praise"; *dogma*, "thought"; *didaskein*, "to teach") and in Latin (*decet*, "it is fitting"; *decus*, "ornament"; *doceo*, "to teach"; *disco*, "to learn"; *dignus*, "worthy"; *dexter*, "right", as opposed to "left"). In both languages, forms that have *g* instead of *c* or *k* owe it to assimilation by a following nasal consonant. *Doxa* leads to *doxology, paradox, orthodox, heterodox* and similar forms and derivatives (*paradoxical, orthodoxy*). *Didaskein* leads to *didactic*. Stemming from *dogma* are *dogmatic, dogmatism*, etc. Latin *decet* and *decus* produce *decent, indecent, decency, decorum, decorate, decorous, decorator, decoration, decorative*, etc., while a French descendant appears in *décor*. *Doceo* gives us *docile* ("teachable, easy to teach"), *docility*, as well as *doctor* (originally "teacher") with its many derivatives (*doctoral, doctorate*, etc.). It also leads to *doctrine* ("that which is taught"), with *doctrinal, indoctrinate*, etc. A *document* is something that serves to teach or show, and here we have *documentary, documentation*, etc. *Disco* leads to *disciple* (appearing in Anglo-Saxon in the form *discipul*), and also *discipline, disciplinary*, etc. *Dignus* gives us *dignity, indignity, indignant, indignation, dignify, dignitary*;

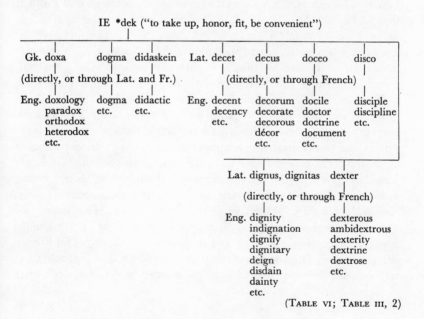

IE *dek ("to take up, honor, fit, be convenient")

Gk. doxa	dogma	didaskein	Lat. decet	decus	doceo	disco
(directly, or through Lat. and Fr.)			(directly, or through French)			
Eng. doxology	dogma	didactic	Eng. decent	decorum	docile	disciple
paradox	etc.	etc.	decency	decorate	doctor	discipline
orthodox			etc.	decorous	doctrine	etc.
heterodox				décor	document	
etc.				etc.	etc.	

Lat. dignus, dignitas　　dexter

(directly, or through French)

Eng. dignity	dexterous
indignation	ambidextrous
dignify	dexterity
dignitary	dextrine
deign	dextrose
disdain	etc.
dainty	
etc.	

(TABLE VI; TABLE III, 2)

in French development, it also gives us *deign, disdain, disdainful,* and even *dainty* (the story behind this is curious: *dignitas,* "dignity", was used in Low Latin as a euphemism for "testicles", the "dignity" of the male; the testicles of a stag were considered the choicest morsel, a "dainty"; the noun ultimately turned into an adjective in English, with the meaning of "choice, refined, delicate"). *Dexter* gives us *dexterity, dexterous, ambidextrous,* and even *dextrine* and *dextrose.* The **dek* root was productive in Germanic, with a Gothic *taihswa,* a modern German *Zeche,* "reckoning, bill", and an Anglo-Saxon *teohh* and *teohhian,* but the Anglo-Saxon forms did not survive. There is even an Indo-Iranian relative in *Deccan* or *Dekkan,* the southern region of India, which gets its name from Sanskrit *dahśina,* "right", transferred to mean "south" (the south is on your right hand as you face east to pray). But since this place name gives rise to no common noun, it will be best to exclude it from our tree.

A two branch family with vast ramifications in Greek and Latin is that of IE **dō, *də,* "to give". In Greek it produces the verb *didomi* and the nouns *dosis,* "a giving", and *doron,* "gift". The first gives us *dose, dosage.* From the participial stem of *didomi, dotos,* we get the *-dote* of *antidote* and *anecdote* (the latter literally means "not given out, unpublished, one you haven't heard yet"). *Doron* appears in such first names as *Theodore* and *Dorothea* or *Dorothy* (both mean "God's gift"), as well as *Isidore* ("the gift of Isis"). On the Latin side, we have the verb *do,* "to give", with a past participle *datus* and a very large number of compounds which appear in Latin itself; an extension of *do* in the form of *dono*; and the noun *dos* (genitive *dotis*), "dowry". The last gives us the French-derived *dot* and *dotal, dowry, endow, endowment, dowager. Dono* gives us *donate, donation, donative, donor, condone, condonation, pardon, pardonable, impardonable.* The participial *datum,* with a plural *data,* and often appearing as *-ditum* in compounds, gives us *datum, data, dative, die* and its plural *dice* (through Old French *dé,* from *datum,* "that which is given or allotted by fate"); it also gives us *date* (the Romans used to describe a letter as *data,* "given", on a certain day); with *date* go *dateless, date line, predate, postdate,* even the teenagers' *to date.* Through *-ditum* forms, we get *extradite, extradition; recondite; edit, edition, editor, editorial; perdition; add, addition, additional, addend, addendum, additive; tradition, traditional,* with less learned French forms *treason* (*trahison,* from Latin *traditionem*), *treasonable, traitor* (French *traître* from Latin *traditor*), *traitorous, betray, betrayer, betrayal; vend* (Latin *vendo,* "to sell", is formed from *venum-do,* "to give in sale", the first element being the same one we find in *venal, venality*), with *vendition, vender, vending machine; render, surrender, rendition* (Latin *reddo,* "to give back", acquires a nasal infix as it passes into French *rendre*), also *rent* (French *rente,* from Latin *reddita,* "that which is returned, a return on an investment"), with *rental, rentable, renter* and the straight French *rentier,* "one who lives on the return of investments"; *abscond* (*abs-,* "away from", and *condo,* "with-give", or "offer"), which in French development gives us *sconce* and *ensconce.* Slavic forms include the Russian *blagodaryu,* "I give blessings, thank you", and the participial *dana,* sometimes used in English as a first or family name.

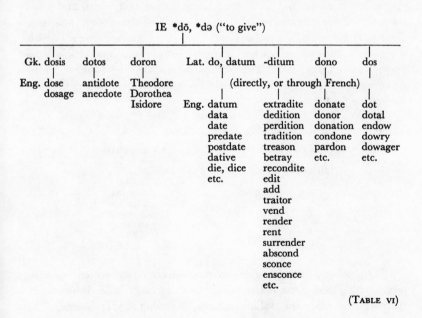

IE *dō, *də ("to give")

Gk. dosis	dotos	doron	Lat. do, datum	-ditum	dono	dos
Eng. dose	antidote	Theodore	(directly, or through French)			
dosage	anecdote	Dorothea				
		Isidore	Eng. datum	extradite	donate	dot
			data	dedition	donor	dotal
			date	perdition	donation	endow
			predate	tradition	condone	dowry
			postdate	treason	pardon	dowager
			dative	betray	etc.	etc.
			die, dice	recondite		
			etc.	edit		
				add		
				traitor		
				vend		
				render		
				rent		
				surrender		
				abscond		
				sconce		
				ensconce		
				etc.		

(TABLE VI)

D. LATIN-GERMANIC

Latin-Germanic combinations form the most numerous group of English word-families. This is quite natural, since we have on the one hand our basic Anglo-Saxon, reinforced by the Scandinavian of the Danes, plus a fair number of Frankish (Old High German) words (brought in by the French-speaking Normans) which had acquired French citizenship before the Norman conquest of England, plus a few German, Dutch, and Scandinavian words borrowed by English at a later period; on the other hand, Latin words borrowed by the Anglo-Saxons, French words imported by the Normans and at all later periods, and Latin words of a learned nature appropriated by English scholars from the early Renaissance onward, plus independent borrowings from the other Romance languages (Italian, Spanish, Portuguese).

To begin with some of the simple and obvious Latin-Germanic combinations, there is the IE root *peisk, "fish", which appears in Anglo-Saxon as *fisc* and *fiscian* (the latter if used as a verb), and gives us *fish* and its derivatives and compounds (*fishy, fishery, fisherman, fishmonger, fish story*, etc.). In Latin, the root produces *piscis*, which gives us a number of rather learned forms (*piscatorial, piscine*, the constellation *Pisces*, etc.). The French *poisson*, derived from a diminutive form of *piscis, piscionem*, made no headway whatsoever against the native *fish*.

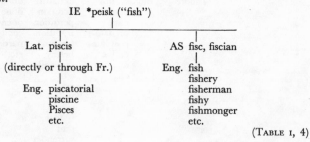

IE *peisk ("fish")

Lat. piscis   AS fisc, fiscian
(directly or through Fr.)   Eng. fish
                                                fishery
Eng. piscatorial   fisherman
     piscine   fishy
     Pisces   fishmonger
     etc.   etc.

(TABLE I, 4)

IE *(s)poimno, "foam", gives in Anglo-Saxon *fām*, which leads to *foam* (with *foamy, foam rubber*, etc.). On the Latin side, it produces *spuma* (*spume, spumy*, the Italian *spumante*, "foaming or sparkling wine") ; also *pumex*, which becomes *pumice*.

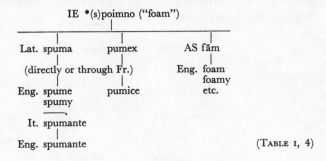

IE *(s)poimno ("foam")

Lat. spuma	pumex	AS fām
(directly or through Fr.)		Eng. foam
Eng. spume	pumice	foamy
spumy		etc.

It. spumante

Eng. spumante

(TABLE I, 4)

An extremely simple IE root is that of *ghdhyes*, or *ghyes*, "yester-day" (in Greek it produces *chthes*). In Latin, the more simple variant produces *hesi* which becomes *heri*, by reason of the change of *s* between vowels, to *r*, normal in Latin. The adjective *hesternus*, "of yesterday", gives us a little-used *hesternal*. In Anglo-Saxon, the root produces *geostra* and *gioster-dæg*, which become *yester* (with *yesteryear*, etc.) and *yesterday*.

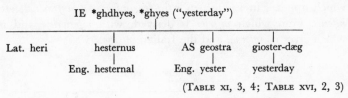

IE *ghdhyes, *ghyes ("yesterday")

Lat. heri	hesternus	AS geostra	gioster-dæg
	Eng. hesternal	Eng. yester	yesterday

(TABLE XI, 3, 4; TABLE XVI, 2, 3)

The root *nokʷt*, "night", produces in Anglo-Saxon *neaht*, *niht*, leading to English *night* and its many compounds: *nightly*, *midnight*, *benighted*, *nightcap*, *nighthawk*, *nightingale* ("night singer", with the *-gale* part coming from the same root as *yell*), *nightmare*, *nightwalker*, *nightshade*, *night club*, *night owl*, etc. The Latin form is *nox* (root *noct-*), and here, in addition to the name of the night goddess *Nox*, we have *nocturne*, *nocturnal*, *equinox*, *equinoctial*, *noctule* (a learned name for the bat). The Greek form is *nykt-*, and it appears in *nycteris* (another learned name for the bat), *nyctophobia* ("fear of the night"), etc.

But since these terms are learned, we may be justified in treating our tree as a two-branch one.

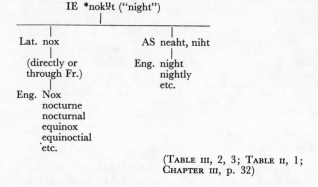

IE *nok*u*t ("night")

Lat. nox	AS neaht, niht
(directly or through Fr.)	Eng. night nightly etc.
Eng. Nox nocturne nocturnal equinox equinoctial etc.	

(TABLE III, 2, 3; TABLE II, 1; CHAPTER III, p. 32)

From the IE root *ṇdhos* or, by extension, *ṇdheri*, "under", Anglo-Saxon obtains *under* (*undaro* in Gothic), which gives us compounds too numerous to list (*underneath, understand, underhand, underwrite, underclothes,* abbreviated to *undies,* are only a few). Latin gets *infra,* which appears in English in *infra-red, infracostal, infrarenal,* etc.; and *inferus,* from which *inferior* is derived, with *inferiority,* and *infernus,* which gives us *infernal* and the Italian *inferno.*

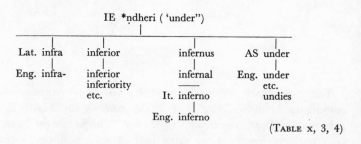

IE *ṇdheri ('under")

Lat. infra	inferior	infernus	AS under
Eng. infra-	inferior inferiority etc.	infernal ——— It. inferno	Eng. under etc. undies
		Eng. inferno	

(TABLE X, 3, 4)

The root *swer,* "to speak", produces Anglo-Saxon *swerian* and *and-swaru* ("against-swear"), which give us *swear, answer, answerable,* etc. The Latin form appears in *sermo* (*sermon, sermonize, Sermon on the Mount*). If there is a link between *sermo* and *series* (but this is doubtful), then we have another line of descendants including *series, serial, serialization, sort, sorcerer, sortilege, assort, consort, resort, assert, desert, dissertation, exert, insert,* etc.

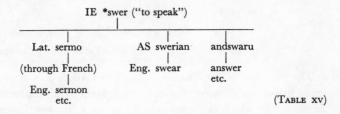

IE *swer ("to speak")

Lat. sermo	AS swerian	andswaru
(through French)	Eng. swear	answer etc.
Eng. sermon etc.		

(TABLE XV)

The root *ar(ə), "plow, to plow", becomes the Latin *aro,* "to plow", from which we get *arable.* With an extension, it produces Anglo-Saxon *earth, ierth,* leading to *earth,* with *unearth, earthen, earthenware, earthquake, earthly, earth-bound, earth-worm, earthling,* etc. In the Dutch form *aard,* the Germanic root appears in *aardvark* and *aardwolf,* the first of which (literally "earth-pig") is from the Afrikaans of the South African Boers.

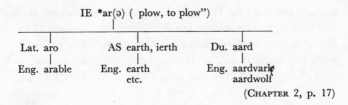

IE *ar(ə) (plow, to plow")

| Lat. aro | AS earth, ierth | Du. aard |
| Eng. arable | Eng. earth etc. | Eng. aardvark aardwolf |

(CHAPTER 2, p. 17)

A case in which there is some reasonable doubt is that of the IE root *genu,* "chin", which in Anglo-Saxon produces *cinn,* later palatalized into *chin* (compare the German *Kinn*). In Latin, the root yields *gena,* "jaw", with a derivative *genuinus (dens),* "jaw-tooth", from which we get *genuine.* The doubt lies in the semantics. *Genuinus* in Latin is used in the combination described above, but also in the sense of "genuine"; hence some authorities prefer to take the two identical forms separately, and derive the one meaning "genuine" either from the root of *genu,* "knee" (see p. 155), or from that of *genus,* "kind, sort, species". If the *genuinus* that develops into *genuine* is from *gena*, the tree is:

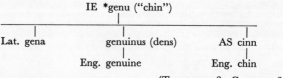

IE *genu ("chin")

Lat. gena	genuinus (dens)	AS cinn
	Eng. genuine	Eng. chin

(TABLE VII, 2; CHAPTER 2, p. 17)

The root *erə* or *rē*, "to row", produces Anglo-Saxon *rōwan*, which leads to *row* (with *rower, rowboat*, etc.), and, by an extension, Anglo-Saxon *rōthor*, which becomes *rudder*. On the Latin side is *remus*, "oar", appearing in *bireme* and *trireme*, Roman ships with two and three banks of oars.

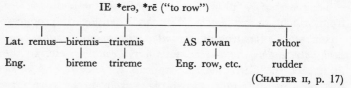

IE *erə, *rē ("to row")

Lat. remus—biremis—triremis			AS rōwan	rōthor
Eng.	bireme	trireme	Eng. row, etc.	rudder

(CHAPTER II, p. 17)

The root *awos* means "grandfather on the mother's side". In Anglo-Saxon, this comes out as *ēam*, surviving in the somewhat archaic *eme*. In Old High German, the form is *ōheim*, later shortened to *Ohm*, appearing as the family name of a physicist, from which we get *ohm*, the unit of electrical resistance, with *ohmmeter* and other technical compounds. In Dutch form, the word is *oom*, and this was part of the nickname of Kruger, leader of the Boer forces in the South African war (*Oom Paul*, "Uncle Paul"). In Latin, *awos* comes out as *avus*, with *avuncular*, and through a diminutive *avunculus*, produces French *oncle*, which becomes English *uncle*.

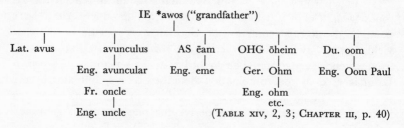

IE *awos ("grandfather")

Lat. avus	avunculus	AS ēam	OHG ōheim	Du. oom
	Eng. avuncular	Eng. eme	Ger. Ohm	Eng. Oom Paul
	Fr. oncle		Eng. ohm	
	Eng. uncle		etc.	

(TABLE XIV, 2, 3; CHAPTER III, p. 40)

The root *swesor*, "sister", produces in Anglo-Saxon *sweoster*, but this appears influenced by a Scandinavian form to produce English *sister* (with *sister-in-law, sisterly, sisterhood, sissy, sis, sissified,* etc.; the Anglo-Saxon form, uninfluenced, would have produced **swester*). It also produces the Latin *soror,* from which we get *sororal, sorority, sorosis, soroptimist.* Through a derivative, **cum-sobrinus* or *consobrinus,* it passes into French in the forms *cousin, cousiner* (the latter means "to treat as a cousin, to deceive through pretext of relationship"), from which we get *cousin* and *cozen.*

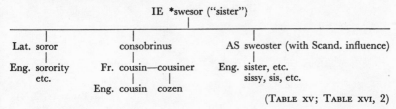

IE **swesor* ("sister")

Lat. soror	consobrinus	AS sweoster (with Scand. influence)
Eng. sorority etc.	Fr. cousin—cousiner	Eng. sister, etc. sissy, sis, etc.
	Eng. cousin cozen	

(TABLE XV; TABLE XVI, 2)

The IE root **bhardhā,* "beard", produces Anglo-Saxon and English *beard,* and also a German *Bart* which, through Middle High German *helmbarte,* "a beard-like weapon designed to split helmets", passes into Italian, then into French, and finally into English in the form *halberd.* On the Latin side, there is a highly irregular *barba* (it should have been **farba,* and it is possible that a similar form appeared in Oscan and Umbrian, as seems indicated by developments in some South Italian dialects; several explanations for the Latin irregularity are offered, none fully satisfactory). *Barba* gives us *barber, barbate, barb, barbed, barbel,* and even *barbiturate.* It is of interest that *barbatus,* "bearded", has become in Rumanian the regular word for "man" (*bărbat*). The root appears also in Slavic (Russian *boroda,* "beard"). *Borodino,* scene of a great battle in Napoleon's Russian campaign, and *Barbados,* in the West Indies (named after the bearded fig-trees, *higos barbados,* that abound on the island), are two place names based on this root.

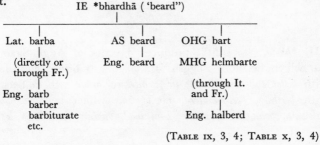

IE **bhardhā ('beard")

Lat. barba	AS beard	OHG bart
(directly or through Fr.)	Eng. beard	MHG helmbarte
Eng. barb barber barbiturate etc.		(through It. and Fr.) Eng. halberd

(TABLE IX, 3, 4; TABLE X, 3, 4)

An IE root *bhares*, "barley", comes into Anglo-Saxon as *bere*, and with the suffix *-līc*, "-like", becomes *barley*, with a few compounds like *barley-corn*. The *bere* root also produces Anglo-Saxon *bern*, "a place to store barley", which becomes *barn*, with *barnyard*, *barnstorming*, etc. The Latin form is *far*, with derivatives *farina* (*farina*, *farinaceous*, etc.), and *farrago*, which comes into English unchanged.

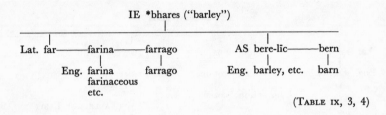

IE *bhares ("barley")

Lat. far——farina——farrago		AS bere-līc——bern
Eng. farina farrago		Eng. barley, etc. barn
farinaceous		
etc.		

(TABLE IX, 3, 4)

IE *bhēdh*, "to bury, dig", gives Anglo-Saxon *bedd* and English *bed* (with *bedroom*, *bedtime*, *bedside*, *bedstead*, *bedding*, *bed-pan*, *bedclothes*, *bedbug*, *bedfellow*, *bed-chamber*, etc.). It also gives Latin *fodio*, "to dig", with its past participle *fossus*, from which we derive *fossa*, *fossil*, *fossilize*, etc.

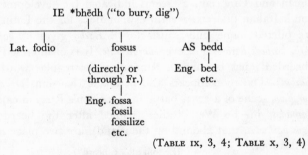

IE *bhēdh ("to bury, dig")

Lat. fodio	fossus	AS bedd
	(directly or through Fr.)	Eng. bed etc.
	Eng. fossa fossil fossilize etc.	

(TABLE IX, 3, 4; TABLE X, 3, 4)

IE *bheid*, "to split", produces a series of Anglo-Saxon words: *bita*, which becomes English *bit*; *bītan*, "to bite"; *biter*, later *bitter* (with *bitter end*, *bittersweet*, etc.); *bitel* or *bitula*, which become *beetle* (with *beetling*, *beetle-browed*, etc.); *bāt*, which becomes *boat* (with *boatswain*, *boatman*, *boathouse*, *boat load*, *boating*, *boat hook*, etc.). The

Latin form is *findo*, "to split", with a root *fid-* and a past participle *fissus*, from which come *fission, fissionable, fissile,* etc.

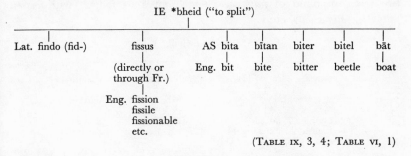

IE *bheid ("to split")

Lat. findo (fid-)	fissus	AS bita	bitan	biter	bitel	bāt
	(directly or through Fr.)	Eng. bit	bite	bitter	beetle	boat
	Eng. fission fissile fissionable etc.					

(TABLE IX, 3, 4; TABLE VI, 1)

The root **bhlē*, "to howl, cry", gives Anglo-Saxon *blǣtan* and English *bleat* and *blatant*, with a Scandinavian variant *blathra* which produces *blather*. There is a possibility that *blare*, described by some as echoic (that is, formed in imitation of the sound it betokens), by others as derived from Low German or Dutch, may also belong here. There is another possibility that this root may be connected with that of *bellow, bell, belch*. On the Latin side, we have *fleo*, "to weep", and *flebilis*, "weepable, weak", which produces in Old French *feible* and *foible* (later *faible*), taken over by English as *feeble* and *foible*, respectively. Taking only assured forms:

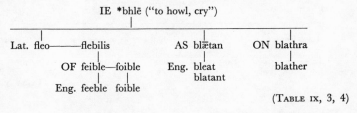

IE *bhlē ("to howl, cry")

Lat. fleo———flebilis	AS blǣtan	ON blathra
OF feible—foible	Eng. bleat blatant	blather
Eng. feeble foible		

(TABLE IX, 3, 4)

The root **dhē*, "to dwindle", produces an Old Norse *dasask* (*dasa* plus a reflexive suffix *-sk*), which appears in Middle English as *dasen*, "to grow weary", and ultimately gives us *daze*, with a frequentative form *dazzle* ("frequentative" means that the form of the verb in question indicates a frequent or repeated occurrence of the action described by the main verb). Old Norse *dasathr*, "weary", seems to give rise to English *dastard, dastardly*, also appearing in late Middle

English. On the Latin side, we have _fames_, "hunger", which through French gives us _famine_ and _famish_; also perhaps _fatigo_, "to weary, to tire", a compound of _fatim ago_, which gives us _fatigue_, with _indefatigable_, _fatigue duty_, etc.

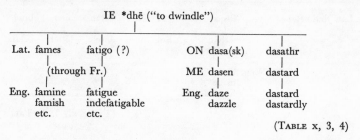

IE *dhē ("to dwindle")

Lat. fames	fatigo (?)		ON dasa(sk)	dasathr
	(through Fr.)		ME dasen	dastard
Eng. famine	fatigue		Eng. daze	dastard
famish	indefatigable		dazzle	dastardly
etc.	etc.			

(Table x, 3, 4)

The IE root *_dheu_, "to die", produces Old Norse _deyja_, from which English gets _die_, and this relegates _starve_, from Anglo-Saxon _steorfan_, "to die", to specialized uses ("to die by hunger", or "to die from cold", as in Scottish usage). It also produces Anglo-Saxon _dēad_, _dēath_, and possibly _dwīnan_, from which we get _dead_, _death_ and _dwindle_, with all their derivatives and compounds (_deadly_, _deaden_, _dead beat_, _dead end_, _deadline_, _deadlock_, _dead pan_, _deadwood_, _deathbed_, _deathly_, _death warrant_, _death watch_, etc.; _undying_ is the one outstanding derivative of _die_). The Latin form is _funus_, which gives us _funeral_ and _funereal_.

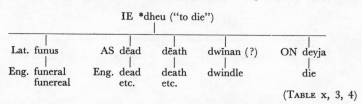

IE *dheu ("to die")

Lat. funus	AS dēad	dēath	dwīnan (?)	ON deyja
Eng. funeral	Eng. dead	death	dwindle	die
funereal	etc.	etc.		

(Table x, 3, 4)

The root *_geus_, "to taste", appears in Gothic as _kausjan_, in Old High German as _kiosan_, and in Anglo-Saxon as _cēosan_. The last produces the verb _choose_ (Anglo-Saxon palatalizes _c_ before _e_; see Chapter 3, p. 35). The noun _choice_, however, comes through Old French _chois_ (modern French _choix_). Since French palatalizes _c_ into _ch_ only before _a_ (see Chapter 3, p. 41), it seems that a form like Gothic _kausjan_ (possibly from East Germanic Burgundian) was more likely to produce Old French _chois_ than Old High German _kiosan_. On the Latin side, we have *gustum*, with English *gustatory*, *disgust*, etc.; also *gusto*, through Italian, and *ragout* (a "re-adding of taste through combination with other ingredients") through French. The same root, in Celtic, produces the proper name *Fergus*, but no common noun in English.

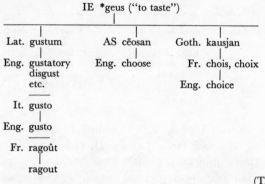

IE *geus ("to taste")

Lat. gustum	AS cēosan	Goth. kausjan
Eng. gustatory	Eng. choose	Fr. chois, choix
disgust		Eng. choice
etc.		

It. gusto

Eng. gusto

Fr. ragoût

ragout

(TABLE VII, 2)

An IE root *treud*, "to crush, press, strike", produces in Anglo-Saxon *thrēatnian* and *thrēat*, which become *threaten* and *threat*. Two additional and fairly likely possibilities are Anglo-Saxon *gethryscan*, *threscan*, which give us *thrash* and *thresh*, with *threshold*, and Old Norse *thrȳsta*, which becomes *thrust*. The Latin cognate is *trudo*, "to push", which with its past participle *trusus*, gives, in compound forms, *protrude*, *intrude*, *intruder*, *intrusion*, *obtrude*, *abstruse*, *extrude*, etc.

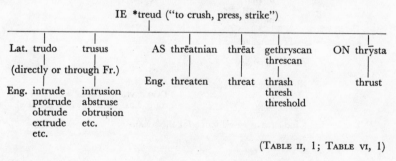

IE *treud ("to crush, press, strike")

Lat. trudo	trusus	AS thrēatnian	thrēat	gethryscan threscan	ON thrȳsta
(directly or through Fr.)		Eng. threaten	threat	thrash	thrust
Eng. intrude	intrusion			thresh	
protrude	abstruse			threshold	
obtrude	obtrusion				
extrude	etc.				
etc.					

(TABLE II, 1; TABLE VI, 1)

The IE root *dakru*, "tear", becomes in Anglo-Saxon *tæhher*, *tægor*, leading to English tear, with *tearless*, *tearful*, *tear gas*, *tear jerker*, etc.

In archaic Latin *dacruma* appears, but in classical Latin, perhaps through Sabine influence (initial *d* of Italic becomes *l* in Osco-Umbrian), we have *lacrima* or *lachryma*, leading to *lachrymal* and *lachrymose*.

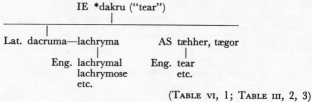

IE *dakru ("tear")

Lat. dacruma—lachryma   AS tæhher, tægor

Eng. lachrymal   Eng. tear
lachrymose   etc.
etc.

(TABLE VI, 1; TABLE III, 2, 3)

In similar fashion IE *dn̥ghū*,[1] "tongue", becomes in Anglo-Saxon *tunge*, leading to *tongue* (with *tongue-tied*), and, possibly, *tongs*, while Old Norse *tangi*, "projecting point", gives *tang*. Latin *lingua*, evidently a Sabine variant of *dingua*, gives us *lingual, linguist, linguistic, bilingual, multilingual, plurilingual*, the modern *linguistician*, and *lingua franca*. From French *langue, langage*, comes *language*, while a Provençal form of the word gives us *lingo*. Note, from the same root, German *Zunge* and Russian *yazyk*.

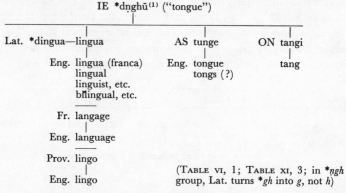

IE *dn̥ghū[1] ("tongue")

Lat. *dingua—lingua   AS tunge   ON tangi

Eng. lingua (franca)   Eng. tongue   tang
lingual   tongs (?)
linguist, etc.
bilingual, etc.

Fr. langage

Eng. language

Prov. lingo

Eng. lingo

(TABLE VI, 1; TABLE XI, 3; in *n̥gh group, Lat. turns *gh into g, not h)

[1] The symbol *n̥* indicates a vowel value for the sonant *n*.

A Latin-Germanic combination of interest is presented by the IE root *ayos*, "metal", which appears in Anglo-Saxon *īsen, īren*, from which we get *iron*, with derivatives and compounds like *ironmonger*, *ironclad, iron horse, Iron Curtain.* In the form *ār*, it also develops into *ore*, and a similar Scandinavian form produces *öre* and *øre*, coins of various Scandinavian countries, while an Old High German form gives the *Erz-* of *Erzgebirge*, a mountain range. The Latin form appears in *aes* (root *aer-*), the word for "bronze", from which we get on the one hand *era* (the plural *aera*, "brass counters", used for counting and measuring); on the other the verb *aestimari* ("bronze" plus the verb "to cut", used in the sense of "measure, appraise"), which eventually appears in English *esteem, estimate, estimable, estimation,* and the British first name *Esmé,* which is the past participle of the Old French verb *esmer,* "to esteem", later replaced in French by the learned *estimer.* An important Latin compound of *aestimari,* the verb *existimo,* "to think", fails to appear in English.

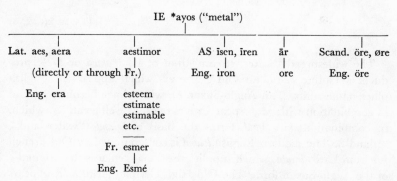

IE *ayos ("metal")

Lat. aes, aera	aestimor	AS īsen, īren	ār	Scand. öre, øre
(directly or through Fr.)		Eng. iron	ore	Eng. öre
Eng. era	esteem estimate estimable etc.			
	Fr. esmer			
	Eng. Esmé			

(TABLE XIII; TABLE XVI, 2, 3)

IE *wiros,* "man", produces in Anglo-Saxon a form *wer,* of which the only ostensible present-day survivors are *werewolf* and *wergild,* the money paid in Anglo-Saxon times for taking a man's life. In highly disguised form, however, *wer* survives also in Anglo-Saxon *weorold,* literally "man-age", which becomes *world,* with *worldly, worldliness, unworldly,* etc., while the German cognate of *world, Welt,* gives us loan-words such as *Weltpolitik, Weltanschauung, Weltschmerz, Weltansicht.* The Latin *vir,* "man", appears in *virile, virility, virago, triumvirate, quadrumvirate,* and an extension of *vir, virtus,* "manly quality, virtue", which results in *virtue, virtual, virtuous, virtually,* and the Italian-derived *virtuoso, virtuosity.*

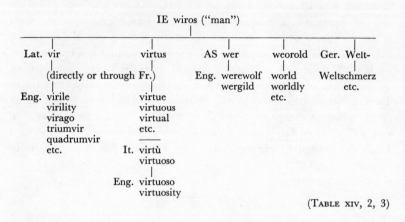

	IE wiros ("man")			
Lat. vir	virtus	AS wer	weorold	Ger. Welt-
(directly or through Fr.)		Eng. werewolf	world	Weltschmerz
		wergild	worldly	etc.
Eng. virile	virtue		etc.	
virility	virtuous			
virago	virtual			
triumvir	etc.			
quadrumvir	———			
etc.	It. virtù			
	virtuoso			
	Eng. virtuoso			
	virtuosity			

(TABLE XIV, 2, 3)

The widespread "water, stream" root of IE, **akwā* or **ēkŭ*, produces a Gothic *ahwa,* an Old Norse *ey,* which appears in English place-name suffixes, an Anglo-Saxon *ēa,* which later becomes *ea,* and in combination with *gār,* "spear", gives *eagre,* as well as an *īeg,* which, in combination with *land,* forms the basis of *īgland* ("water-land", "island"). The modern English *island* is contaminated by Old French *isle* from Latin *insula,* which supplies the *s* that replaces the original *g* of the Anglo-Saxon form. The Old High German form, *ache,* appears in the name of the German city of *Aachen,* which translates the French *Aix,* derived from Latin *Aquis(grana).* Lastly, there is the place name *Scandinavia,* in which the -*av*- portion comes from the "water" root. The Latin form is *aqua,* and this produces, directly or through French or Italian, *aquamarine, aquarelle, aquarium, aquarian, Aquarius, aquatint, aqueduct, aquaplane, aquavit,* and the modern American *aquacade,* along with straight Latin forms like *aqua fortis, aqua regia, aqua vitae.* Through the French descendant of *aqua, eau,* we get *eau de vie, eau de Cologne;* through *évier,* the French descendant of *aquarium,* we get *ewer,* as well as *sewer* (with *sewage, sewerage*), from *ex-aquarium,* "outlet for water". *Osier* may also come from this root, through the Celtic *av,* but there are other theories to the effect that it comes from Low Latin *ausaria* or Greek *oisos,* so it is best omitted.

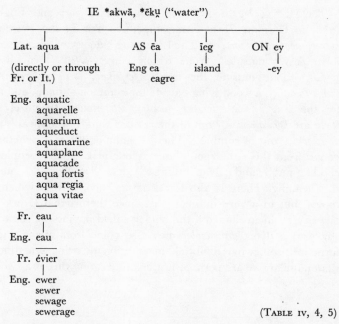

IE *akwā, *ēku̯ ("water")

Lat. aqua	AS ēa	īeg	ON ey
(directly or through Fr. or It.)	Eng ea eagre	island	-ey
Eng. aquatic aquarelle aquarium aqueduct aquamarine aquaplane aquacade aqua fortis aqua regia aqua vitae			
Fr. eau			
Eng. eau			
Fr. évier			
Eng. ewer sewer sewage sewerage			(TABLE IV, 4, 5)

A slightly doubtful family is that of *kāu, *kəu, "hew, strike", which produces an Anglo-Saxon hēawan that eventually becomes hew (with hewer). Latin shows incus, "anvil", from the stem of in-cudo, "to strike", and this is used in English to designate scientifically one of the bones of the ear; also codex, from which we derive code, codex, codicil, encode, decode, codify. The doubts reside in the possible connection, on the Germanic side, with hack; on the Latin side, with cauda, "tail", which would lead to caudal, coda, coward, etc. There seems to be an assured connection with Slavic forms represented by kovač and kuznets, "blacksmith". Limiting ourselves to reasonably sure forms, we have:

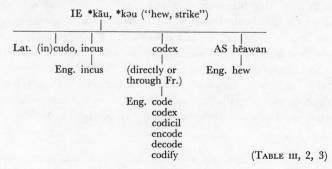

IE *kāu, *kəu ("hew, strike")

Lat. (in)cudo, incus	codex	AS hēawan
Eng. incus	(directly or through Fr.)	Eng. hew
	Eng. code codex codicil encode decode codify	(TABLE III, 2, 3)

The IE *dhwĕr, "door", gives Anglo-Saxon *duru* and English *door* (akin to German *Tor*), with compounds like *doorstep, doorway, doorkeeper, indoors, outdoors,* etc. The Latin *fores,* "doorway", has a secondary form *foris,* "outside", from which come *forfeit* (through French *forfait,* "done outside the law"), *forfeiture, foreign, foreigner, forest* (*silva forestis,* "a wood lying outside the common domain, and reserved for the king"), with *forester, forestry, reforestation.* In purely French form are *hors d'oeuvre,* "out of the regular work of the meal", and *hors de combat,* "out of combat". There is some doubt as to whether *forum* comes from the same root ("an outdoor place where people met to conduct public and private business"); if so, *forensic* would come under this heading. There is also Greek *thyra,* "door", from which we get *thyroid,* but in a very indirect way, since the original Greek word is *thyreoidos,* "shield-shaped", the oblong shield having the same general shape as a door; *dithyrambic* may also come from *thyra;* since these forms are somewhat doubtful, in addition to being scientific rather than popular, we are perhaps justified in treating this as a two-branch root.

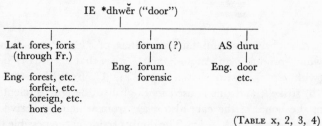

IE *dhwĕr ("door")

Lat. fores, foris (through Fr.)	forum (?)	AS duru
Eng. forest, etc. forfeit, etc. foreign, etc. hors de	Eng. forum forensic	Eng. door etc.

(TABLE X, 2, 3, 4)

The root *ghostis,* "foreign, guest", produces Anglo-Saxon *giest* and English *guest.* The Latin *hostis* shows in its semantics a predominance of the idea of "foreign", therefore "enemy, hostile", and it is from this meaning that *host,* "army" and *hostile,* with *hostility,* descend. *Host* in the sense of "Communion wafer" seems to come from the idea of "enemy" extended to that of "expiatory offering". Latin also has *hospes,* which some authorities analyze as *hosti-pots,* "the one who has power over the guest or enemy"; but Latin shows, from the very beginning, the same confusion between the two meanings of "guest" and "host" that appears today in the languages descended from it. *Hospes,* with root *hospit-,* gives rise to *hospital, hospitality, hospitable, hospitalize, hospice, host, hostess, hostage, hostel, hostelry* or *ostelry, hostler, hotel*; it is probably *hostage* which, despite its late formation, holds the semantic key; the *hostage* is both a guest and an enemy. Some dictionaries also list a Rumanian *hospodar* which comes from the Slavic development of the root as it appears in Russian *gospod'*, "lord", *gospodin*, "Mr., sir", *gospodar*, "nobleman", etc.

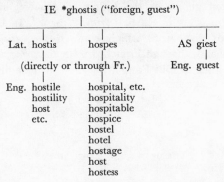

IE *ghostis ("foreign, guest")

Lat. hostis	hospes	AS giest
(directly or through Fr.)		Eng. guest
Eng. hostile	hospital, etc.	
hostility	hospitality	
host	hospitable	
etc.	hospice	
	hostel	
	hotel	
	hostage	
	host	
	hostess	

(TABLE XI, 3, 4)

A root *aweg*, "to increase", gives in Anglo-Saxon *ēacan, ēcan*, (*ēa* is a normal Anglo-Saxon development of *aw*), and also *weaxan*. This first gives us *eke*, the second *wax* (in the sense of "increase") and also *waist*, with *waistline, waistcoat*, etc. In Latin, we have *augeo*, "to increase", from which come *augment, augmentation, augmentative*, with extensions like *augurium (augur, augury, inaugurate, inauguration); augustus (august, August, Augustan, Augustine, Austin); auxilium (auxiliary); auctio (auction, auctioneer); auctor (author, authoress, authorship, authority, authoritative, authoritarian, authorize*, etc.), and a French development *octroi*, which comes from Vulgar Latin *auctoricare*, becoming *octroyer*. There is question whether *autumn* also belongs to this root, or is from Etruscan.

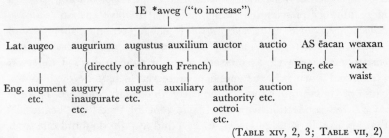

IE *aweg ("to increase")

Lat. augeo	augurium	augustus	auxilium	auctor	auctio	AS ēacan	weaxan
	(directly or through French)					Eng. eke	wax
							waist
Eng. augment	augury	august	auxiliary	author	auction		
etc.	inaugurate	etc.		authority	etc.		
	etc.			octroi			
				etc.			

(TABLE XIV, 2, 3; TABLE VII, 2)

A somewhat doubtful, yet picturesque family is that of IE *bhrēi, "to cut with a sharp tool". Through Anglo-Saxon brȳne it gives us brine, with a semantic difficulty. It is also possible that it gives Anglo-Saxon priccian, leading to prick, prickle, prickly, prig, priggish, but here we encounter a phonological difficulty, since IE *bh should produce Germanic b, not p. There is the French briser, coming from a Celtic development and giving us the little-used brisance; also the Slavic development appearing in Russian britva, "razor". In Latin, the root yields frico, "to rub", from which come friction, fricative, dentifrice, frivolous, frivolity and, through French, friable, fray, frazzle, with (small) fry attributed either to Old French froi or to a Scandinavian source.

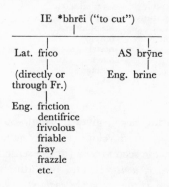

IE *bhrēi ("to cut")

Lat. frico	AS brȳne
(directly or through Fr.)	Eng. brine
Eng. friction dentifrice frivolous friable fray frazzle etc.	

(TABLE IX, 3, 4)

An IE root *ker(ə), "to burn, glow, heat", gives Anglo-Saxon heorth and English hearth, with hearthstone, etc. For Latin, we have carbo, "coal", and cremo, "to burn, cremate", from which come cremate, cremation, crematorium, cremator, etc. The carbo root appears in a large number of scientific compounds that involve carbon (carbonic, carbohydrate, carbide, carbonate, carbolic, which combines the roots of "coal" and "oil", carborundum, a trade name, carbon monoxide, carburetor, etc.), as well as carbuncle and the Italian-derived Carbonari ("charcoal burners", the name of a secret society devoted to the cause of Italian unification in the early nineteenth century). There is an assured connection with the Slavic root for "red" or "beautiful" that appears in Russian krasny, krasivy, and a quite doubtful one with Greek keramos, "earthenware", from which we get ceramics.

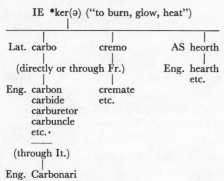

IE *ker(ə) ("to burn, glow, heat")

Lat. carbo	cremo	AS heorth
(directly or through Fr.)		Eng. hearth
		etc.
Eng. carbon	cremate	
carbide	etc.	
carburetor		
carbuncle		
etc. ·		

(through It.)

Eng. Carbonari   (TABLE III, 2, 3)

IE *pek is "to pluck wool or hair". On the Germanic side, we have Anglo-Saxon *feohtan*, "to pick on, fight", which becomes *fight* with its derivatives (*fighter plane*); Anglo-Saxon *feoh*, which gets crossed with *fieu*, brought in by the Normans and derived by Old French from Old High German *fiu*, to give us *fee*. The Old High German-Old French word alone produces *fief*, while an Old High German extension, *fēhida*, leads to *feud* and *feudal*, *feudalism*. Other Germanic relatives are Old Norse *fēlagi*, "partner", which gets into Anglo-Saxon as *fēolage* and ultimately becomes *fellow* (with *fellowship*, *fellow traveler*, etc.); and the Scandinavian name of the *Faroe* ("sheep") islands. Latin shows the root in *pecus*, "sheep", from which we get, through the idea of sheep or cattle as a medium of exchange, *peculate*, *peculiar*, *pecuniary*, *impecunious*, etc., as well as the Italian *pecorino*, "a cheese made with sheep's milk". There is also *pecten*, "comb", which appears in English as a scientific term, along with its adjective *pectinate*.

IE *pek ("to pluck wool or hair")

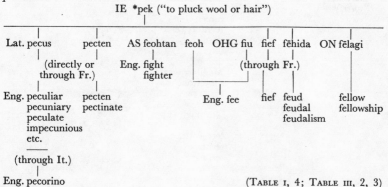

Lat. pecus	pecten	AS feohtan	feoh	OHG fiu	fief	fēhida	ON fēlagi
(directly or through Fr.)		Eng. fight fighter		(through Fr.)			
Eng. peculiar	pecten			Eng. fee	fief	feud	fellow
pecuniary	pectinate					feudal	fellowship
peculate						feudalism	
impecunious							
etc.							

(through It.)

Eng. pecorino   (TABLE I, 4; TABLE III, 2, 3)

The root *ters* means "dry, arid, thirst". In Anglo-Saxon this produces *thurst* and *thyrstig*, which become *thirst* and *thirsty*. In Latin, we have the verb *torreo*, "to burn", with past participle *tostus*, and *terra*, "land, earth" (presumably dry land as opposed to the sea; in Latin *rr* often replaces *rs*). *Torreo* gives rise to *torrid*, *torrefaction*, *torrefy*, and *torrent*, with *torrential* (*torrens*, the present participle of *torreo*, was at first applied to the drying-up bed of a seasonal stream; but since the latter, in times of heavy rains, becomes a rushing stream, this meaning finally took the upper hand). The past participle *tostus* yields *toast*, "bread heated over a fire to the point of drying up"; then, from the custom of dipping pieces of toasted bread into wine drunk in someone's honor, we get the secondary meaning of *toast*. *Terra* appears in Latin form in *terra firma*, in Italian form in *terracotta* ("cooked earth"), and, generally through French, goes on to produce *terrestrial*, *terrain*, *terrier* (a dog used to burrow in the earth after small game); *terrine* (with its variant *tureen*, something made of earthenware); *terrace* and the Italian *terrazzo*; *territory*, with *territorial*, *extra-territoriality*, etc.; the French *parterre*, ("on the ground"); *inter* and *disinter*; *Mediterranean* ("in the midst of lands", the Internal Sea of the ancients), *subterranean*; and even *turmeric*, from *terra merita*, "deserving earth".

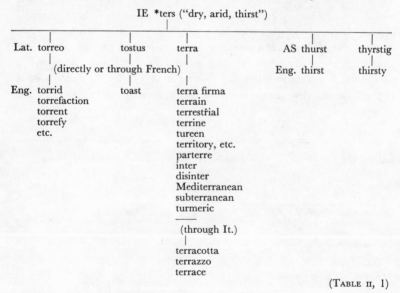

IE *ters ("dry, arid, thirst")

Lat. torreo	tostus	terra	AS thurst	thyrstig
(directly or through French)			Eng. thirst	thirsty
Eng. torrid	toast	terra firma		
torrefaction		terrain		
torrent		terrestrial		
torrefy		terrine		
etc.		tureen		
		territory, etc.		
		parterre		
		inter		
		disinter		
		Mediterranean		
		subterranean		
		turmeric		

(through It.)

terracotta
terrazzo
terrace

(TABLE II, 1)

The IE root *lou, "to wash", has certain doubtful ramifications. On the Germanic side, Anglo-Saxon *lēathor* gives *lather*, and *lēah* gives *lye*. In Latin, we have the verb *lavo*, "to wash", with a secondary form in *lu-* and a past participle *lotus*. *Lavo* produces, directly or through French or Italian, *lave, lava, lavender, laundry, laundress, latrine* (from an original *lavatrina*), *lavabo* (Latin for "I shall wash"), *lavatory, lavish, lavasse* ("a heavy rain"). The *lu-* variant appears in compounds, and gives rise to such forms as *ablution, dilute, dilution, alluvial, deluge, ante-diluvian, pollute, pollution* (*porro-luere*, "to wash from afar", though some authorities prefer to derive this from *lutum*, "mud"). The participial *lotus* appears in *lotic* and *lotion*. There is a possibility of connection, on the Germanic side, with Anglo-Saxon *lapian*, which becomes the verb *lap*, and *lippa*, which produces *lip*, and if this connection is accepted, it also involves Latin *labium* or *labrum*, "lip", and *lambo*, "to lap, lick", with consequent involvement of *labial, candelabrum, lambent*, and even *lampoon* (from the French *lapons, lampons*, "let us lap it up"). Restricting ourselves to the surer forms, we have:

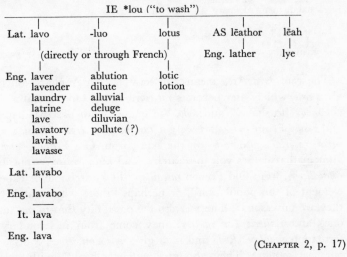

IE *lou ("to wash")

Lat. lavo	-luo	lotus	AS lēathor	lēah
(directly or through French)			Eng. lather	lye
Eng. laver	ablution	lotic		
lavender	dilute	lotion		
laundry	alluvial			
latrine	deluge			
lave	diluvian			
lavatory	pollute (?)			
lavish				
lavasse				

Lat. lavabo
|
Eng. lavabo

It. lava
|
Eng. lava

(CHAPTER 2, p. 17)

An IE root *mori, "sea," produces Anglo-Saxon *mōr, merisc*, and *mere*, which work out in English as *moor, marsh* (with *marshy, marshmallow*), and *mere* (with *mermaid, merman*). The Latin form is *mare*, which directly or through French produces *marine, submarine, mariner*, *marinade, maritime*, etc. *Ros marinus*, "sea dew," is misunderstood (another case of popular etymology) and becomes *rosemary*. There is the French *mal de mer*, "seasickness," and the Italian *maremma*, "marshland." *Morass* comes originally from Latin *mariscus*, appropriated by Frankish (Old High German) in the form *marisk*, then passed on to Old French as *marais* and to Dutch as *moeras*, from which it comes into English. A Celtic extension appears in *Armorica*, the ancient name of Brittany, and a Slavic one in *Pomerania* (*Pommern* in German, *Pomorze* in Polish); both mean "by the sea."

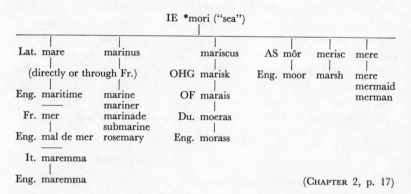

IE *mori ("sea")

Lat. mare	marinus		mariscus	AS mōr	merisc	mere
(directly or through Fr.)		OHG marisk		Eng. moor	marsh	mere
Eng. maritime	marine	OF marais				mermaid
	mariner					merman
Fr. mer	marinade	Du. moeras				
	submarine					
Eng. mal de mer	rosemary	Eng. morass				
It. maremma						
Eng. maremma						

(CHAPTER 2, p. 17)

The root *rēd*, *rōd* means "to scratch." In Anglo-Saxon form, it gives *rætt*, which later becomes *rat* (with *ratty*). On the Latin side, we get *rado*, "to shave", and *rodo*, "to gnaw", with past participles *rasus* and *rosus*. From *rado-rasus* we get *rase* or *raze*, *erase*, *abrasion*, *abrasive*, *razor*, *rasorial;* also *rash* (on the skin), from Old French *rasche*, "the ailment that causes you to scratch"; and *rascal*, *rascally* (possibly also *rapscallion*), from Old French *rascaille*, "the scratchable or expendable element of the population", or perhaps "those who scratch because they are unwashed". There is also the possibility that to *rail* (at someone) and *raillerie* (or *raillery*) may come from a secondary Latin formation *radulare*. *Rodo* and *rosus* give us *rodent*, *erode*, *erosion*, *corrode*, *corrosion*, *corrosive*. They also give *rostrum*, "beak", with *rostral* and *rostrate* (the rostrum from which Roman orators spoke in the Forum was so called because it was adorned with *rostra*, ships' prows or beaks, used in ramming and sinking enemy ships; these rostra had been taken by the Romans from the Volscians at the battle of Antium, later Anzio, where another big battle was fought in the Second World War).

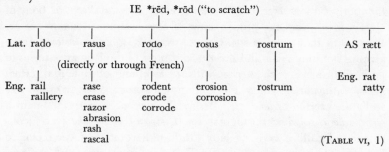

IE *rēd, *rōd ("to scratch")

Lat. rado	rasus	rodo	rosus	rostrum		AS rætt
	(directly or through French)					
					Eng. rat	
Eng. rail	rase	rodent	erosion	rostrum		rat
raillery	erase	erode	corrosion			ratty
	razor	corrode				
	abrasion					
	rash					
	rascal					

(TABLE VI, 1)

The IE root *pleu*, "to run, swim, flow", produces in Anglo-Saxon *flōwan*, which leads to *flow*; *flotian*, which comes out as *float*, with *floterian*, which becomes *flutter*; *fleoge* and *flēogan*, which become the noun and the verb *fly* (with *flywheel*, *flyweight*, *fly-by-night*, *flying saucer*, *flying column*, etc.); *flyht*, which becomes *flight*; and *flugol*, *fugol*, which turns into *fowl*. There is doubt whether *fleet* comes from Anglo-Saxon *flēte, flēotan, flēot* (the last means "ship"), or from Old Norse *floti* through French *flotte* (the French form definitely gives us *flotation* and *flotsam* from *flotaison*, and, with a Spanish extension, *flotilla*). As against all these Germanic forms, all that Latin has to offer is *pluvia*, "rain", from which we get *pluvial*, *pluviometer*, (*Jupiter*) *Pluvius*, and the name of the French Revolutionary month *Pluviôse*; also, through French *plovier*, "the rain-bird", *plover*.

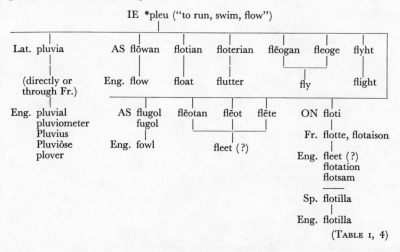

IE *pleu ("to run, swim, flow")

Lat. pluvia	AS flōwan	flotian	floterian	flēogan	fleoge	flyht
(directly or through Fr.)	Eng. flow	float	flutter	fly		flight
Eng. pluvial	AS flugol	flēotan	flēot	flēte	ON floti	
pluviometer	fugol					
Pluvius					Fr. flotte, flotaison	
Pluviôse	Eng. fowl		fleet (?)			
plover					Eng. fleet (?)	
					flotation	
					flotsam	
					Sp. flotilla	
					Eng. flotilla	

(TABLE I, 4)

The root *seno*, "old", gives us, through Old High German *sini-skalk*, "elder servant," and French *sénéchal*, English *seneschal*. In Latin, the root produces *senex*, "old", *senior*, "elder", *senatus*, "senate, body of elderly men", and the proper name of *Seneca*, famous Roman orator. *Senex*, with its adjective *senilis*, gives us *senile, senility, senescent. Senior* gives us not only *senior* and *seniority*, but most of the Romance terms of polite address: French *seigneur*, with *seignorial* and other feudal terms; also *Monseigneur, Monsieur* and its plural *Messieurs, Sieur, sire*, and *sir;* Italian *signor(e), Monsignor, Messer(e), signora, signorina;* Spanish *señor, señora, señorita;* Portuguese *senhor, senhora, senhorinha* (the inconsistency of calling a young lady "little old woman" never seems to have struck Romance speakers). There are even *surly* and *surliness*, derived from an earlier *sirly*, "behaving like an aristocrat".

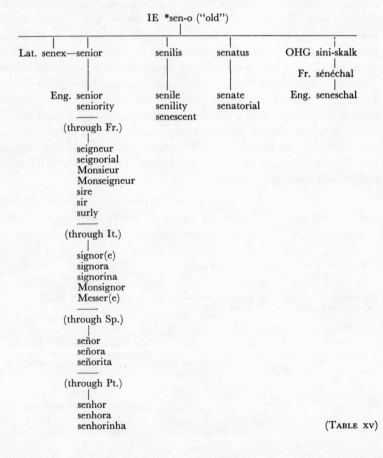

IE *sen-o ("old")

Lat. senex—senior	senilis	senatus	OHG sini-skalk
			Fr. sénéchal
Eng. senior	senile	senate	Eng. seneschal
seniority	senility	senatorial	
	senescent		

(through Fr.)

seigneur
seignorial
Monsieur
Monseigneur
sire
sir
surly

(through It.)

signor(e)
signora
signorina
Monsignor
Messer(e)

(through Sp.)

señor
señora
señorita

(through Pt.)

senhor
senhora
senhorinha

(TABLE XV)

The IE root *al, "to grow, nurture", gives in Anglo-Saxon *eald*, which turns into *old* (with *older, oldish, oldster*, etc.); *ealdorman*, which becomes *alderman; yldo, yldra*, which become *eld* and *elder; weorold* (literally, "man-age"), which becomes *world* (with *worldly, unworldly, world-wide*, and even *World's Series*). A High German form which becomes modern German *Welt* gives us *Weltpolitik, Weltschmerz, Weltansicht, Weltanschauung*. There is even a Scandinavian form *elska*, "to love", but it does not get into English. The two main Latin developments are *alo*, "to nourish", and *altus*, "high, tall". The former has many derivatives and compounds, among them the *alma* of *Alma Mater; alumnus* and *alumna; ailment* and *alimentary; alimony; coalesce* and *coalition; adult* and *adolescent* (not, however, *adultery* and *adulterate*, which come from the root of *alter*, "other"); *abolish*, with *abolition* and *abolitionist; proletarian, proletariat, prolific, proliferate;* possibly *indolent* and *indolence* (but there is a chance that these come from *doleo*, "to grieve"). *Altus* gives us *altitude, altimeter, exalt, exaltation;* numerous Italian forms, like *alto, contralto, altissimo, alto rilievo;* French forms like *haut relief, hautboy* (or *oboe*), *haughty, haughtily, haughtiness* (in French the Latin root of *altus* gets crossed with the Germanic *h* of *high, hoch*, and by reason of the fact that *l* following a vowel and preceding a consonant becomes *u*, turns into *haut*). There is the possibility that *altar* may also come from *altus*, but the picture is obscured by the presence of *ara*, also meaning "altar".

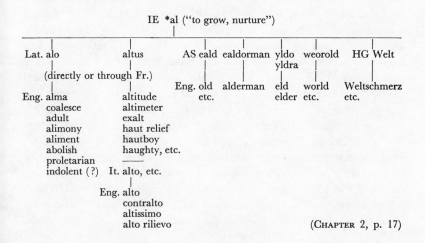

IE *al ("to grow, nurture")

Lat. alo	altus	AS eald	ealdorman	yldo yldra	weorold	HG Welt
(directly or through Fr.)						
Eng. alma	altitude	Eng. old	alderman	eld	world	Weltschmerz
coalesce	altimeter	etc.		elder	etc.	etc.
adult	exalt					
alimony	haut relief					
aliment	hautboy					
abolish	haughty, etc.					
proletarian	———					
indolent (?)	It. alto, etc.					
	Eng. alto					
	contralto					
	altissimo					
	alto rilievo				(CHAPTER 2, p. 17)

The IE root *yeu, "young", produces in Anglo-Saxon the adjective *geong* and the noun *geoguth*, leading to *young* and *youth* (with derivatives like *youngster*, *youthful*). There is also a Dutch form, *jonkheer*, from which we get a little-known *younker* (but also the name of the city of *Yonkers*), and its German counterpart, *Junker* ("young gentleman", in both cases). The German *Hitlerjugend*, or "Hitler Youth" movement, is not altogether forgotten. In Latin, the root takes the form *juvenis* (leading to *juvenile*, *rejuvenate*, etc., as well as the name of the poet *Juvenal*), and its comparative *junior*, which reaches us unchanged, with *juniority*, etc. The goddess Juno also seems to take her name from this root, and this would give us *June* and all its compounds (*June bug, June bride*, etc.)

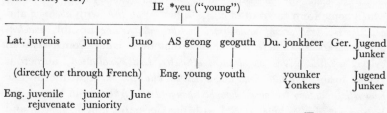

IE *yeu ("young")

Lat. juvenis	junior	Juno	AS geong	geoguth	Du. jonkheer	Ger. Jugend Junker
(directly or through French)			Eng. young	youth	younker Yonkers	Jugend Junker
Eng. juvenile rejuvenate	junior juniority	June				

(TABLE XIII, 2, 3)

Kan is the IE root that means "to sing, sound". On the Anglo-Saxon side, it gives *hano*, "rooster" (German *Hahn*), and *henn*, which becomes *hen* (with *henpeck*, *henbane*, etc.). The Latin form is *cano* or *canto*, "to sing". There is also *carmen*, "song", which appears in the name of an opera, as well as in *charm, charmer, charming* (with normal palatalization of *c* before *a* in French *charme*). Derivative forms include *accentum*, "a singing upon, accent", indicating that the accent was originally viewed as primarily of the musical or pitch variety rather than of the stress variety (here we get *accent, accentuation*, etc.); and *incino*, "to strike up a tune", from which we get *incentive*. *Canto*, the more popular of the two Latin forms, appears as *chant*- when it comes to us from standard French, as *cant*- when it comes from Norman-Picard or Italian. Hence we have *chant, chanty, chantry, enchant, enchantment, enchanter, enchantress, disenchantment, chanticleer* (the clear-singing rooster that is France's national symbol), the recently imported *chanteuse*, the older *chanson* (*de geste*); while from *cant*- we have *cant, decant, recant, cantor, canticle, cantilene*, all on the French (Norman-Picard) side, and Italian gives us (*bel*) *canto, cantata, cantabile, canzone*, *canzonet*, and even *cantaloupe*, from the name of the Calabrian town of *Cantalupo* ("Singing Wolf"), renowned for the fruit.

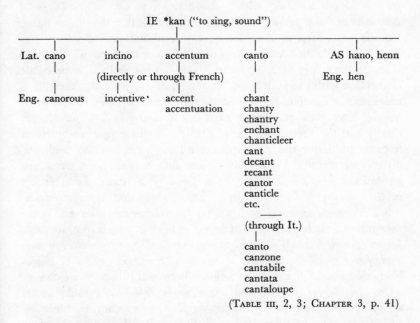

IE *kan ("to sing, sound")

Lat. cano	incino	accentum	canto	AS hano, henn
		(directly or through French)		Eng. hen
Eng. canorous	incentive·	accent	chant	
		accentuation	chanty	
			chantry	
			enchant	
			chanticleer	
			cant	
			decant	
			recant	
			cantor	
			canticle	
			etc.	

(through It.)

canto
canzone
cantabile
cantata
cantaloupe

(TABLE III, 2, 3; CHAPTER 3, p. 41)

It is a commonplace that when the same root appears in both the Germanic and the Latin branches, its extensions and ramifications will normally be far greater in the latter than in the former. This is due to the greater number and productivity of the Latin prefixes and suffixes as compared with the Germanic, for what concerns English. German is there to attest that a similar productivity can be achieved by the Germanic counterparts of the Latin elements. In English, however, the Anglo-Saxon development was partly arrested after the Norman Conquest, and the French-Latin formations took over. This explains why the Germanic words in our tongue are usually (by no means always) shorter, more terse, more direct-sounding than the French or Latin. It is of interest to note, however, that where the Latin root, and particularly its French development, is uncomplicated by prefixes and suffixes, it is usually just as monosyllabic as the Anglo-Saxon. A good example of this is the IE *dheig͜u*, "to stick, set fast", which on the Germanic side yields Anglo-Saxon _dic_ and English _dike_, with its extension _ditch_. Through Dutch _dijk_ and French _diguer_, English gets on the one hand _dig_, with its few derivatives, such as the _Digger_ of Australia and the _gold-digger_ of the U.S., on the other the proper name Van Dyke, which appears in several combinations, of which _Van Dyke beard_ is the best known. In Latin, we have the verb _figo_, "to fix", with its participle _fixus_, and the noun _finis_, as well as a probable connection with the verb _fingo_, "to shape, mold, pretend", showing a nasal infix in the root. _Fixus_ yields _fix, fixation, prefix, suffix, infix, transfix, crucifix_, and their numerous extensions: _suffixation, crucifixion_, etc. _Crucify_ and the French _fichu_ are from the infinitive _figere_ rather than from the participle _fixus_. _Finis_ appears in Latin form, but also produces, directly or through French, an almost infinite variety of secondary formations: _fine, finery, finial, finesse, finish, final, finale, finite, finality infinite, infinity, infinitesimal, affinity, confine, confinement, define, definition, refine, refinement, superfine_, even _finicky, finance, financier, financial_. If we accept the likely hypothesis that _fingo_ also belongs to this root, we have _figment, fiction, fictional, fictitious, feign, feint, faint, figure, figurative, figurehead, figure of speech, disfigure, configuration, transfigure, effigy_. It is less likely that _filum_, "thread", also belongs here, but if it does, we can go on to _file, filament, filigrain_ and _filigree, defile, defilement, enfilade, profile_, and with the alternative form _hilum_ for _filum_, we can add _nihil, nihilist, annihilation_, etc. Omitting the less likely _filum_, but including the more probable _fingo_, we have:

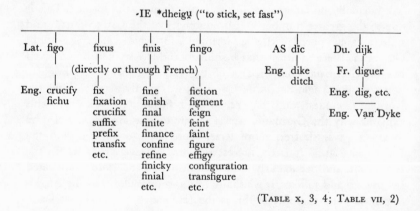

·IE *dheigu̯ ("to stick, set fast")

Lat. figo	fixus	finis	fingo		AS dīc	Du. dijk
	(directly or through French)				Eng. dike	Fr. diguer
					ditch	
Eng. crucify	fix	fine	fiction			Eng. dig, etc.
fichu	fixation	finish	figment			
	crucifix	final	feign			Eng. Van Dyke
	suffix	finite	feint			
	prefix	finance	faint			
	transfix	confine	figure			
	etc.	refine	effigy			
		finicky	configuration			
		finial	transfigure			
		etc.	etc.			

(TABLE X, 3, 4; TABLE VII, 2)

The IE root *eu or *wā means "to lack", "empty". With extensions that in part coincide, it produces both Germanic and Latin roots. For the former, we have Anglo-Saxon *wan* and *wanian*, leading to *wan* and *wane*, as well as Old Norse *vanta*, which produces *want;* and, by combining *wane* with Anglo-Saxon *togen*, "drawn", which is the past participle of the verb that eventually gives us *tow*, the form *wanton* is produced, originally meaning "lacking in drawing out (education)" or "illmannered". There is also an Anglo-Saxon *wēste*, "waste, lay waste"; its Old High German cognate *wuosti* combines with Latin *vasto*, which has the same meaning and ultimate origin, to produce Old French *guastier* (*wastier* is the Walloon-Norman form; see Chapter 3, p. 42), and English *waste*, with *wasteful, wastage, wastrel*. More directly derived from Old French *guastier*, modern French *gâter*, is *enfant gâté*, "spoiled child". Latin forms coming from the same root, in addition to the verb *vasto*, are the adjective *vastus*, from which we get, directly or through French, *vast, vastness, vastity, vastly, devastate, devastation; vanus*, which in various incarnations gives us *vain, vanity, vainglory, vanish, evanesce, vaunt* and *vaunted* (French *vanter* from Latin **vanitare*), *inane, inanition*, and *inanity* (from Latin **invanum*, with fall of *v*); *vaco*, "to empty", and *vacuus*, "empty", which give *vacant, vacancy, vacate, vacation, vacuum, vacuity, vacuous, evacuation, evacuee*. There is also an alternative Latin form with *o* instead of *a*, *vocitus*, which produces French forms that lead to *void, avoid, avoidance*.

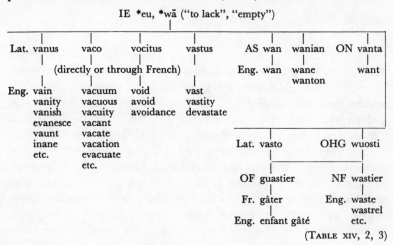

(Table XIV, 2, 3)

The root *gel(ə), "cold, to freeze", appears in Anglo-Saxon *calan,
ceald*, which come out as *cold;* in *cōl, cōlian*, which give us *cool*, both
adjective and verb, with *coolant, cooler, coolness*, etc.; and in *ciele, cēlan*,
which become *chill*, noun and verb, with *chilliness*. The Latin forms
are *gelu*, "frost", and *gelidus*, "cold", on the one hand, *glacies*, "ice",
on the other. *Gelu* and *gelidus* go on to French forms (*geler*, etc.) which
ultimately give us *gelid, gel, jelly* (with *jell* and *jellyfish*), *gelatine* (through
Italian; with *gelatinous*), *congeal;* while *glacies* produces *glacial, glacier,
glacis* (so called because it is slippery like ice), and the directly French
glacé, glacée. Note that French palatalizes Latin *g* before *e* and *i* without
change of spelling, while Anglo-Saxon usually palatalizes *c* before *e*
to *ch;* but the spelling change occurs only after the Norman Conquest
(see Chapter 3, pp. 42, 35).

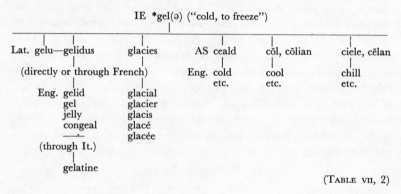

IE *gel(ə) ("cold, to freeze")

Lat. gelu—gelidus	glacies	AS ceald	cōl, cōlian	ciele, cēlan
(directly or through French)		Eng. cold	cool	chill
		etc.	etc.	etc.
Eng. gelid	glacial			
gel	glacier			
jelly	glacis			
congeal	glacé			
	glacée			
(through It.)				
gelatine				

(TABLE VII, 2)

A family that is somewhat doubtful, for reasons that will be presented
shortly, yet accepted by most authorities, is IE *ghĕrdh*, "to enclose,
fence in". In Anglo-Saxon, this gives *geard* and ultimately *yard* (with
yardarm, yardstick, barnyard, etc.). It also produces Anglo-Saxon *gyrdel*
and *gyrdan*, which give us *girdle* and *gird*, while the closely related
Old Norse *girthi, györth* produces *girth*. Old High German *gardo*,
passing into French, becomes *jardin* (English *jardinière*), but the
northern French dialects, not palatalizing *g* before *a*, give us *garden*
(with *gardener*, etc.; *gardenia* is from a family name *Garden*). The
doubtful Latin relative is *hortus*, "garden", with *horticulture, horti-
culturist*, and even the proper name *Hortense*, as well as *ortolan* (a
species of bird), which comes from Provençal via French. In the Latin

compound *cohors*, this root gives us *cohort*, but in contracted form it becomes Old French *cort*, *court* (modern French *cour*), and here we acquire *court* with its numerous compounds (*courthouse*, *courtroom*, *courtship*, *courtyard*, etc.), along with *courteous*, *courtesy*, *curtsy*, *courtly*, *courtier*, *courtesan* (this comes by way of Italian *cortigiano*); negative forms in *dis-* (*discourteous*), even *curtain*, and *cortège*, which comes from Italian *corteggio* through French. The phonological difficulty lies in the fact that IE **dh* before or after *r* normally gives Latin *b*, not *t* (compare Latin *verbum*, English *word*). This leads some authorities to link *yard* and *gird* with Latin *urbs* rather than with *hortus* (but *urbs* lacks the initial *h* called for by IE **gh*), and this would lead us to *urban*, *suburb*, *urbane*, etc. The Slavic form is the *grad* or *gorod* of *Leningrad*, *Novgorod*, but so far as English is concerned, this appears only in place names (the semantics would go with *urbs* rather than with *hortus*, but both a garden and a town could in origin be an enclosure). Assuming *hortus* to be nearer right than *urbs*, we have:

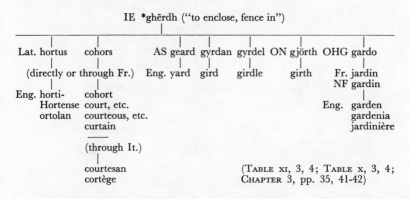

IE **ghērdh* ("to enclose, fence in")

Lat. hortus	cohors	AS geard	gyrdan	gyrdel	ON gjörth	OHG gardo
(directly or through Fr.)		Eng. yard	gird	girdle	girth	Fr. jardin / NF gardin
Eng. horti- / Hortense / ortolan	cohort / court, etc. / courteous, etc. / curtain					Eng. garden / gardenia / jardinière
	(through It.)					
	courtesan / cortège			(TABLE XI, 3, 4; TABLE X, 3, 4; CHAPTER 3, pp. 35, 41-42)		

One of the most productive IE roots is **deuk*, "to draw, pull". On the Germanic side come Anglo-Saxon *togian*, *tēon*, which become *tow*, with *towline*, *towboat*, etc., and with the compound *wan togen*, "poorly drawn or educated", which becomes *wanton;* *tiegan*, which gives us *tug; toht*, yielding *taut; tīeman*, becoming *teem; tēam*, becoming *team* (*teamster*, *teamwork*, *team-mate*, etc.); *tūdor*, becoming Middle English *teder* and modern English *tether; tūccian*, becoming *tuck; tyge*, *tēh* and *tīegan*, giving *tie;* with *tight* coming either from Anglo-Saxon *tyht* or from a kindred Scandinavian form (*tighten*, *tights*, *tightrope*, *tightwad*, etc.).

In addition, we have *toy* from Dutch *tuig, speeltuig*, "play-gadget", and the High German *heritogo, herizogo*, which becomes *Herzog*, "army-puller, army leader" (in modern German, this root gives *Zug*, "train"). Latin forms comprise *duco*, "to lead", with past participle *ductus*, and *dux*, "leader". The latter gives us *duke, duchess, duchy, archduke, grand duke, ducal, ducat*, the *doge* of Venice and the *Duce* of Fascism. The verbal forms lead to our numerous compounds in *-duce*, *-duct, -ducate*, all of which involve the idea of leading, conducting; as well as to the Italian *condottiere;* the French *conduit;* the French *douche* from Italian *doccia;* the French *endue* and *subdue; redoubt*, with a *b* from *dubito*, "to doubt", thrown in by mistake (French *redoute*, Italian *ridotto*, from *reductus*). Among *-duce* forms are *adduce, conducive, deduce, introduce, produce, producer, reproduce, seduce, traduce; -duct* forms from the participial stem include *duct, duction, ductile, ductless, viaduct, aqueduct, abduct, abduction, conduct, conductor, deduct, deduction, introduction, product, production, productive, reproduction, reduction, seduction, seductive;* while *-ducate* produces *educate, education, educational, educator*, etc.

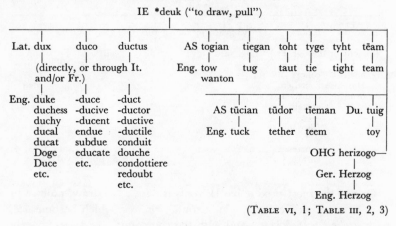

IE *deuk ("to draw, pull")

Lat. dux	duco	ductus	AS togian	tiegan	toht	tyge	tyht	tĕam
(directly, or through It. and/or Fr.)			Eng. tow wanton	tug	taut	tie	tight	team
Eng. duke	-duce	-duct	AS tūcian	tūdor	tīeman	Du. tuig		
duchess	-ducive	-ductor						
duchy	-ducent	-ductive	Eng. tuck	tether	teem	toy		
ducal	endue	-ductile						
ducat	subdue	conduit	OHG herizogo—					
Doge	educate	douche						
Duce	etc.	condottiere	Ger. Herzog					
etc.		redoubt						
		etc.	Eng. Herzog					

(TABLE VI, 1; TABLE III, 2, 3)

Another immensely productive root is that of IE *dherāgh*, "to sleep on the ground, draw". It presents a major phonological difficulty, since the Latin forms we shall soon see ought to have initial *f* instead of *t* from IE *dh*. In view of the clear semantic connection, however, this discrepancy is minimized by the experts, who attribute the *t* instead of *f* to a dissimilation of one of the two spirants in the word, or to an alternative IE form *terāgh. On the Germanic side, we have Anglo-Saxon *dragan* becoming *draw* (with *withdraw, drawing-room, drawer, drawers, drawing, drawl,* as well as *draught* or *draft, draughts, drafty, draftsman*); an Anglo-Saxon noun *dræge,* leading to *dray,* and possibly also to *dredge* and *dredger* (these may, however, represent a Dutch development of the Germanic root); and an Old Norse *draga* which gives us *drag, draggle, bedraggled* (note that the *-g,* which in Anglo-Saxon development turns into *-y* or *-w,* remains in words borrowed late from Scandinavian; see Chapter 3, p. 35). From Dutch *trek,* which seems to have been borrowed from High German (Dutch would keep the same initial *d-* as English, while High German, by the second consonant shift, would turn it to *t-*), we have *trek* and *track, voortrekker* (the original Boers of South Africa who moved north from Capetown into the African hinterland), and *trigger.* The Latin form, showing the questionable *t-* for *f-,* is *traho,* "to draw", with its past participle *tractus* (for **trahtus; ht* and *gt* both shift to *ct* in Latin), and from this we get all our compounds in *-tract-, -treat-, -trait-, -trace-, -trail-, -train,* and even *trawl* and *trawler; tract, traction, tractable, tractile, tractor, retractile, abstract, abstraction, attract, attraction, contract, contractor, detract, detraction, distract, distraction, extract, extraction, protract, retract, retraction, subtract, subtraction, intractable,* along with the Italian *trattoria,* "restaurant"; *treat, entreat, entreaty, maltreat, treatment, retreat, treatise, treaty; trait, portrait, portray; trace, tracer, traces, retrace; trail, trailer; train, entrain, training;* and other forms too numerous to list. A Slavic cognate appears in Russian *doroga,* "road".

IE *dherāgh, *terāgh(?) ("to sleep on the ground, draw")

Lat. traho	tractus	AS dragan	dræge	ON draga	Du. trek
	(directly or through Fr.)	Eng. draw	dray	drag	trek
		draught	dredge (?)	draggle	track
	Eng. -tract-	draft			voortrekker
	-trace-				trigger
	-trait-				
	-tray				
	-trail				
	-train				
	-treat				
	treaty				
	trawl				
	etc.				

(TABLE X, 3, 4; TABLE XI, 3, 4)

The IE root *ghend, *ghed, "to seize, grasp", produces an Old Norse geta and an Anglo-Saxon begietan, bigetan, which combine in English get, beget, forget, misbegotten, and lead to such modern English forms as getaway and go-getter. The form guess, coming from Middle English gessen, is said to go back to Low German or Scandinavian (get-sian is suggested to account for the English ss instead of t). On the Latin side, we have praehendo (prae-hendo), with a past participle praehensus, which in French ultimately becomes pris, prise; there is also a noun praeda (from *prae-henda), from which, directly or through French, we get prey, predator, predatory, (de)predation. The Latin verb, in compound form, gives prehensile, apprehend, apprehension, apprehensive, misapprehension, comprehend, comprehension, reprehend, reprehensible, while various French developments, mostly from the French past participle pris, prise, lead to prise, prize, pry, apprise, comprise, enterprise, surprise, reprisal, prison (from prae-hensio), with emprison, prisoner, etc. There are also apprentice, impregnable, and the straight French entrepreneur.

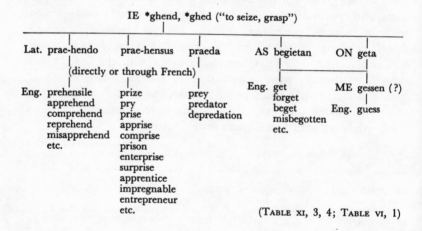

IE *ghend, *ghed ("to seize, grasp")

Lat. prae-hendo	prae-hensus	praeda	AS begietan	ON geta
(directly or through French)				
Eng. prehensile apprehend comprehend reprehend misapprehend etc.	prize pry prise apprise comprise prison enterprise surprise apprentice impregnable entrepreneur etc.	prey predator depredation	Eng. get forget beget misbegotten etc.	ME gessen (?) Eng. guess

(TABLE XI, 3, 4; TABLE VI, 1)

The next two families seem intimately related, and it is difficult to unscramble their descendants in spots. IE *kap, "to seize", gives us Anglo-Saxon habban and English have (with behave, behavior, behaviorism, etc.); also Anglo-Saxon *hæfen* and English *haven* (with such foreign place names as *Habana*, *Le Havre*, *København* or *Copenhagen*, from the same Germanic root); Anglo-Saxon *hefe* and English *heft;* Anglo-Saxon *hebban* and English *heave;* Anglo-Saxon *behōfian* and English *behoove;* Anglo-Saxon *hefig* and English *heavy* (with *heavily*, *heaviness*); Anglo-Saxon *hæft* and English *haft;* Anglo-Saxon *heafoc* and English *hawk*, and, from the same word-root, but with development through Old French *crier havot*, "to cry pillage", *havoc*. There is a further possibility, through Old Nórse *happ*, "good luck", of tying to the same root *hap*, *happen*, *happenstance*, *haphazard*, *happy*, *happiness*. The Latin form, *capio*, "to take", with past participle *captus*, which in compound

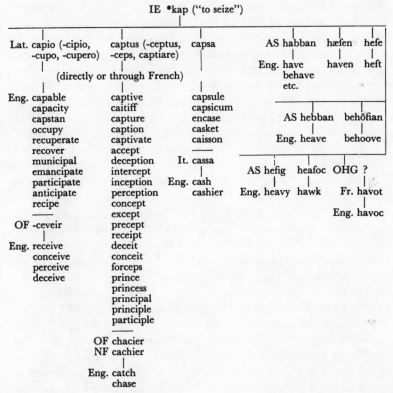

IE **kap* ("to seize")

Lat. capio (-cipio, -cupo, -cupero)	captus (-ceptus, -ceps, captiare)	capsa	AS habban hæfen hefe
	(directly or through French)		Eng. have haven heft behave etc.
Eng. capable	captive	capsule	
capacity	caitiff	capsicum	AS hebban behōfian
capstan	capture	encase	
occupy	caption	casket	Eng. heave behoove
recuperate	captivate	caisson	
recover	accept		
municipal	deception	It. cassa	AS hefig heafoc OHG ?
emancipate	intercept		
participate	inception	Eng. cash	Eng. heavy hawk Fr. havot
anticipate	perception	cashier	
recipe	concept		Eng. havoc
———	except		
OF -ceveir	precept		
	receipt		
Eng. receive	deceit		
conceive	conceit		
perceive	forceps		
deceive	prince		
	princess		
	principal		
	principle		
	participle		
	OF chacier		
	NF cachier		
	Eng. catch		
	chase		

(TABLE III, 2, 3; TABLE I, 4; CHAPTER 3, pp. 34, 41)

forms become -*cipio* and -*ceptus*, give us forms in *cap-, capt-, -cept, -cup-* or -*cupy, -ceipt, -ceive, -cip-, -cipate,* of which only a few can be listed: *capable, capacity, capability, capacious, incapable, capstan; captive* (with its northern French variant *caitiff*), *caption, captious, capture, captivate; accept, acceptance, deception, deceptive, intercept, inception, perception, perceptive, concept, conceptual, except, precept, receptacle, susceptible; occupy, occupant, occupation, recuperate* (and its variant *recover*, which has nothing to do with *cover*); *deceit, receipt, conceit; receive, deceive, perceive, conceive, conceivable, receiver; forceps; municipal, municipality, participle; prince* (which is *primi-ceps, "the one who takes first place"), with *princess, principal, principality, principle; emancipate, emancipator, anticipate, participate, participation, anticipation*. But this is only a beginning. *Recipe* is an imperative form of *re-cipio*, "receive, take". *Catch* and *chase* are respectively the Norman-Picard and the Francien version of a Vulgar Latin *captiare*, built on the participial root of *captus*, and *purchase* is "to chase through" (*porchacier* in Old French). In addition, there is the noun *capsa*, from the root of *capio*, meaning "receptacle, that which takes", from which we get on the one hand *capsule* and *capsicum*, on the other *case* (in the sense of "receptacle"), *encase, encasement, casket, caisson,* and, through Italian, *cash* and *cashier*. For a few other words, there is doubt whether they belong with *kap or with the following *kaput, "head".

IE *kap-ut, "head", may be related to *kap, "seize", through semantic use as "vessel, receptacle for the brain". On the Germanic side, it gives Gothic *haubith*, German *Haupt*, and Anglo-Saxon *hēafoth*, which turns into *head*, a word that has many compounds and derivatives (*ahead, behead, heading, heady, headache, headstrong, headlong, headcheese, headland, headless, headline, headlight, head-on, headquarters, headstone, headway* are only a few). Through Latin *caput* we get *cap* and *cape* (the first form comes through Anglo-Saxon *cæppe*, though it was later joined by the French descendants of *caput*). Words with regular French form (French turns *c* to *ch* before *a*) appear in *chief, chieftain, chef* (a later development of Old French *chief*, and English borrows the word twice), with *chef d'oeuvre*; also *kerchief* (*couvre-chief*, or "cover-head", which makes *handkerchief* slightly nonsensical), *mischief* and *mischievous, achieve* (*achever*, or "bring to a head") and *achievement*. A conflict between the Francien and the Norman-Picard development of the Latin *capitalis*, "pertaining to a head", appears in *chattel* vs.

cattle; but we also have learned treatment in *capital, capitalism, capitulate, capitulary, recapitulation, decapitate.* A Provençal (southern French) form appears in *cadet,* with *cad* and *caddie.* Other forms appear in *captain, biceps* ("double-headed"), *chapter* (from *capitulum,* which also gives the Spanish *cabildo), caudillo* (the Spanish development of *capitellum,* "little head"), *occipital, precipice, precipitate* ("to hurl headlong") *caparison. Capillary,* from *capillum,* "hair", may also belong here. *Cape,* which in the meaning of "headland" definitely comes from *caput,* in the sense of "cloak" stems from *cappa,* a "covering for the head", later a "cloak". Here we have *capote* (with its German adaptation *kaput*) and *capuchin* (the latter from Italian); *escape* (getting out of a cloak that someone has thrown over your head; compare the native English *hoodwink*) and *escapade;* possibly *cope* and *coping* (but these may also come from French *couper,* "to cut off"); and the clearly French *chapeau, chapel, chaplain, chaplet* and *chaperon.* The story of *chapel* is to the effect that St. Martin of Tours, who was an officer in the Roman army, cut his military cloak (*cappa*) in two to give half to a beggar, who turned out to be Christ, and that a shrine erected to commemorate

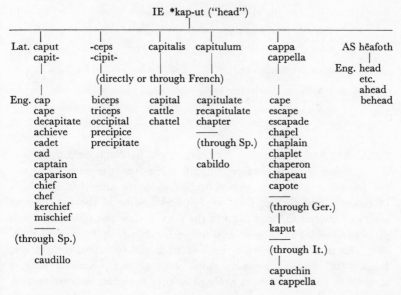

IE *kap-ut ("head")

Lat. caput	-ceps	capitalis	capitulum	cappa	AS hēafoth
capit-	-cipit-			cappella	
					Eng. head
	(directly or through French)				etc.
					ahead
Eng. cap	biceps	capital	capitulate	cape	behead
cape	triceps	cattle	recapitulate	escape	
decapitate	occipital	chattel	chapter	escapade	
achieve	precipice		——	chapel	
cadet	precipitate		(through Sp.)	chaplain	
cad				chaplet	
captain			cabildo	chaperon	
caparison				chapeau	
chief				capote	
chef					
kerchief				(through Ger.)	
mischief					
——				kaput	
(through Sp.)				——	
caudillo				(through It.)	
				capuchin	
				a cappella	

(TABLE III, 2, 3; TABLE I, 4; TABLE II, 1)

his act of charity bore the name of "little cloak" or "half cloak", *cappella;* a more prosaic explanation is that the chapel, being covered, afforded shelter similar to that of a cloak. The Italian *a cappella* singing comes from the Italian form, which is identical with the Latin. *Chaperon* was in origin a "cloak" or "protection", and the term was applied to the elderly lady who by her presence gave protection (and perhaps even a figurative cloak) to a younger woman in the company of the other sex.

The IE root **kel*, "to hasten, drive cattle", leads to Anglo-Saxon *healdan* and English *hold* (with such derivatives as *holder, holdover* and *beholden*). The High German form appears in German *halten*, from which French takes the military command passed on to English as *halt*, and generalized both as a verb and a noun. The Latin form appears in *celer*, "swift", of *celerity, accelerate, deceleration*, etc., which some authorities prefer to derive from non-Indo-European Etruscan; and in *celeber*, "frequented", later "famous", which appears in *celebrate, celebrity, celebration*, etc.

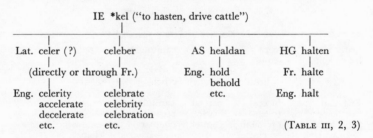

IE *kel ("to hasten, drive cattle")

Lat. celer (?)	celeber	AS healdan	HG halten
(directly or through Fr.)		Eng. hold	Fr. halte
Eng. celerity	celebrate	behold	
accelerate	celebrity	etc.	Eng. halt
decelerate	celebration		
etc.	etc.		(TABLE III, 2, 3)

Another **kel* root means "to call, cry". In Anglo-Saxon, it produces *hlōwan*, which modern English turns into the verb "to low" (all initial *hl-* and *hr-* groups of Anglo-Saxon are simplified into *l-*, *r-* in modern English; see Chapter 3, p. 34). Some of the Latin forms insert *a* between the initial *c* and the *l*, as in *Kalendae, Calendae*, which gives us *Calends* and *calendar*, and the verb *calo*, which gives us *intercalation*. The majority, however, present an initial *cl-; clamo* and *clamor*, leading to *clamor, clamorous, claim*, with *claimant, acclaim, declaim, declamation, disclaim, reclaim, reclamation, exclaim, exclamation, exclamatory, proclaim, proclamation, nomenclature; clarus*, which gives us *clarity, clarify*, *declare, declaration, declarative, clarinet, éclair, clairvoyant, clear, clearance, clear-cut, clearing-house, clarion, claret; classis,* which gives us *class, classic, classical, classify, classification, classroom, classmate,* and the French *déclassé.* There are also forms in which the *a* of *calo,* unstressed, becomes *i,* as in *concilium,* giving us *council, councilor, ⸗conciliate, reconcile, reconciliation, conciliatory.* In Slavic the root produces, among other things, the Russian *kolokol,* "bell" (*Tsar Kolokol,* the "Emperor Bell").

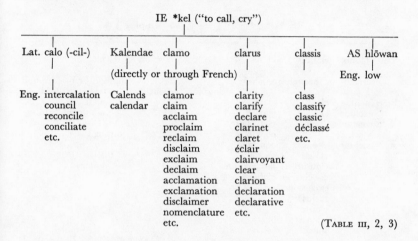

IE *kel ("to call, cry")

Lat. calo (-cil-)	Kalendae	clamo	clarus	classis	AS hlōwan
	(directly or through French)				Eng. low
Eng. intercalation	Calends	clamor	clarity	class	
council	calendar	claim	clarify	classify	
reconcile		acclaim	declare	classic	
conciliate		proclaim	clarinet	déclassé	
etc.		reclaim	claret	etc.	
		disclaim	éclair		
		exclaim	clairvoyant		
		declaim	clear		
		acclamation	clarion		
		exclamation	declaration		
		disclaimer	declarative		
		nomenclature	etc.		
		etc.			

(TABLE III, 2, 3)

The IE root *klēu,* with a possible extension *klēud,* means "hook, wooden plug". In Anglo-Saxon it gives us *hlēotan, hlot,* which become *lot.* French, receiving the Germanic root from Old High German (Frankish) *hlōt,* combines it with the Latin preposition *ad,* "to", in the form *aloter,* which is passed on to English as *allot, allotment.* Italian receives it as *lotto, lotteria,* which are passed on to English as *lotto, lottery.* With an *s-* prefix, the word appears in Middle English as *slot.* A similar formation in High German is *slōz,* which eventually becomes *Schloss,* "castle". The connection of German *Schloss* with the verb *schliessen,* "to close", leads to a suspicion that *lot* and *slot* may have a connection with *slit* (Anglo-Saxon *slītan*), and possibly with *slice* and *slat.* The chief Latin forms are *claudo,* "to close", with its past participle *clausus,* and *clavis,* "key". The latter gives us *clavicle, claviform, clavichord, clavier, conclave, enclave, laticlavium,* and the French *clef.* From the verb *claudo* and its participle *clausus* we get *close, enclose, disclose, enclosure, disclosure, closet, closure* or *cloture, clause, include, conclude, preclude, occlude, exclude,* with derivatives in *-clusion,* such as *inclusion* and *exclusion; recluse, cloister, claustrophobia* (a hybrid, since it combines Latin *claustrum,* "closed space", with Greek *phobia,* "fear"). Lastly, there is *sluice,* coming from the French *escluse,* which in turn comes from Latin *exclusa (aqua),* "shut-out water". Spanish *clavel,* "carnation", comes from still another Latin form, *clavus,* "nail".

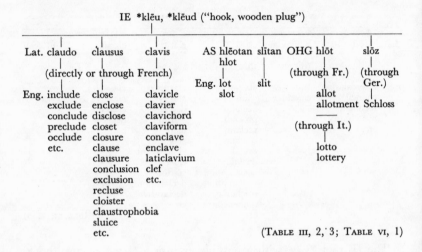

IE *klēu, *klēud ("hook, wooden plug")

Lat. claudo	clausus	clavis	AS hlēotan hlot	slītan	OHG hlōt	slōz
	(directly or through French)				(through Fr.)	(through Ger.)
			Eng. lot	slit		
Eng. include	close	clavicle	slot		allot	
exclude	enclose	clavier			allotment	Schloss
conclude	disclose	clavichord			———	
preclude	closet	claviform			(through It.)	
occlude	closure	conclave				
etc.	clause	enclave			lotto	
	clausure	laticlavium			lottery	
	conclusion	clef				
	exclusion	etc.				
	recluse					
	cloister					
	claustrophobia					
	sluice					
	etc.					

(TABLE III, 2, 3; TABLE VI, 1)

The IE root *pā, *pā-t,* "to nurture, feed", appears in Anglo-Saxon *fōda, fēdan, fōthor* and *fōstor,* which develop respectively into *food, feed, fodder,* and *foster,* with such compounds as *foodstuffs, feeder, feedback, foster-parent,* etc. In Latin, we have *pasco,* "to feed, graze", with past participle *pastus; panis,* "bread"; and *pabulum,* "fodder". The participial root of the verb produces, directly or through French, *pastor, pastoral, pasture, repast, pastourelle, pasteurize* and *pasteurization* (through *Pasteur,* the family name of the scientist after whom the process was named); also *paste, pastry,* the French *pâtisserie* and *pâté, pasty, patty,* the Italian *pasta, pastel, pastiche, pasticcio.* There are compound forms like *pasteboard, pâté de foie gras, pasta asciutta.* From the root of *panis,* we get *panification* and *pastille; panel* and *empanel* (but these may also come from *pannus,* "cloth"); *pantry* (Old French *paneterie,* "place where bread is made or kept"); *appanage* (originally "an allowance for bread" and other necessities); *companion, company, companionate, accompany, accompanist* (here we have a Latin loan-translation from the Germanic *ga-hlaifs*, "with-loaf", "one who shares bread with you"; just as *comrade* is in origin "one who shares a room (*camera*) with you", a "room-mate"). There are also the Spanish *panada* and *empanada*.

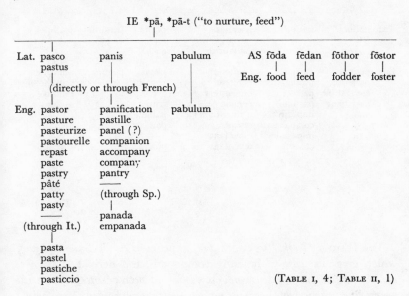

IE *pā, *pā-t ("to nurture, feed")

Lat.	pasco pastus	panis	pabulum	AS	fōda	fēdan	fōthor	fōstor
				Eng.	food	feed	fodder	foster

(directly or through French)

Eng.	pastor	panification	pabulum
	pasture	pastille	
	pasteurize	panel (?)	
	pastourelle	companion	
	repast	accompany	
	paste	company	
	pastry	pantry	
	pâté	———	
	patty	(through Sp.)	
	pasty		
	———	panada	
	(through It.)	empanada	
	pasta		
	pastel		
	pastiche		
	pasticcio		

(TABLE I, 4; TABLE II, 1)

The IE root *pē(i)*, "abuse, sorrow, illness", appears in Anglo-Saxon in *fēond*, leading to *fiend*, the producer of such manifestations, with *fiendish, fiendly* (note that in German *Feind*, the same form is extended to mean "enemy, foe" in general, rather than the specific "Enemy of Mankind"). On the Latin side, we have *patior*, with past participle *passus*, "to suffer, endure, undergo"; *paenitet*, "it causes repentance, regret"; *poena*, "penalty"; *penuria*, "penury, lack"; *punio*, "to punish". From *patior* and its participle come *patient, patience, impatient, compatible; passion, passible, passive, passionate, compassion, impassioned* (with such compounds as *passion flower, Passion play, passive resistance,* etc.); *paenitet* yields *penitence, penance, penitential, penitentiary, impenitent, repent, repentance, repentant; poena* gives *penal, penalty, penalize, pain, painful, painless, painstaking,* the Latin *subpoena,* and, through *pīnian,* an Anglo-Saxon development of the Latin *poena, pine* and *repine; penuria* yields *penury* and *penurious;* and *punio* gives *punish, punishment, punitive, impunity.*

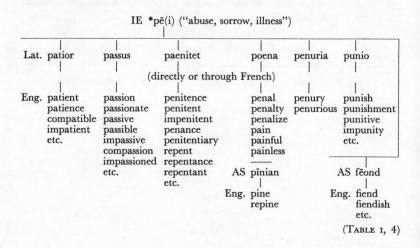

IE *pē(i) ("abuse, sorrow, illness")

Lat.	patior	passus	paenitet		poena	penuria	punio
			(directly or through French)				
Eng.	patient	passion	penitence		penal	penury	punish
	patience	passionate	penitent		penalty	penurious	punishment
	compatible	passive	impenitent		penalize		punitive
	impatient	passible	penance		pain		impunity
	etc.	impassive	penitentiary		painful		etc.
		compassion	repent		painless		
		impassioned	repentance		———		
		etc.	repentant	AS	pīnian		AS fēond
			etc.				
				Eng.	pine	Eng.	fiend
					repine		fiendish
							etc.

(TABLE I, 4)

The IE root *wegh,* "to go, draw", appears in Anglo-Saxon as *weg,* which gives us *way,* with many compounds and derivatives: *away, always, wayfarer, waylay, wayward,* etc.); *wægn,* which becomes *wain,* with *wainscoting, wainwright; wagian,* which leads to *wag, waggle, waggish; wegan, wǣg,* which becomes *weigh,* with *weighty, weightless,* etc. The same root that appears in Anglo-Saxon *wægn* appears in Dutch as *wagen,* and eventually becomes *wagon* (with *wagonette, wagon train,* the French *wagon-lit,* etc.), while the same root in German produces the proper name *Wagner.* The Latin forms are *veho,* "to carry", with past participle *vectus,* from which we derive *vehicle, vehicular, inveigh,* etc.; *vector, vection, convector, convection, convex, invective; vehemens,* which gives us *vehement, vehemence,* etc.; *velox,* which leads to *velocity, velocipede, velodrome,* and the Italian musical *veloce; via,* from which come, mostly through French, *viable, viability, viaduct, viaticum, deviate, devious, deviation, deviationist, obviate, obvious, previous, impervious, trivia, trivial, trivium,* and *triviality, quadrivium, convey, conveyor, conveyance, convoy, envoy, invoice* (Old French *envois,* "things sent", from the verb *envoyer,* from *in-viare,* "to send on its way"), *renvoi, voyage, voyager* (the last two are developments of *viaticum*, "that which is necessary for the way or journey").

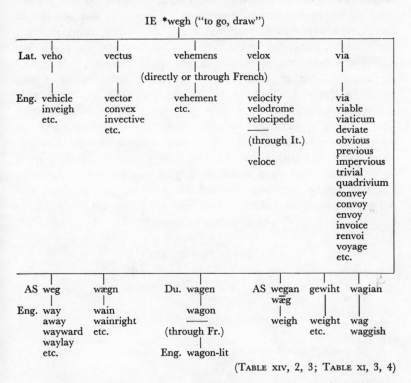

IE *wegh ("to go, draw")

Lat.	veho	vectus	vehemens	velox	via
			(directly or through French)		
Eng.	vehicle	vector	vehement	velocity	via
	inveigh	convex	etc.	velodrome	viable
	etc.	invective		velocipede	viaticum
		etc.		———	deviate
				(through It.)	obvious
					previous
				veloce	impervious
					trivial
					quadrivium
					convey
					convoy
					envoy
					invoice
					renvoi
					voyage
					etc.

AS	weg	wægn	Du. wagen	AS wegan	gewiht	wagian
				wæg		
Eng.	way	wain	wagon		weight	wag
	away	wainright	———	weigh	etc.	waggish
	wayward	etc.	(through Fr.)			
	waylay					
	etc.		Eng. wagon-lit			

(TABLE XIV, 2, 3; TABLE XI, 3, 4)

The IE root *ghabh*, "to seize, take", appears in Latin *habeo*, "have", with its contracted compounds *debeo* (*de-habeo*), "owe", and *praebeo* (*prae-habeo*), "offer", as well as numerous other compounds in which contraction does not occur, but *-habeo* appears in modified form as *-hibeo* (*prohibeo, exhibeo, adhibeo, inhibeo*, etc.). There is also an adjective *habilis*, "able", often appearing as *-hibilis, -ibilis* in compounds. There are secondary formations like *habito* and *habitus*, and an adjective *debilis*, "feeble", from *debeo*. *Habeo* itself, which provides the Romance languages with their verbs meaning "to have" (*avoir, haber, avere*, etc.), gives us the legal *habeas corpus* ("you may have the body"). *Debeo* supplies *debit, debt, debtor, indebtedness, debenture, due, duty*, and *endeavor*.

Praebeo supplies *prebend* and *provender*. Compounds in *-hibeo* give us *adhibit*, *exhibit*, *exhibition*, *exhibitionist*, *inhibit*, *inhibition*, *prohibit*, *prohibition*. *Habilis*, in addition to giving the suffixes *-able* and *-ible* (as in *capable*, *capability*, *sensible*, *sensibility*), forms *able*, *unable*, *ability*, *inability*, *enable*, *disable*, *able-bodied*; in the verb-form *habilitare*, it gives us *habilitate*, *rehabilitate*, *habiliment*, *déshabillé*. *Debilis* gives *debilitate*, while *male habitus* ("holding or held badly") produces the French *malade*, *maladie* and the English *malady*. *Habitus* by itself produces *habit*, *habitual*, *habituate*, *habitué*. *Habitare* gives the Latin *habitat* (literally "he inhabits"), *habitation*, *inhabit*, *inhabitant*, *uninhabited*, while a derivative *habitaculum*, through Portuguese *bitácola*, becomes *binnacle*. Germanic forms appear in Anglo-Saxon *giefan*, probably derived from Scandinavian or a northern English dialect, which becomes *give*, with *forgive*, *forgiveness*, *give and take*, *givaway*; *giefu* and *gift*, also probably taken from Scandinavian, with *gift* and *gifted*; *gafol*, which becomes *gavel*; and possibly *gabelle* (though this may come from

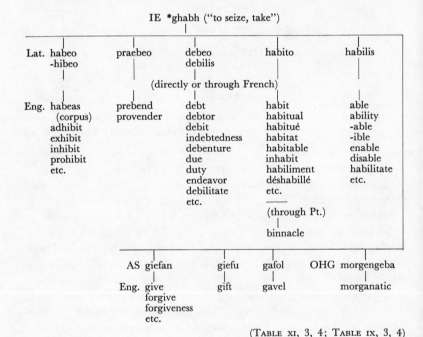

IE *ghabh ("to seize, take")

Lat.	habeo -hibeo	praebeo	debeo debilis	habito	habilis
			(directly or through French)		
Eng.	habeas (corpus) adhibit exhibit inhibit prohibit etc.	prebend provender	debt debtor debit indebtedness debenture due duty endeavor debilitate etc.	habit habitual habitué habitat habitable inhabit habiliment déshabillé etc. (through Pt.) binnacle	able ability -able -ible enable disable habilitate etc.

	AS giefan	giefu	gafol	OHG morgengeba
Eng.	give forgive forgiveness etc.	gift	gavel	morganatic

(TABLE XI, 3, 4; TABLE IX, 3, 4)

Celtic *gabagla* or Arabic *qābalah*). There is also *morganatic*, which comes from the first part of Old High German *morgengeba*, "morning gift" (it was customary for the aristocrat who married beneath his station to make an endowment of worldly goods to his lower-class bride on the morning following their wedding night). As to the semantic difference between the Latin *habeo* and the Germanic *give*, it is explained as representing the same act from opposite points of view.

CHAPTER 6

Three–Branch Families

Three-branch families are, in their overwhelming majority, of the Greek-Latin-Germanic persuasion. This is quite natural, since these three branches supply English with most of its vocabulary. The Greek contribution is, for the most part, of the learned or scientific variety, and, though built on the most anciently recorded of the three members, it is likely to be the most modern so far as English is concerned. This, however, is not invariably the case, since numerous Greek words entered Latin and were then passed on to English either directly or through an intermediate French or other Romance stage.

A. MIXED GROUPS

It is only occasionally that in a three-branch family Indo-Iranian or Celtic replaces Greek, Latin, or Germanic. The first example is widespread throughout all the Indo-European branches, but only four are productive so far as English is concerned; and one of them, Greek, gives us only an obsolete word, justifying its exclusion. The root is that of IE *bhrāter, "relative, brother", which in Greek produces the little-used *phrater* and *phratria* (*adelphos*, "from the same womb", is the replacement preferred by Greek); in English, this gives us *phratry*, but the word is practically obsolete today. In Indo-Iranian, the Sanskrit form is *bhrātr*, which eventually develops into Romany Gypsy *pral*, corrupted by English slang usage into *pal*. The Latin form, *frater*, gives us *fraternal*, *fraternity*, *fraternize*, *fratricide*, and, through French development, *friar* and *friary*, as well as *confrère*, while a Spanish development gives *Fray* (as in *Fray Luis de León*) from *fraile*. Anglo-Saxon *brothōr* produces *brother*, with *brotherly*, *brotherhood*, *brother-in-law*, and the irregular plural *brethren*, as well as the *br'er* of the U.S. South.

There is a suspicion that *boy* (Middle English *boi*) may come from the same root, from an Old Norse *bofi*, "rogue", with a development similar to that of German *Bube* from Old High German *buobo*, but this is uncertain.

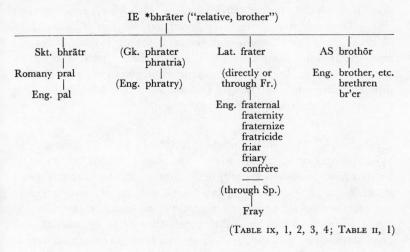

IE *bhrāter ("relative, brother")

Skt. bhrātr	(Gk. phrater phratria)	Lat. frater	AS brothōr
Romany pral		(directly or through Fr.)	Eng. brother, etc. brethren br'er
Eng. pal	(Eng. phratry)		
		Eng. fraternal fraternity fraternize fratricide friar friary confrère	
		(through Sp.)	
		Fray	

(TABLE IX, 1, 2, 3, 4; TABLE II, 1)

The root *kei*, "to lie, home, camp", produces in Anglo-Saxon the form *hām*, which appears on the one hand in place-name endings in *-ham* (*Birmingham, Durham,* etc.), as well as in *hamlet;* on the other hand, under the stress, it becomes *home* with its many compounds and derivatives (*homeless, home brew, homework, homespun, homesick, homemaker, home run, homestead, homely, homeliness,* etc.). *Haunt,* which with

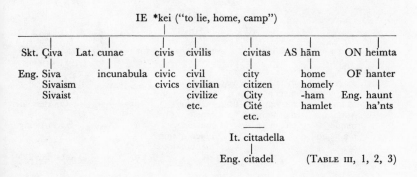

IE *kei ("to lie, home, camp")

Skt. Çiva	Lat. cunae	civis	civilis	civitas	AS hām	ON heimta
Eng. Siva Sivaism Sivaist	incunabula	civic civics	civil civilian civilize etc.	city citizen City Cité etc.	home homely -ham hamlet	OF hanter
						Eng. haunt ha'nts
			It. cittadella			
			Eng. citadel		(TABLE III, 1, 2, 3)	

the dialectal U.S. *ha'nts* goes back to Old French *hanter*, may have as its Germanic progenitor either Old Norse *heimta*, "to bring the cows home, to frequent", or Anglo-Saxon *hāmettan*, "to house". On the Latin side, the root gives rise to *civis*, "citizen", from which come *civic, civil, uncivil, civilian, civics, civilize, civilization*, and, through *civitas*, "city, city state", *city, citizen, citizenship*, the *City* of London, the *Ile de la Cité* of Paris. *Citadel*, from the same source, is directly derived from the Italian *cittadella*. There is also the Latin *cunae*, from which we get *incunabula*. In Indo-Iranian, the root gives rise, among other things, to the name of the god *Çiva* or *Siva*, "the friendly one, the preserver", from which we get *Sivaism, Sivaist*, etc.

IE **magh*, "can, help, might", produces in Indo-Iranian the Sanskrit forms *māyā*, "magic power" and *magha*, "might", and an Old Persian form from which Latin derives *magus*, the word that appears in *Magi, magic, magician, magical*. Greek *mekhane* (*mechane*) gives us *mechanic, mechanical, mechanism, mechanistic, mechanize*, etc., while the Doric variant *makhana* (*machana*) comes into Latin as *machina*, and gives us *machine, machinist, machination, machinery, machine gun, machine shop, machine tool, etc*. In Germanic, Anglo-Saxon *magan, mæg* give English *may*, and, through a French development of the Germanic root (*de-ex-*magare* to *desmaier*), *dismay*, while Anglo-Saxon *meahte* produces *might, mighty*. (In the Indo-European period, **gt* was shifted to **kt* by assimilation; then the first Germanic sound shift turns **kt* to *ht*). The Slavic word for "to be able" (Russian *moch'*, with present *mogu*) is also from this root, but does not appear in English.

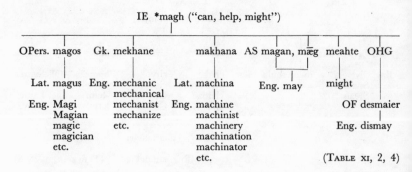

IE *magh ("can, help, might")

OPers. magos	Gk. mekhane		makhana	AS magan, mæg	meahte	OHG
Lat. magus	Eng. mechanic	Lat. machina			might	
	mechanical			Eng. may		
Eng. Magi	mechanist	Eng. machine				OF desmaier
Magian	mechanize	machinist				
magic	etc.	machinery				Eng. dismay
magician		machination				
etc.		machinator				
		etc.				(TABLE XI, 2, 4)

One three-branch family in which Celtic replaces Greek presents certain phonological complications. This is IE *perkᵘs, "oak". Through Old Norse *fyri*, English acquires *fir*. The Cymric (Welsh, Brythonic) branch of Celtic produces the place-name *Perth* (from a word meaning "hedge" or "bush"; "a place of hedges or bushes"), and from this comes the name of the little-known mineral found in Ontario called *perthite*. Note that in order to achieve *Perth*, we must postulate for *perkᵘs in Celtic (as we must also in Latin) a shift from initial IE *p-, which would fall in Celtic and remain in Latin, to *kw, which in Latin becomes *qu-* and in the Brythonic branch of Celtic becomes *p-* (in the Irish or Goidelic branch of Celtic, *kw-* would come out as *c-*; the fact that Perth is in Scotland, which is today Goidelic territory, need not perturb us, as many Brythonic place names appear there, and it is probable that Brythonic speakers preceded the Goidelic speakers in that area). This shift is accounted for by the assimilative pull exerted on the initial *p-* by the *kw that appears later in the word, and is of the same nature as the one we see in the case of the root *penkᵘe, "five", where, corresponding to Sanskrit *panca*, Greek *pente*, Slavic (Russian) *pyat'*, English *five*, etc., we have Latin *quinque* (but Oscan *pump*), Irish *cuig* (but Welsh *pimp*). In the case of *perkᵘs, Latin, with the same shift caused by assimilation from initial *p to *kw, gives us *quercus*, "oak", from which we get *quercine, quercitron*,

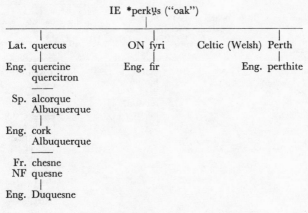

```
                    IE *perkᵘs ("oak")
                          |
_____
      |                   |                        |
Lat. quercus         ON fyri          Celtic (Welsh) Perth
      |                   |                        |
Eng. quercine        Eng. fir                Eng. perthite
     quercitron

Sp. alcorque
    Albuquerque
      |
Eng. cork
     Albuquerque

Fr. chesne
NF  quesne
      |
Eng. Duquesne
```

(TABLE IV, 4; TABLE I, 4)

Albuquerque ("white oak"; used as a Portuguese and Spanish family name), and *cork* (through Spanish *alcorque*, where the Arabic article *al-* is prefixed to the native descendant of *quercus*). A secondary derivative of *quercus* seems to have been **quesnus*, from which Old French may have derived *chesne* (modern French *chêne*); although *Casinum*, the progenitor of Monte Cassino, seems more likely from a phonological point of view; other authorities offer a hypothetical **cassanus*, phonologically unsatisfactory. This in the Norman-Picard dialects comes out as *quesne*, and as a proper name leads to *Fort Duquesne*, the old name of Pittsburgh.

IE **bhāt*, **bhau*, "to beat, strike" (but the connection of the two postulated root-forms is quite doubtful) also shows a Latin-Germanic-Celtic combination if it is accepted. Through Anglo-Saxon *bēatan* we get *beat* (with *beatnik*), while Anglo-Saxon *batt* gives us *bat* (with *batter*, *batting average*) and Anglo-Saxon *buttuc* gives *buttock*, with the possibility that it may also give us *butt* in the sense of "stump, end", and *butte*, with perhaps some participation by French *bout* and *but*, which seem to stem from a Germanic source. (If this participation

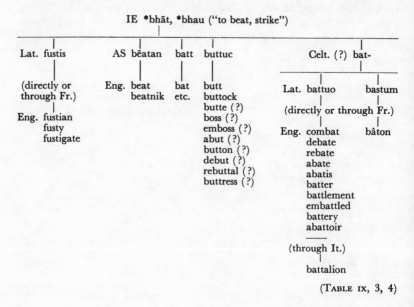

IE *bhāt, *bhau ("to beat, strike")

Lat. fustis	AS bēatan	batt	buttuc	Celt. (?) bat-	
(directly or through Fr.)	Eng. beat beatnik	bat etc.	butt buttock butte (?) boss (?) emboss (?) abut (?) button (?) debut (?) rebuttal (?) buttress (?)	Lat. battuo (directly or through Fr.)	bastum
Eng. fustian fusty fustigate				Eng. combat debate rebate abate abatis batter battlement embattled battery abattoir	bâton
				(through It.) battalion	

(TABLE IX, 3, 4)

holds true, we have also a link with *boss* in the sense of "protuberance", *emboss, abut, abutment, boutade, button, debut, rebut, rebuttal, buttress,* etc.) Latin gives us *fustis*, "stick", from which come *fustian*, "vegetable cloth, cloth from a wooden source", *fustigate* and *fustigation, fusty*; there is a remote possibility that *fatuous*, with *infatuate, infatuation*, and *confute, refute, refutation, irrefutable*, may come from this source, but for the first group a link with *vapidus* is suggested, for the second with *fundo*. Latin also has the verb *battuo* which is said to come to it from a Celtic source (but the borrowing may also have gone the other way); this gives us *combat, non-combatant, debate, debatable, rebate* and the archaic *rabbet, abate, abatement, abattoir, abatis, batter, battering-ram, bâton* and *Bâton Rouge* (here Latin had *bastum*, from the same source as *battuo*), *battle* (with *battle-ax, battle cruiser, battleship*) and *battlement, embattled, battery*, and the Italian-derived *battalion*. Limiting ourselves only to the more probable elements of a family whose unity is not at all certain, we have the family shown on page 150.

B. GREEK-LATIN-GERMANIC ROOTS

The IE root *ank*, *ang*, "bend", comes into Greek in the form *ankylos*, "crooked", and gives us scientific terms like *ankylosis;* but in the form *ankyra* it passes into Latin as *anchora* and ultimately reaches us as

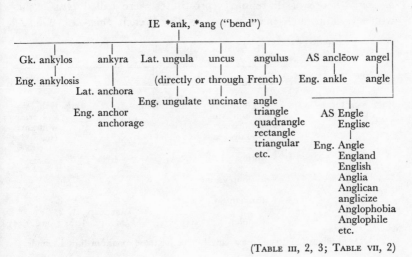

IE *ank, *ang ("bend")

Gk. ankylos	ankyra	Lat. ungula	uncus	angulus	AS ancléow	angel
Eng. ankylosis		(directly or through French)			Eng. ankle	angle
	Lat. anchora					
		Eng. ungulate	uncinate	angle triangle quadrangle rectangle triangular etc.		
	Eng. anchor anchorage				AS Engle Englisc	
					Eng. Angle England English Anglia Anglican anglicize Anglophobia Anglophile etc.	

(TABLE III, 2, 3; TABLE VII, 2)

anchor, with *anchorage*. Native Latin forms are *uncus*, "hook", of *uncinate;* *ungula*, "nail, hoof", of *ungulate* (French *ongle*, Italian *unghia*, Spanish *uña* do not come into English); and *angulus*, "angle, corner". The last gives us, directly or through French, *angle, triangle, quadrangle, rectangular* and similar forms. There is also the proper name of *Ancus Martius*, one of Rome's early kings, and there is the name of the city of *Ancona* (though this may have come from the Illyrian or Albanian branch). Anglo-Saxon gets the root in the forms *anclēow*, "ankle"; *angel*, which gives us *angle* in the fishing sense, with *angler, angleworm*, etc.; and *Angle, Engle, Englisc*, the name of the region and people, said to be derived from the fact that the original Anglo-Saxons came from the angle or bight of Holstein; these, in native form, give us *England* and *English;* latinized into *Anglii*, they give us *Anglia, Anglic, Anglican, anglicize, anglomaniac, anglophobia*, and similar forms.

The root *wĺkᵘos*, *wĺp*,[1] "wolf", is quite widespread, appearing in Sanskrit *vrkas*[1] and Slavic *volk*. In Greek, through a dialectal development, it produces *lykos*, from which we get *lycanthrope* and *lycanthropy*, "the state of being a werewolf". The Latin *lupus* shows a Sabine (Oscan) development, with *p* replacing the *qu* that would be normal in Latin. Here we get *lupine, lupiform*, the French *loup garou*, "werewolf", the proper name *Ulpius*, the feast of the *Lupercalia*, the Latin *lupanar*, "house of ill repute" (prostitutes were called *lupae*, "she-wolves"), and such place names as the French *Saint-Leu, Saint-Lô*

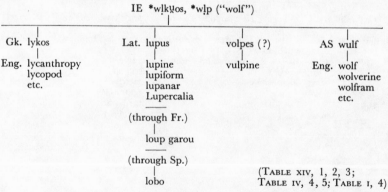

IE *wĺkᵘos, *wĺp ("wolf")

Gk. lykos　　　　　Lat. lupus　　　　volpes (?)　　　　AS wulf

Eng. lycanthropy　　lupine　　　　　vulpine　　　　　Eng. wolf
　　　lycopod　　　　lupiform　　　　　　　　　　　　　　wolverine
　　　etc.　　　　　lupanar　　　　　　　　　　　　　　wolfram
　　　　　　　　　Lupercalia　　　　　　　　　　　　　etc.

　　　　　　　　　(through Fr.)

　　　　　　　　　loup garou

　　　　　　　　　(through Sp.)
　　　　　　　　　　　　　　　　　　　　(TABLE XIV, 1, 2, 3;
　　　　　　　　　lobo　　　　　　　　　TABLE IV, 4, 5; TABLE I, 4)

[1] The symbols *ḷ* and *ṛ* denote a vowel value for these sonant or liquid sounds.

(*Lupus* was currently used as a first name in Low Latin times, and people bearing that name became saints); through Spanish, we get the *lobo* of our Southwest. There is also a likelihood that *volpes*, "fox", from which we get *vulpine*, comes from the identical root. Anglo-Saxon offers *wulf*, from which comes *wolf*, with *wolfish*, *wolfbane*, *wolfhound*, *wolverine*, *wolfram* (this, in the original Germanic, is "wolf-raven", not "wolf-ram"), *wolframite* (the normal Germanic *wh* becomes *f* in final position).

The IE root **sweid*, "sweat", produces in Greek the noun *hidron*, "sweat" (not to be confused with *hydor*, "water"), which gives us *hidrosis*, a medical term used to describe a sweating condition. Latin *sudor* gives us *sudoriferous* and *sudorific*, as well as *exude*. Anglo-Saxon *swāt*, *swēt*, *swǣtan*, produce our noun and verb *sweat*, with such compounds as *sweatband*, *sweatbox*, *sweatshirt*, *sweatshop*.

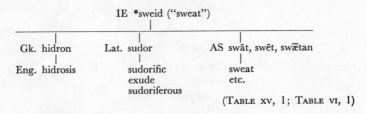

IE *sweid ("sweat")

Gk. hidron	Lat. sudor	AS swāt, swēt, swǣtan
Eng. hidrosis	sudorific exude sudoriferous	sweat etc.

(TABLE XV, 1; TABLE VI, 1)

A root **sp(h)er*, "to jerk, kick away", appears in Greek as *sphaira*, from which come *sphere*, *spherical*, *spheroid*, *hemisphere*, *planisphere*, *atmosphere*. In Latin, there is, in addition to the verb *sperno*, "to reject",

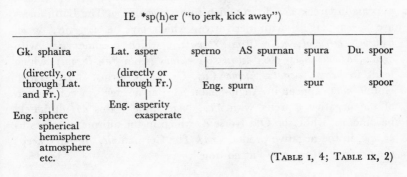

IE *sp(h)er ("to jerk, kick away")

Gk. sphaira	Lat. asper	sperno	AS spurnan	spura	Du. spoor
(directly, or through Lat. and Fr.)	(directly or through Fr.)		Eng. spurn		
Eng. sphere spherical hemisphere atmosphere etc.	Eng. asperity exasperate			spur	spoor

(TABLE I, 4; TABLE IX, 2)

the adjective *asper*, from which come *asperity, exasperate, exasperation*. Anglo-Saxon *spura, sporettan*, produce the noun and verb *spur*, while Anglo-Saxon *speornan, spurnan*, with perhaps an assist from Latin *sperno*, give us *spurn*. In addition, English borrows from Dutch the form *spoor*, "track, footprint".

The root **bhel*, "beam, plank, stem", gives Greek *phalanx*, which appears in English, with a derivative *phalanstery*. It also produces, in French development, *planche*, which in Norman-Picard form gives us *plank*, and with a direct borrowing, *planchette*. The Latin form, from the verb *fulcio*, "to prop", is *fulcrum*, which is borrowed directly. Anglo-Saxon has *bealca, balca*, "ridge", from which we get *balk*. Old High German *bloh*, entering French as *bloc*, eventually reaches us as *bloc, block, blockade, blockhouse, blockhead, blockbuster*, etc. Old Norse *bolr*, coming into English as *bole*, "trunk", which is antiquated, still survives in *bulrush*.

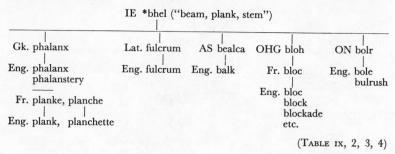

IE *bhel ("beam, plank, stem")

Gk. phalanx	Lat. fulcrum	AS bealca	OHG bloh	ON bolr
Eng. phalanx phalanstery	Eng. fulcrum	Eng. balk	Fr. bloc	Eng. bole bulrush
Fr. planke, planche			Eng. bloc block blockade etc.	
Eng. plank, planchette				

(TABLE IX, 2, 3, 4)

The IE root **ayu*, "life strength", with a variant **aew*, "duration", appears in Greek *aion*, from which comes *aeon* or *eon*. The Latin forms are *aevum*, "age", with derivatives which give us *longevity, coeval, medieval, primeval*; *aetas* (from **aev-itas*), which becomes *age*, with *ageless, Middle Ages*, etc., *aeternus* or *eternus* (from **aev-iternus*), which leads to *eternal, eternity, Eternal City*. Germanic forms, starting with Gothic *aiws*, appear in Anglo-Saxon *nā*, "at no age", a contraction of the negative *n*-prefix with *āwa*, "age, time"; this *nā* ultimately becomes *no*, while the Old Norse *ei*, which in the affirmative gives us *ay, aye*, in the negative produces *nay*. The German *nie*, "never", keeps the original meaning of "at no time".

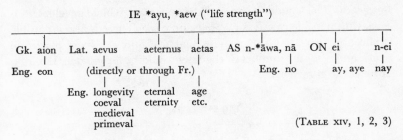

IE *ayu, *aew ("life strength")

Gk. aion	Lat. aevus	aeternus	aetas	AS n-*āwa, nā	ON ei	n-ei
Eng. eon	(directly or through Fr.)			Eng. no	ay, aye	nay
	Eng. longevity	eternal	age			
	coeval	eternity	etc.			
	medieval					
	primeval			(Table xiv, 1, 2, 3)		

The root *genu, *gneu, "knee", produces in Greek gonia, "angle", which gives us all our learned forms in -gon; hexagon, polygon, octagonal, goniometry, diagonal, trigonometry, etc. The Latin genu, "knee", gives us genuflect, genuflection, and possibly genuine (the story goes that a father would recognize a new-born child as genuinely his by holding it on his knee; but see p. 105). Anglo-Saxon cnēo, cnēowlian, give us knee and kneel (with kneecap, knee-deep, kneepan, knee action, etc.). In addition, there are the place names Genoa and Geneva, said to come from an Illyrian form, Genusia.

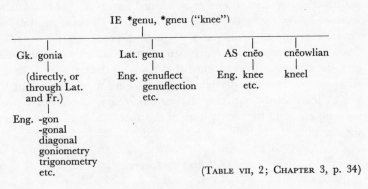

IE *genu, *gneu ("knee")

Gk. gonia	Lat. genu	AS cnēo	cnēowlian
(directly, or through Lat. and Fr.)	Eng. genuflect genuflection etc.	Eng. knee etc.	kneel
Eng. -gon -gonal diagonal goniometry trigonometry etc.			
		(Table vii, 2; Chapter 3, p. 34)	

The root *ger, *gere, "to unite", produces in Greek agora, "market-place", and kindred compounds from which we get agoraphobia, allegory, allegorical, category, categorical, phantasmagoria, panegyric. The Latin grex, "flock, herd", gives egregious ("one who stands out from the herd"), gregarious ("one who likes to belong to the herd"), with aggregate, aggregation, congregate, congregation, congregational, segregate, *segregation.* The Anglo-Saxon form is *crammian*, which develops into *cram*, with possible relatives in *cramp* and *crimp*. There is also a possible connection between this root and that of Latin *ago* (past participle *actus*), and if so, the number of cognates would be far greater. Limiting ourselves to surer forms:

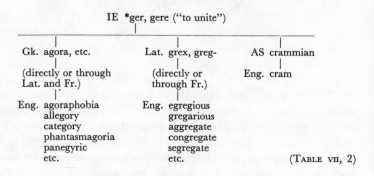

IE *ger, gere ("to unite")

Gk. agora, etc.	Lat. grex, greg-	AS crammian
(directly or through Lat. and Fr.)	(directly or through Fr.)	Eng. cram
Eng. agoraphobia allegory category phantasmagoria panegyric etc.	Eng. egregious gregarious aggregate congregate segregate etc.	

(TABLE VII, 2)

The root *$g^u her$*, "warm, hot", gives Greek *thermos*, from which we get a variety of learned and semi-learned forms: *thermos bottle, thermal, diathermy, thermometer, thermotherapy, thermostat, Thermidor.* Latin *furnus*, "oven", produces *furnace* and, through French, *petits fours*. Anglo-Saxon *wearm, wearman* (used in substitution for an original **gwarm*) give *warm, warmth*. It is claimed that *Germani*, the name of a Teutonic tribe, comes from an Illyrian form belonging to this root, but there are at least four competing derivations. *Gorky*, the Russian writer, owes his name to the Slavic form of this root, which in Slavic assumes the meaning of "bitter".

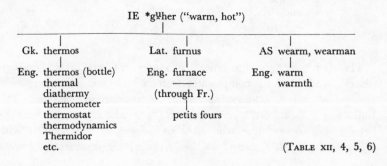

IE *$g^u her$ ("warm, hot")

Gk. thermos	Lat. furnus	AS wearm, wearman
Eng. thermos (bottle) thermal diathermy thermometer thermostat thermodynamics Thermidor etc.	Eng. furnace ——— (through Fr.) petits fours	Eng. warm warmth

(TABLE XII, 4, 5, 6)

IE *kwon, *kun, "dog", gives Greek kyon, from which we get such forms as cynic, cynical, cynicism (originally applied to a philosophical school nicknamed the "dogs, snarlers"), cynosure (originally the name of a constellation, "Dog's Tail", shifted in meaning because it is eye-attracting), cynegetics (the art of dog-leading, or hunting), cynocephalous ("dogheaded", like the Egyptian god Anubis). Latin canis, "dog" (for *kwanis), gives us canine, canicular ("dog-days", which occur when the constellation of the Big Dog, Canis Major, is in the ascendant). From a Norman-Picard French development we get kennel (kenil, for Francien chenil); regular French gives us chenille (from canicula, originally "little bitch"; here the doubtful explanation for the semantic transfer is that the head of a caterpillar was reminiscent of the head of a small dog; then the material is reminiscent of caterpillars). Italian canaglia, "dog pack", through French, gives us canaille. There is also canary, a bird pertaining to the islands which were found to be infested with wild dogs and therefore named by Columbus Islas Canarias, "Dog Islands". Anglo-Saxon hund gives us hound, and from a closely related High German root we get such hound names as Dachshund, "badger-hound". There is a Slavic cognate represented by Russian sobaka, but it does not get into English.

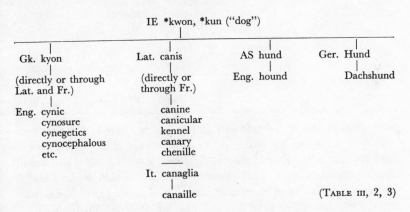

IE *kwon, *kun ("dog")

Gk. kyon	Lat. canis	AS hund	Ger. Hund
(directly or through Lat. and Fr.)	(directly or through Fr.)	Eng. hound	Dachshund
Eng. cynic cynosure cynegetics cynocephalous etc.	canine canicular kennel canary chenille		
	It. canaglia canaille		(TABLE III, 2, 3)

The root *mer, "to die", produces in Greek a form brotos, "mortal" (from *mr-otos), which in the negative gives us ambrosia, the food of the immortal gods, with ambrosial, ambrotype, the proper name Ambrose, and even the family name of Tito Brož, the Yugoslav dictator.

A minority opinion holds that *martyr* (originally "witness"), with *martyrdom* and *martyrology*, stems from the same root, but the root of *memory* appears more likely. The Latin *mors, mort-*, gives us *mortal, mortality, immortalize, mortgage, mortify, mortification, mortician, mortuary, mortmain, amortize, post-mortem, morbid, moribund*, possibly *morgue*, and, through French *morine*, "plague", *murrain*. In Anglo-Saxon, *morthor, myrthrian, morth*, produce *murder, murderous, murderer*. Other forms that do not appear in English include the Persian-Hindustani (Indo-Iranian) *mard*, "man", and the Slavic (Russian) *smert'*, "death", *myortvy*, "dead" (Rachmaninov's *Myortvy Ostrov*, "The Isle of the Dead").

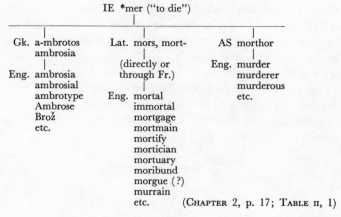

IE *mer ("to die")

Gk. a-mbrotos ambrosia	Lat. mors, mort-	AS morthor
	(directly or through Fr.)	Eng. murder
Eng. ambrosia		murderer
ambrosial		murderous
ambrotype	Eng. mortal	etc.
Ambrose	immortal	
Brož	mortgage	
etc.	mortmain	
	mortify	
	mortician	
	mortuary	
	moribund	
	morgue (?)	
	murrain	
	etc. (Chapter 2, p. 17; Table II, 1)	

The root **ster*, "star", gives in Greek *aster*, from which we derive *aster, asterisk, asterism, asteroid* and similar forms. There is also a variant which is borrowed by Latin in the form *astrum*, from which we get *astronomy, astrology, astral, disaster, disastrous, astrolabe, astrophysics*, and numerous other forms. Latin *stella* gives us *stellar, stellate, constellation*. Anglo-Saxon *steorra* gives us *star, starry, starfish, stargazer, starlet, starlight*, and many compound forms, including *Stars and Stripes, Stars and Bars, Star-Spangled Banner*. *Sterling* is attributed by some authorities to Middle English *sterre* from Anglo-Saxon *steorra*, on the theory that ancient sterling coins bore a star; but others dispute this version, and derive *sterling* from *easterling*.

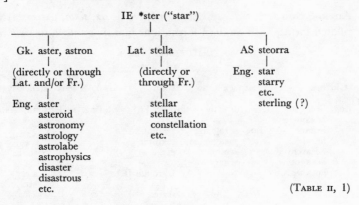

IE *ster ("star")

Gk. aster, astron	Lat. stella	AS steorra
(directly or through Lat. and/or Fr.)	(directly or through Fr.)	Eng. star starry etc. sterling (?)
Eng. aster asteroid astronomy astrology astrolabe astrophysics disaster disastrous etc.	stellar stellate constellation etc.	

(TABLE II, 1)

IE *swād, "sweet", gives in Greek *hedys*, from which we derive *hedonism*, *hedonistic*. The Latin *suadeo*, past participle *suasus*, gives us *persuade*, *persuasion*, *dissuade*, *suasion*, *assuage*, etc., while *suavis* gives *suave*, *suavity*. Anglo-Saxon *swēte* produces *sweet*, with *sweeten*, *sweetheart*, *sweetness*, *sweetbread*, *sweetmeat*, etc.

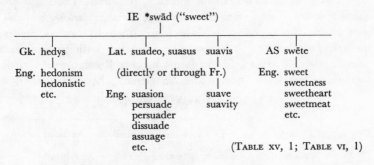

IE *swād ("sweet")

Gk. hedys	Lat. suadeo, suasus	suavis	AS swēte
Eng. hedonism hedonistic etc.	(directly or through Fr.)		Eng. sweet sweetness sweetheart sweetmeat etc.
	Eng. suasion persuade persuader dissuade assuage etc.	suave suavity	

(TABLE XV, 1; TABLE VI, 1)

The IE root *sweks*, "six", gives the Greek *hex*, with *hexagon*, *hexagonal*, *hexameter*, *hexapod*, *hexarchy*, *hexane*, *hexyl*, *hexahedron*, *hexagram*, and other learned and semi-learned forms. Latin *sex* produces *sexagenary*, *sexagesimal*, *sextant*, *sexto*, *sextuple*, *sextuplet*, *semester* and *semestral*, *senary*, and, through Italian, *sextette*, *sestet*, *sestina*, *Sistine* (both Chapel and Madonna, from the papal name *Sixtus* or *Sisto*, "sixth"), while Spanish gives us *siesta* (the sixth hour of daylight, devoted to rest).

Anglo-Saxon *seox, sixta, syxtȳne, sixtig* give us *six, sixth, sixteen, sixty,* and related forms, with modern formations like *six-shooter* and *sixth column.*

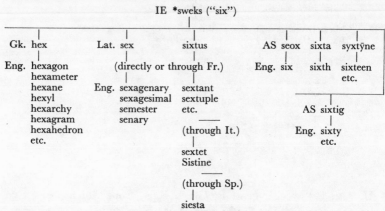

IE *sweks ("six")

Gk. hex	Lat. sex	sixtus	AS seox	sixta	syxtȳne
Eng. hexagon	(directly or through Fr.)		Eng. six	sixth	sixteen
hexameter					etc.
hexane	Eng. sexagenary	sextant			
hexyl	sexagesimal	sextuple			
hexarchy	semester	etc.		AS sixtig	
hexagram	senary	———			
hexahedron		(through It.)		Eng. sixty	
etc.				etc.	
		sextet			
		Sistine			
		(through Sp.)			
		siesta			

(TABLE XV, 1; TABLE III, 3; Anglo-Saxon *x* may stand for *hs* as well as *ks*)

An IE root *wer,* *werdh,* "to say, speak", appears in Greek in the form of *rhetor* (directly derived from the verb *eiro* for *werio,* "to say"), and this gives us *rhetor, rhetoric, rhetorical, rhetorician.* The Latin *verbum* produces *verb, verbal, verbalize, verbatim, verbiage, verbose,* as well as *verve* from the plural *verba;* also derivatives like *adverb, adverbial, proverb, proverbial.* Anglo-Saxon gives us *word,* with *wordy, wordless, wording, byword, reword.* Slavic forms include Russian *vrat',* "to lie", and *vrach,* "physician" (originally "magician", therefore "liar").

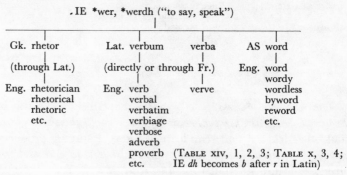

.IE *wer, *werdh ("to say, speak")

Gk. rhetor	Lat. verbum	verba	AS word
(through Lat.)	(directly or through Fr.)		Eng. word
Eng. rhetorician	Eng. verb	verve	wordy
rhetorical	verbal		wordless
rhetoric	verbatim		byword
etc.	verbiage		reword
	verbose		etc.
	adverb		
	proverb	(TABLE XIV, 1, 2, 3; TABLE X, 3, 4;
	etc.	IE *dh* becomes *b* after *r* in Latin)

The IE root *de,* *do,* "this", generally used in the formation of demonstrative pronouns and adverbs, appears in Anglo-Saxon in the form *tō*, which gives rise to English *to* and *too*, with such compounds as *tomorrow*, *tonight*, *too much*, etc. There is also the military *tattoo*, which comes from Dutch *tap toe*, "tap shut". One Greek derivative appearing in English in compound form is the *-do-* of *endo-* in such words as *endocrinology*. In Latin, the form *-de-* appears in many variants: *indigenous*, the *de-* which also serves as an English prefix, the *-dam*, *-dem* of *quondam*, *tandem*, *idem*, the last of which leads to *identical*, *identity*, *identify*. The oft-repeated story of how *tandem*, "finally, at length", came to have its current English meaning goes back to the days of horse vehicles, when a carriage drawn by two horses placed end to end was jocularly described as being "at length". The root appears in other Latin words, such as *dum*, *donec*, *inde*, *quando*, from some of which come very well-known Romance forms (French *en*, *donc*, *quand;* Italian *ne*, *dunque*, *quando;* Spanish *ende* (archaic), *cuando*).

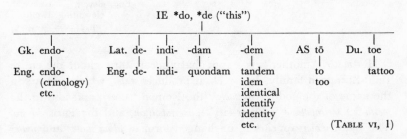

IE *do, *de ("this")

Gk. endo-	Lat. de-	indi-	-dam	-dem	AS tō	Du. toe
Eng. endo- (crinology) etc.	Eng. de-	indi-	quondam	tandem idem identical identify identity etc.	to too	tattoo

(TABLE VI, 1)

The IE root *leikʉ*, "to leave behind", produces Greek *leipo*, "to leave", from which proceed *eclipse* (from *ekleipo*, "to abandon"), and *ellipse*, with *ellipsis*, *elliptical*. The Latin form is *linquo*, with a nasal infix which disappears in the past participle *lictus;* the form with the nasal gives us *relinquish*, *delinquent*, *delinquency*, etc.; the participial form leads to *relic* and *reliquary*, *relict*, *derelict*, *dereliction*. Other suggested connections, with doubtful features, are *limpidus* (*limpid;* this would have to come through Oscan-Umbrian to justify its *p* for *qu*); and *liquidus* (*liquid*, *liquefaction*, *liquefy*, *liquor*, *liqueur*, *liquidate*, *liquidation*, etc., as well as *prolix*, *prolixity*). On the Germanic side, we have Anglo-Saxon *leihan*, *lǣnan*, *lǣn*, *lēon*, as well as Old Norse *lān*, which, losing *h* between vowels,[2] eventually develop into *loan* (with *loanword*, *loan*

[2] Note that *h* is already a reduction from an earlier *hw*, indicated by Gothic *leihwan*.

translation) and *lend* (with such modern formations as *lend-lease*). There are also *endleofan*, "(ten) one-leave", *twelf*, "two-leave", which give us *eleven* with *eleventh* and *twelve* with *twelfth;* but to justify this interpretation, we have to assume an alternative form **leip*, perhaps borrowed from the Brythonic branch of Celtic, which turns **kw* into **p*. The tree, for reasonably sure forms, is:

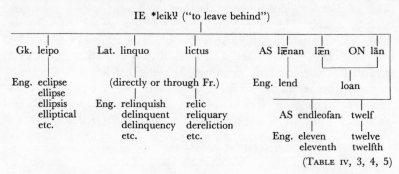

IE **leikʷ* ("to leave behind")

Gk. leipo	Lat. linquo	lictus	AS lǣnan	lǣn	ON lān
Eng. eclipse	(directly or through Fr.)		Eng. lend		loan
ellipse					
ellipsis	Eng. relinquish	relic			
elliptical	delinquent	reliquary	AS endleofan		twelf
etc.	delinquency	dereliction			
	etc.	etc.	Eng. eleven		twelve
			eleventh		twelfth

(TABLE IV, 3, 4, 5)

IE **mātēr*, "mother", is a root that appears throughout the entire Indo-European family. In Greek, it produces *meter*, which appears in the name of the goddess *Demeter* (the Roman *Ceres*), and also in the *metro-* of *metropolis* ("mother-city"), *metropolitan*, and the Paris *Métro*. The Latin *mater* appears in unchanged form in *alma mater* and *mater familias*, in the *mater-* of *maternal, maternity*, in the *matro-* of *matronymic* (but this could also be a dialectal form of the thoroughly Greek *metronymic*), in the *matri-* of *matrix, matriculate, matriculation, matriarch. matrimony, matrimonial, matricide*, etc. An augmentative form, *matrona*, gives *matron, matronly*, and probably the name of the French river *Marne*. A Latin derivative is *materies* or *materia*, which produces *matter* (with *matter of fact, matter of course*), *material, immaterial, materiel, materialize, materialism, materialist, materiality, materia medica*, and the Portuguese *madeira*, with a shift in meaning from "matter" in general to "wood", then to the wooded island of Madeira, lastly to the wine which is one of the island's products. *Madre* may be Italian or Spanish; *madrepore* is a combination of Italian *madre* with Greek *poros*, "stone", and there is a French *commère* that occasionally appears in English. There is doubt concerning *madrigal*, which could be connected with Spanish *madrugar*, "to rise early", or with the root of *mandria*, "herd, flock", which would make it a pastoral song. Anglo-Saxon *mōdor* crossed with Old Norse *mōðir* produces *mother*, with *stepmother, motherhood, mother-in-law*, etc.

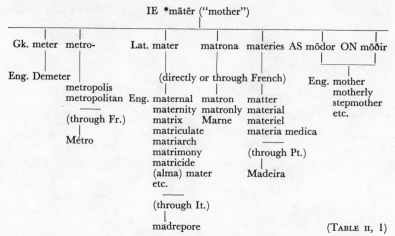

IE *mātēr ("mother")

| Gk. meter metro- | Lat. mater | matrona | materies | AS mōdor | ON mōðir |

Eng. Demeter

metropolis
metropolitan Eng. maternal matron matter
(through Fr.)   maternity matronly material
Métro   matrix   Marne   materiel
                   matriculate   materia medica
                   matriarch   ————
                   matrimony   (through Pt.)
                   matricide   Madeira
                   (alma) mater
                   etc.

(directly or through French)   Eng. mother
                                      motherly
                                      stepmother
                                      etc.

————
(through It.)
madrepore   (TABLE II, 1)

Mē-nōt is the IE root for "month, moon". Anglo-Saxon has *mōna*, "moon", from which we get *moon* (with *moonbeam, moonlight, moonstone, moonshiner, moonstruck*, etc.) and also *Monday* from Anglo-Saxon *mōnandæg;* while Anglo-Saxon *mōnath* produces *month, monthly*. There is also Anglo-Saxon *mæl*, which gives *meal, mealy, mealtime, piecemeal*, etc. In Greek, the root appears with the meaning of "measure", and Greek *metron* gives us *meter* (or *metre*), *metric, metric ton, metrics, metronome, metrical, hexameter, diameter, diametrically, perimeter, pentameter, symmetry, symmetrical, geometry, trigonometry, thermometer, barometer, centimeter, millimeter, kilometer, micrometer, hygrometer*, and a host of other scientific measures and measuring instruments. In Latin, we have on the one hand *mensis*, "month" (the variant *mesis* appears in the Romance languages because Vulgar Latin regularly drops *n* before *s*); here come *semester, trimester, semestral, menstrual, menstruate, menstruation*. On the other hand, the verb *metior*, "to measure", with its Vulgar Latin noun *mensura, mesura*, gives rise to *measure, measurement, measureless, measurable, incommensurable, mensuration, dimension, dimensional, immense, immensity*. Two additional forms coming through other languages are the German *Mensur* (from *mensura;* the regulated duel of German university fraternities); and the Spanish *mesa* (from Latin *mensa*, "table, that which has been measured off"). If the root is connected, as some authorities suppose, with that of Latin *mederi*, "to heal", and Latin *modus*, "mode, way", then we have a large further ramification including *medical, medicine, mode, mood, meditate, modest, moderate, remedy, model, modern, modify, mold, accommodate, incommode*, etc.

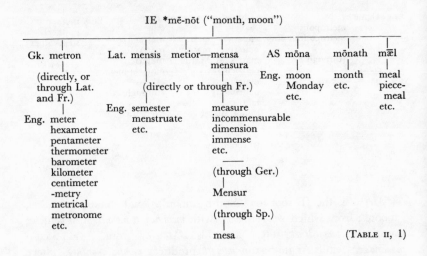

IE *mē-nōt ("month, moon")

Gk. metron	Lat. mensis metior—mensa mensura	AS mōna	mōnath	mæl
(directly, or through Lat. and Fr.)	(directly or through Fr.)	Eng. moon Monday etc.	month etc.	meal piece-meal etc.
Eng. meter hexameter pentameter thermometer barometer kilometer centimeter -metry metrical metronome etc.	Eng. semester menstruate etc.	measure incommensurable dimension immense etc.		
		(through Ger.) Mensur		
		(through Sp.) mesa		

(TABLE II, 1)

The root *en(o)mn, *nomn, "name", appears in Greek as *onoma*, "name", which gives us a large variety of words: *onomastic, onomato-pœia, anonymous, anonymity, synonym, pseudonym, antonym, eponym, homonym, patronymic, toponymy, metonymy.* The Latin *nomen*, in Latin form, gives us *agnomen, praenomen, cognomen, nomenclature;* then there are *nominal, nominate, nominative, nominee, nomination, denominate, denomination, denominator, nuncupate, ignominious, misnomer*, etc. In forms derived through French we have *noun, pronoun, renown, renowned, nom de guerre, nom de plume*. The Anglo-Saxon *nama* gives us *name, surname, nameless, namesake, namely*, etc. *Nome*, in Alaska, gets its name from a misreading of the word "name" (the head of a government bureau in Washington had scribbled "Name?" on the map of the region that showed a locality without a name, and this was later interpreted as being the actual name of the place). There is a possible link between this root and that of Latin *nosco*, "to know" (see p. 206) and if this is correct the family becomes much larger. The tree, for what is assured, is:

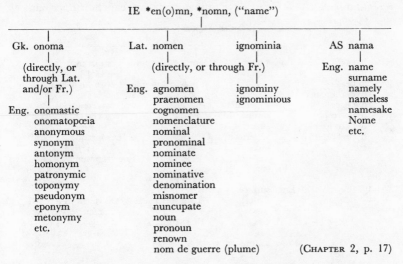

IE *en(o)mn, *nomn, ("name")

Gk. onoma	Lat. nomen	ignominia	AS nama
(directly, or through Lat. and/or Fr.)	(directly, or through Fr.)		Eng. name surname
	Eng. agnomen	ignominy	namely
	praenomen	ignominious	nameless
Eng. onomastic	cognomen		namesake
onomatopœia	nomenclature		Nome
anonymous	nominal		etc.
synonym	pronominal		
antonym	nominate		
homonym	nominee		
patronymic	nominative		
toponymy	denomination		
pseudonym	misnomer		
eponym	nuncupate		
metonymy	noun		
etc.	pronoun		
	renown		
	nom de guerre (plume)	(Chapter 2, p. 17)	

An IE root *uper*, *uperi*, "over", gives Greek *hyper*, which appears as a prefix in numerous English words, among them *hyperborean*, *hyperbole*, *hypertrophy*, *hypercritical*, *hypertension*. Latin has *super*, used as a prefix in *superintendent*, *superabundant*, *superannuated*, *supercargo*, *super-fluous*, *supervise*, *supercilious*, *superstition*, *supersede*, *superlative*, *superman*, *supernatural*, etc. There are also forms like *supernal*, *insuperable*, the Italian *soprano*, the French *soubrette*, the French-derived *sovereign*, *sovereignty*. The Latin *superior* passes into English without change of form, forming *superiority*, and Latin *superbus* gives us *superb*. Latin *supra* appears in a number of learned compounds (*suprarenal*, *supra-liminal*, *suprailiac*, etc.) and *supremus* gives us *supreme*, *supremacy*. The French descendant of *super* is *sur*, which appears in *surface*, *survive*, *surfeit*, and other forms, including *sirloin*, where it is misspelt by popular etymology. There is some question whether *summus*, the alternative form of Latin *supremus*, comes from the same root; if it does, we have *sum*, *summary*, and a host of other forms. The Anglo-Saxon cognate is *yferra*, *ofer*, which becomes *over*, with very numerous compounds (*overall*, *overbearing*, *overboard*, *overcoat*, *overcome*, *overflow*, *overhead*, *overdue*, *overly*, *overnight*, *overpower*, *overseer*, *oversight*, *overtime*, *overweening, overwrought*, to cite only a few). The same Anglo-Saxon root produces *efes*, "eaves", and *yfesdripe*, "overdrip", from which we get *eaves* and *eavesdrop*. A Celtic development, *ver-*, appears in proper names, like *Vercingetorix*.

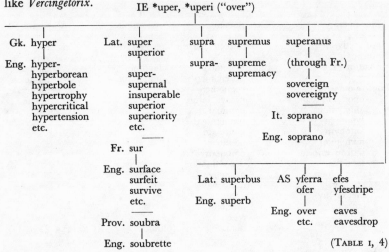

IE *uper, *uperi ("over")

Gk. hyper	Lat. super	supra	supremus	superanus
Eng. hyper-	superior			
hyperborean		supra-	supreme	(through Fr.)
hyperbole	super-		supremacy	
hypertrophy	supernal			
hypercritical	insuperable			sovereign
hypertension	superior			sovereignty
etc.	superiority			
	etc.			It. soprano
Fr. sur				Eng. soprano
Eng. surface				
surfeit	Lat. superbus	AS yferra	efes
survive		ofer	yfesdripe
etc.	Eng. superb		
		Eng. over	eaves
Prov. soubra		etc.	eavesdrop
Eng. soubrette			(Table i, 4)

IE *plēk*, "to weave together", gives us in Anglo-Saxon *fleax* (*flax, flaxen*) and *fealdan* (*fold, twofold, manifold, folder*, etc.). Greek adds the prefix for "two" to its *plo-* and gets the *diplo-* that we inherit in *diploid, diplodocus, diploma, diplomat, diplomacy* (the original idea was that of a document that could be folded in two, a *diploma*; people dealing in such documents were then said to engage in diplomacy). Latin has *plecto*, with a past participle *plexus*, and a secondary formation in *plico*. These ultimately produce in English numerous forms in *-plex, -ply, -plicate, -plicit, -ploy, -play, -plice, -pli-, -plet, -ple*, of which only a few examples can be given: *plexus, complex, complexity, duplex, simplex, perplex; comply, reply, multiply* and *multiplier, apply, imply* (but not *supply*, which comes from the root of *plenus*, "full"; see p. 230), with *compliance, pliant, pliable, suppliant, complicate, complication, multiplication, application, applicant, implication, implicate, explication, duplicate, triplicate, duplication, applicable, inexplicable; duplicity, complicity, accomplice, implicit, explicit, explicitly; exploit, exploitation, employ, deploy, deployment, employment, employer, employee; display, plait, pleat; simple, double, triple, quadruple, simplify, simplification, simplicity, doublet, duplicity, triplet, quadruplet,* *quintuplet, dubloon*, the Italian *replica*, etc. Doubt attaches to *flask*, the Italian *fiasco*, and *flagon*, which by reason of their initial *f-* would have to come from the Germanic branch, but which some authorities prefer to derive from the root of Latin *vasculum, vas*, which gives us *vase*. There is also a hypothetical connection with the root of Latin *flecto*, "to bend", but this would call for an alternative IE root in **bhlek*.

IE *plēk ("to weave together")

Gk. (di)plo-	Lat. plecto, plexus	plico		AS fleax	fealdan
Eng. diploid	(directly or through Fr.)			Eng. flax	fold
diplodocus				flaxen	folder
diploma	Eng. plexus	-ply			twofold
diplomat	-plex	-plicate			manifold
diplomacy	-plexity	-plication			etc.
etc.	etc.	-plicant			
		-plicit			
		-plice			
		-plicity			
		-ploy			
		-ployment			
		-ployer			
		-ployee			
		-plicable			
		-plier			
		-pliant			
		-play			
		-ple			
		-plet			
		-ploit			
		-ploitation			
		-ploiter			
		double			
		doublet			
		doubloon			
		plait			
		pleat			

(through It.)

replica

(TABLE I, 4; TABLE III, 2, 3; Anglo-Saxon *x* may stand for *hs* as well as for *ks*)

The IE root **nem*, "to divide, take", produces in Greek the name of *Nemesis*, goddess of retribution, along with a verb *nomeno*, "to let graze", from which we get *nomad, nomadic*, and the *nomos*, "law", that gives us *-nome* and *-nomy* (*metronome, astronomy, autonomy, economy, economic, economize, economical, binomial, Deuteronomy, gastronomic*, etc.). A by-product of *nomos* is *nomisma*, "that which is regulated by law, or sanctioned by custom"; this is applied to coins, and gives us *numismatic* and *numismatist*. The Latin *numerus*, "number", produces *numeral*, *enumerate*, *numerous*, *numerical*, *numerator*, *innumerable*, *supernumerary*, *numerology*, and, through Italian *numero*, the $N°$ we occasionally use, while *nombre*, the French descendant of *numerus*, gives us *number*, *numberless*, and the popular *numbers game*. The Germanic branch produces Anglo-Saxon *niman*, "to take", which was displaced by the Scandinavian *take*, but still appears in German *nehmen*. However, other forms survive: *numen*, the past participle of *niman*, gives us *numb* and *numbness* ("seized, taken", therefore "dazed, deprived of feeling"); *numskull* is a compound of *numb*. There is also *nimble*, which appears only in Middle English, and originally meant "quick to take or seize".

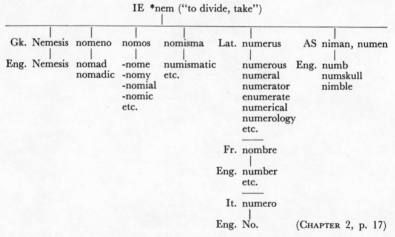

IE *nem ("to divide, take")

Gk. Nemesis	nomeno	nomos	nomisma	Lat. numerus		AS niman, numen
Eng. Nemesis	nomad	-nome	numismatic	numerous	Eng.	numb
	nomadic	-nomy	etc.	numeral		numskull
		-nomial		numerator		nimble
		-nomic		enumerate		
		etc.		numerical		
				numerology		
				etc.		

Fr. nombre

Eng. number
etc.

It. numero

Eng. No.   (CHAPTER 2, p. 17)

IE *ed, "to eat", gives us Anglo-Saxon *etan*, which becomes *eat*, with *eatable*, *eats*, etc. In compound form, this root enters *t-onth*, *t-ōth*, which eventually becomes *tooth*, ("the eater, or eating tool"), with *toothsome*, *toothache*, *toothpick*, etc. There is a further extension in Anglo-Saxon *tusc*, *tux*, which give us *tush* and *tusk*. Before leaving the Germanic field, it may be worth while to see what happens in High German, since this root is a perfect illustration of both the first and the second consonant shifts of the Germanic languages. English *eat* appears in German as *essen*, with *ss* resulting from a medieval *ezzan*, while *tonth*, the earlier Germanic form, passing through *zand* (*tsand*), ends as

Zahn (Italian borrows this High German form in *zanna*, "tusk"). Greek *odont-* appears in *odonto-, mastodon, odontoid*, and other learned forms. It may also be remarked that Slavic makes extensive use of the root (Russian *yest'*, "to eat"; *yeda*, "meal"; *ob-yed*, "dinner"). Some even claim that Scandinavian *jotunn*, "mythological giant", comes from this root. Latin *edo*, "to eat", gives us *edible, edacious, edacity;* in compound form, we get *comestibles* (this is the same compound that produces Spanish-Portuguese *comer*, "to eat", namely *cum-edo*, "eat with"); and *obese, obesity* (*ob-edo, ob-esus*, "one who has eaten to excess"). *Escarole*, taken from Italian *scarola*, is also probably from the participial root of *edo*. Using the same formation that appears in Germanic and Greek, Latin forms *dent-* for "tooth", and this gives us numerous forms (*dent, dental, dentate, dentifrice, dentine*, the French *dentelle, denticulated, denticle, dentist, dentistry, dentition, denture, edentate, bident, trident, indent, indentation, indentured*, etc.). *Redan* comes from *re-dent; dandelion* is *dent de lion*, "lion's tooth". It is possible that Latin *prandium*, "dinner", which appears in *post-prandial*, may come from *primus* combined with *edo*, "the first meal of the day".

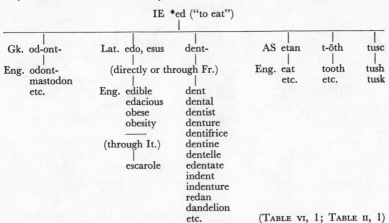

IE *ed ("to eat")

Gk. od-ont-	Lat. edo, esus	dent-	AS etan	t-ōth	tusc
Eng. odont- mastodon etc.	(directly or through Fr.)		Eng. eat etc.	tooth etc.	tush tusk
	Eng. edible edacious obese obesity —— (through It.) | escarole	dent dental dentist denture dentifrice dentine dentelle edentate indent indenture redan dandelion etc.			

(TABLE VI, 1; TABLE II, 1)

An IE root *(aw)es*, "to grow light", produces in Greek *eos*, "dawn", which gives rise to *eocene, eolith, eolithic, eohippus*, and similar forms. The Latin cognate is the word for "dawn", *aurora*, with *aurum*, "gold". These two produce *Aurora Borealis, aureola, aureate, aureomycin, aurous, auriferous, Aurelia*, etc. There is also a form *Auster*, "south wind", from which come the names of *Austria*, *Australia*, and Charlemagne's eastern region of *Austrasia*, along with *austral* and *Aussie* (*austere* and *austerity*, however, come from another root meaning "dry"). The French descendant of *aurum* is *or*, which provides us with the heraldic *or*, *ormolu* (literally, "ground gold"), *oriole* ("the golden bird"), and the *Oriflamme*, or "Golden Flame", which was the battle standard of medieval French kings. The Germanic forms are Anglo-Saxon *ēaste*, "east" (giving us *east*, *eastern*, *easterly*, *eastward*, etc.; *ēa* is a regular Anglo-Saxon development for an original **aw*); *ēastre*, "Easter" (with the possibility that *sterling* may come from *easterling* rather than from the root of *star*); and the *Ostro-*, *Oester-* of *Ostrogoths* ("eastern Goths") and *Oesterreich* ("Austria, eastern realm"). There is also a remote possibility that the German *ur-* of *urgermanisch*, *uralt*, occasionally used in English and meaning "primitive, original", may come from the same source. Slavic gets from this root its word for "morning" (Russian *utro*). The name of *Vesuvius* is also said to contain it. The confusion between the meanings "south" and "east" comes from the direction of the rising sun.

IE **(aw)es* ("to grow light")

Gk. eos	Lat. aurum	Auster	AS ēaste	ēastre	OHG ōstar
Eng. Eos	Aurora		Eng. east	Easter	Ostrogoth
eocene	(directly or through Fr.)		eastern		Oesterreich
eohippus			easterly		
eolith	Eng. Aurora	Austria	eastward		
etc.	aureola	Australia	etc.		
	aureate	Australasia			
	auriferous	austral			
	aureomycin	Aussie			
	Aurelia	etc.			
	or				
	ormolu				
	oriole				
	Oriflamme				
	etc.				

(TABLE XIV, 1, 2, 3; TABLE XVI, 2)

An IE root variously presented as **ghdhem*, **khem*, **ghem*, "earth, soil", gives in Greek *khthōn* (*chthōn*), from which come *chthonian*, *chthonous* and *autochthonous;* also the adverbial *khamai* (*chamai*), "on the ground", from which come *camomile*, *chameleon*, and *germander*, the first being *khamaimelon*, "on-the-ground apple", the second *khamaileon*, "on-the-ground lion", the third *khamai-drys*, "on the-ground tree", the first and last rather radically transformed by their passage through Latin and French. The initial part of *Demeter* is claimed by some to come from this root in Illyrian (or Albanian) form, but others postulate Greek *ge*, "earth". Latin supplies *humus*, "soil", with *humilis*, "pertaining to the soil, humble", and *homo*, "man", with *humanus* (also "pertaining to the soil, human"). *Humus* gives us *humus, humidity, humid, humidify, humidor, exhume, inhume, inhumation;* *humilis* produces *humility, humiliate, humiliation* and, through French, *humble* (but not *humble pie*, changed by popular etymology from *umble pie*, a pie made from the organs of the animal). *Homo* gives us *homo sapiens, homunculus* ("little man"), *hominoid, homicide, homicidal,* Spanish *hombre,* French *homme d'esprit,* and *homage* (from *hominaticum,* "declaring yourself your overlord's man"). In negative form, *ne-homo* contracts into *nemo,* "no one" (*Captain Nemo* of Verne's "Nautilus"). *Humanus* gives us *human, inhuman, humane, inhumane, humanity, inhumanity, humanism, humanist, humanitarian, humanize, humankind, superhuman, subhuman,* etc. The Germanic form appears in Anglo-Saxon *guma*, "man", which survives in the compound *brydguma,* "bride's man", ultimately *bridegroom* or *groom* (the *groom* that attends a horse instead of a bride comes from a different root, which also gives us *gourmand* and *gourmet*, and from this, by popular etymology, *bridegroom* borrows its second *r*). Slavic takes from this root its word for "land" (Russian *zemlya, Novaya Zemlya*).

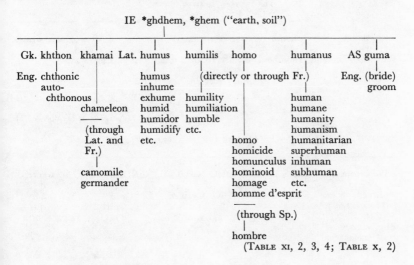

IE *ghdhem, *ghem ("earth, soil")

Gk. khthon	khamai	Lat. humus	humilis	homo	humanus	AS guma
Eng. chthonic		humus	(directly or through Fr.)			Eng. (bride)
auto-		inhume				groom
chthonous		exhume	humility		human	
	chameleon	humid	humiliation		humane	
	———	humidor	humble		humanity	
	(through	humidify	etc.		humanism	
	Lat. and	etc.		homo	humanitarian	
	Fr.)			homicide	superhuman	
				homunculus	inhuman	
	camomile			hominoid	subhuman	
	germander			homage	etc.	
				homme d'esprit		

(through Sp.)

hombre

(TABLE XI, 2, 3, 4; TABLE X, 2)

A family group in which there appears to be confusion of two IE roots is that of *k(w)erp* and *werb*, both of which mean "to twist oneself". Save for their semantics, they might be treated separately. The *werb* root in Greek produces *rhabd-*, "stick" and *rhomb-*, "spinning top", from which come such forms as *rhabdomancy* and *rhombus, rhomboid*, etc. The Latin forms are *verbena*, from which, through French, we get *vervain*, and *verbero*, "to flog", which gives us *reverberate, reverberation*, etc. In Germanic, Anglo-Saxon *weorpan, wearp* gives us *warp*, while the cognate High German *werfen* produces military terms like *Flammenwerfer*, "flame-thrower", and *Minenwerfer*, "mine-thrower". The root with initial *k* and final *p* seems responsible for Greek *karpos*, "wrist", of *carpus, metacarpal*, etc., and for a series of Germanic forms with initial *hw-* (*wh-* in modern English): Anglo-Saxon *hwerf* to *wharf;* Old Norse *hvirfla* to *whir, whirl, whirligig, whirlpool, whirlwind;* Dutch *wervel* to Middle English *whorwyl* and modern English *whorl;* while Germanic *wirbil*, leading to Old French *guerbler* and *werbler* (in the northern French dialects), goes on to *warble*. There is a further possible complication in the root of *-vert, -verse, -vort* (Latin *verto, versus, vortex*), and we could be carried on to many possible extensions, including *wry, wrist, wretch, wriggle, wrong, wrench, wrestle, worm, worth, wrath*, etc. The somewhat hypothetical family trees for both roots are:

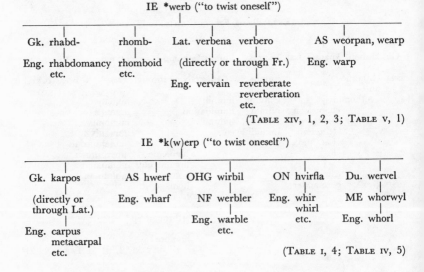

IE *werb ("to twist oneself")

Gk. rhabd-	rhomb-	Lat. verbena	verbero	AS weorpan, wearp
Eng. rhabdomancy etc.	rhomboid etc.	(directly or through Fr.)		Eng. warp
		Eng. vervain	reverberate reverberation etc.	

(TABLE XIV, 1, 2, 3; TABLE V, 1)

IE *k(w)erp ("to twist oneself")

Gk. karpos	AS hwerf	OHG wirbil	ON hvirfla	Du. wervel
(directly or through Lat.)	Eng. wharf	NF werbler	Eng. whir whirl etc.	ME whorwyl
Eng. carpus metacarpal etc.		Eng. warble etc.		Eng. whorl

(TABLE I, 4; TABLE IV, 5)

1,1,1,1,1,1,1,1,1,1,1

Another blend or confusion of two IE roots seems indicated by *(s)teg, "to hide, roof, house", and *tek, *tegh, "to twine, build". Here Greek offers tekton, "carpenter", from which we get architect, architecture; and also the tekhne, "handicraft", of technical, technician, technique, technology, polytechnic, etc. Germanic gives us Anglo-Saxon theccan, thæc, leading to thatch, and Dutch dek, dekken, which produces deck (with deckhand, deckhouse, etc.) Latin gives us the most numerous descendants, with tego, "to cover", (past participle tectus), and texo, "to weave". From the root of tego comes toga, which appears in English in its original form and also as togs; tegmen, and tegumentum, giving us tegument; and tegula, which in learned form gives tegular, but in French development goes on to tuile (appearing in Tuileries, originally "tile works"), and in English development produces Anglo-Saxon tigele and English tile. The participial tectus gives us many forms in -tect (detect, detection, detective, protect, protection, protector, protectionist, protectorate, etc. Tego itself appears in French protéger and its participle protégé, which appears in English. Latin texo, "to weave", gives obvious forms like textile, texture, but also (through the participial textus) text, textual,

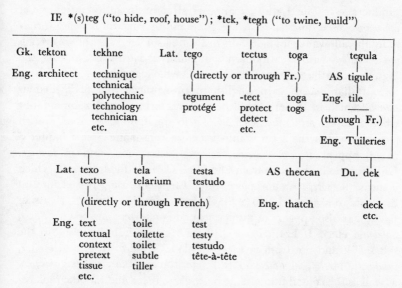

(TABLE II, 1; TABLE VII, 2; TABLE XI, 2; CHAPTER 3, p. 35)

context, *pretext* ("that which you build or weave in front of you, to ward off something unpleasant"), etc. The Latin infinitive *texere* produces Old French *tistre*, with a past participle *tissu*, and this becomes our *tissue*. Ramifications of *texo* are *tela*, "cloth", and possibly *testa*, "earthen vessel". The former gives us *toile*, *toilet* (originally "little cloth"), *toiletry*, *subtle* ("under the cloth"), *subtlety*, *subtleness*. *Telarium*, "weaver's beam", becomes *tiller*, with a shift in use from industry to ships. *Testa* gives *test* (at first a "refining vessel", then the means of refining or testing), *testy*, *tester*, *testudo* (at first a "turtle", similar to a vessel; later a military formation whereby the Roman soldiers joined shields over their heads as they advanced, thus giving themselves protection from missiles from above, but also resembling a moving turtle). In French, *testa* developed into *tête*, "head", from a slangy use of "jug" or "pot" for "head", and the French form appears in *tête-à-tête*.

The IE root **sal*, "salt", appears in Greek as *hals*, from which come the scientific *halogen*, *haloid*, *halophyte*, etc. Anglo-Saxon *sealt*, *sealtan* give us *salt*, and *sealtern* gives us *saltern*, while compound forms appear in *salty*, *saltiness*, *saltcellar*, *saltpeter*. A Scandinavian cognate, *sylt*, produces *silt*. The Latin *sal* appears straight in *sal volatile* and *sal ammoniac*. *Saline* and *salicylate* are compound forms. So is *salary* (originally the allowance for salt paid to Roman soldiers). Through French we get *salad* (with such modern compounds as *salad days*), and *sla*, the Dutch derivative of the French form, which appears in English as *slaw*. Italian *salame* is in English mispronounced and misspelled as *salami*, which in Italian would be a plural form. There is some doubt whether *salmis* and *salmagundi* belong in this family. Various French forms in which the *l* turns into *u* before consonants (see Chapter 3 p. 40) appear in *sauce*, *saucer*, *saucepan*, *saucy*, etc., and in *sausage*. Old French also borrows from Old High German the form *sulz*, which it turns into *solz*, *souz*, and passes on to English as *souse*. It is of interest that this root gives rise to a Slavic form meaning "sweet" (Russian *sladkiy*). It also appears in numerous names of rivers and towns (*Saale*, *Salzburg*, etc.). If Latin *insula*, "island", comes from *in salo* ("in the salt sea"), and not from *in sola* ("in alone"), we have to add *insular*, *insularity*, *insulin*, *insulate* and (through Italian *isola*), *isolate*, *isolation*, as well as the contribution made by *insula* to *island* and *isle* (the replacement of the first part of Anglo-Saxon *iegland* by the French *isle*).

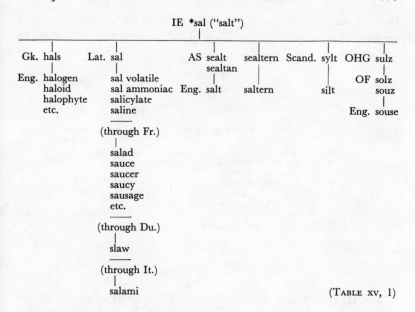

IE *sal ("salt")

Gk. hals	Lat. sal	AS sealt sealtan	sealtern	Scand. sylt	OHG sulz
Eng. halogen	sal volatile	Eng. salt	saltern	silt	OF solz
haloid	sal ammoniac				souz
halophyte	salicylate				
etc.	saline				Eng. souse

(through Fr.)

salad
sauce
saucer
saucy
sausage
etc.

(through Du.)

slaw

(through It.)

salami

(TABLE XV, 1)

IE *newos, "new", appears in Anglo-Saxon nīwe, nēowe, leading to English new, with anew, renew, news, newsboy, newsprint, newspaper, newsletter, new-fangled, newsy, etc. The Greek form is neos, and this gives us the prefix neo- of neolithic, neologism, neophyte, etc., as well as neon; it also appears in various place names (Neapolis, "New City", to Naples, with Neapolitan and Neapolitan ice cream). Slavic novy appears in Novgorod, Novaya Zemlya, "New City", "New Land", and in the Czech family name Novak, but does not otherwise come into English. Latin novus gives us the astronomical nova, the scientific novocain, the compounds renovate, renovation, innovate, innovation, etc., and its Latin derivatives appear in many forms. Novellus gives us novel, novelty, novelette, novelist, the Italian novella, the French nouveau riche and nouveauté, and even creeps into Jespersen's constructed language Novial. Novicius appears in novice, novitiate. Other random Italic and Romance forms are the Oscan Nuvela, which is the modern city of Nola; and Spanish navaja, "razor", from novacula, and novio, novia, "sweetheart, betrothed" (presumably stemming from the idea of a "new interest"). The root *newos appears also in Anglo-Saxon nū, which produces now, in

German *nun*, and in Latin *nunc*, from which we get the humorous *quidnunc* ("what now?"), and which also appears in the religious *nunc dimittis*.

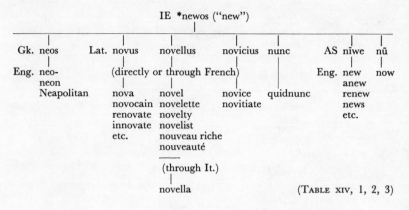

IE *newos ("new")

Gk. neos	Lat. novus	novellus	novicius	nunc	AS nīwe	nū
Eng. neo- neon Neapolitan	(directly or through French) nova novocain renovate innovate etc.	novel novelette novelty novelist nouveau riche nouveauté	novice novitiate	quidnunc	Eng. new anew renew news etc.	now
		(through It.) novella				

(TABLE XIV, 1, 2, 3)

The IE root *sawel*, *swen*, *swo*, "sun", appears in Gothic in the double form *sawil* and *sunno*. Anglo-Saxon offers *sunna*, which gives us *sun* (with *sunny*, *sunstroke*, etc.); *sunnandæg*, which becomes *Sunday* and *sundae;* and *sūth*, *sutherra*, which produces *south*, *southern*, *southward*, *southpaw*, *South Pole*, etc. Compounds of *sun* are numerous: *sunburn*, *sunburst*, *sundial*, *sunspot*, *sun worshiper*, etc. There are also disguised forms in *Suffolk*, *Sussex*, *Southampton*, *Surrey*. The Latin *sol* gives us *solar*, *solar plexus*, *solarium*, *solstice*, *insolation*, *parasol*, as well as the *sol* which is the currency of Peru. Greek *helios* gives us *helium*, *heliotrope*, *heliograph*, *heliacal*, *perihelial*, and other scientific formations.

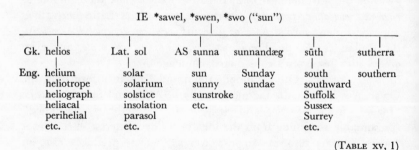

IE *sawel, *swen, *swo ("sun")

Gk. helios	Lat. sol	AS sunna	sunnandæg	sūth	sutherra
Eng. helium heliotrope heliograph heliacal perihelial etc.	solar solarium solstice insolation parasol etc.	sun sunny sunstroke etc.	Sunday sundae	south southward Suffolk Sussex Surrey etc.	southern

(TABLE XV, 1)

IE *(s)nā, "to flow, wetness", produces in Anglo-Saxon a form *gesnott*, which gives us *snotty*, and probably also *snout* and *snooty*, with perhaps an assist from Old High German *snūzen*, which becomes the German *schnauzen*, leading to the name of the breed of dog known as *Schnauzer* (*Schnozzola* is also a derivative of the German form, combining the German root with an Italian ending). In Greek we have *nesos*, "island", which appears in various place names ending in *-nese*, *-nesus*, *-nesia* (*Chersonese*, *Dodecanese*, *Peloponnesus*, *Indonesia*, *Micronesia*, *Polynesia*); there is also a verb *nao*, "to swim", that gives *Naiad*, and the name *Nereis*, which produces *Nereus* and *Nereid*; *naus*, "ship", appears in *nautical*, *Argonaut*, *aeronaut*, *astronautical*, *nautilus*, *nausea* ("ship sickness, seasickness"). The last word in French takes the form *noise* ("that which may cause *nausea*"), passed on to English, with *noisome* as a later formation. Latin forms include *nato*, "to swim", which gives us *natant*, *natatory*, *natation*; *navis*, "ship", with *naval*, *navigate*, *navigator*, *navigable*, *navy*, *navicert*, *navvy*, and the *nave* of a church, likened to a ship; *nutrio*, "nourish", which in more learned Latin form gives us *nutriment*, *nutrient*, *nutrition*, and in French form (*nourrir*, *nourrice*) becomes *nourish*, *nourishment*, and *nurse*, with *nursery* and *nurture*.

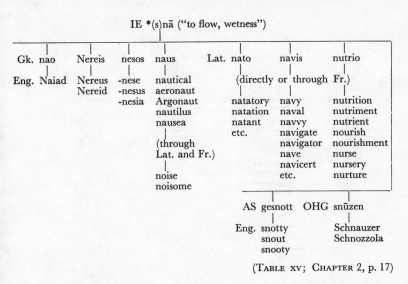

IE *(s)nā ("to flow, wetness")

Gk. nao	Nereis	nesos	naus	Lat. nato	navis	nutrio
Eng. Naiad	Nereus	-nese	nautical	(directly or through Fr.)		
	Nereid	-nesus	aeronaut			
		-nesia	Argonaut	natatory	navy	nutrition
			nautilus	natation	naval	nutriment
			nausea	natant	navvy	nutrient
				etc.	navigate	nourish
			(through		navigator	nourishment
			Lat. and Fr.)		nave	nurse
					navicert	nursery
			noise		etc.	nurture
			noisome			

	AS gesnott	OHG snūzen
	Eng. snotty	Schnauzer
	snout	Schnozzola
	snooty	

(TABLE XV; CHAPTER 2, p. 17)

Better perhaps than any other class of words, numerals illustrate the basically threefold nature of the English vocabulary. The IE root *dekm,[3] *deku, "ten", gives rise to Anglo-Saxon tien, tȳn, and tēotha, from which come ten and tenth, with such secondary forms as the -teen of thirteen, fourteen, teen-age, teen-ager; tenfold, tenpins, tithe, as well as the suffix -tig that appears in English -ty of twenty, forty, etc. The Greek form is deka, from which come our deca- compounds (Decalogue, decade, decahedron, Decameron (something designed for a ten-day period), decapod, decathlon, decasyllabic, and even endecasyllabic, for an eleven-syllable line of verse. Latin decem, "ten" and decimus, "tenth" (with the feminine decima that becomes dime) give us decimal, December, decennial, decimate (to execute one man out of every ten), decibel, decillion, the decanus (originally a leader of a group of ten) that French turns into doyen, adopted by English as dean (with deanery), decurion, decuman. There are also undecim, "eleven", and duodecim, "twelve", from which come undecimal, duodecimal, and dozen (Vulgar Latin duodecina to French douzaine). There is dicker, which comes through German Decker, "a set of ten hides", borrowed from Latin. Deni, "by tens", a derivative of decem) forms denarius, which comes down into English in the double

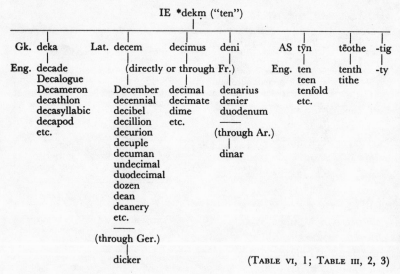

IE *dekm ("ten")

Gk. deka	Lat. decem	decimus	deni	AS tȳn	tēothe	-tig
Eng. decade	(directly or through Fr.)			Eng. ten	tenth	-ty
Decalogue		decimal	denarius	teen	tithe	
Decameron	December	decimate	denier	tenfold		
decathlon	decennial	dime	duodenum	etc.		
decasyllabic	decibel	etc.				
decapod	decillion		(through Ar.)			
etc.	decurion					
	decuple		dinar			
	decuman					
	undecimal					
	duodecimal					
	dozen					
	dean					
	deanery					
	etc.					

(through Ger.)

dicker   (TABLE VI, 1; TABLE III, 2, 3)

[3] The symbol m̥ indicates a vowel value for the sonant m.

form *denier*, used even in hosiery, and *dinar*, a form of currency used in Yugoslavia, Iraq, Iran, etc. It is supposed by some authorities that *dekm gets into the root of *kmtom, "hundred", through an intermediate *dekmtom, and if so, the same basic root would give us *hundred*, *hecatomb*, *cent*, *centime*, *centavo*, *centennial*, *century*, *centurion*, etc., but this is doubtful. The eastern languages of the Indo-European group have *s* corresponding to the general western *k* and the Germanic *h* evidenced by Gothic *taihun*, but lost in Anglo-Saxon (Old High German has *zehan*, and modern German keeps the *h* in spelling, even though it does not pronounce it in *zehn;* see Chapter 3, p. 33); Sanskrit has *daśa*, and Slavic (Russian) has *desyat'*.

The IE root *gᵘ̯ou, "ox", appears in Anglo-Saxon as *cū* (plural *cȳ*), leading to *cow* and *kine* (with compounds such as *cowslip*, *cowboy*, *cowpuncher*, *cowhide*, etc.). Latin *bos*, *bov-*, seems to have been in origin either a Greek or an Oscan loan word, as native Latin development should have given *vos, *vov-. This gives us *bovine* and, through French, *beef* (plural *beeves*), with *beefy*, *beefeater*, *beefsteak*, etc. Latin also offers *bubalus*, for which there is an Oscan doublet *bufalus*, from which Italian derives *bufalo*, passed on to English as *buffalo*, and shortened to *buff*. *Buculus*, "little ox", produces *bugle*, originally a hunting horn. In Greek there is a *bous*, "ox", which appears in *bubalis*, *bucentaur*, *hecatomb* (*hekaton-be*, "a sacrifice of a hundred oxen or cows"), *bucolic* (*boukolikos*, "pertaining to a cowherd"), *boustrophedon* ("as the ox plows", right to left, then left to right, then right to left again; used to describe the early Greek system of writing). There is also a related verb *bosko*, "to graze", which appears in *proboscis* on the one hand, in *botany*, *botanical*, etc., on the other. There is also the possibility that it may have been borrowed by Latin to give *boscus*, from which seem to stem both French *bois* and English *bush*, with such additional English forms as *bosky*, *boscage*, and *haut-bois* or *oboe*. The most far-reaching word, however, is *boutyron*, "ox-cheese", which passes into Latin in the form *butyrum* and gives rise to *butter* and its associated words (*butterfly*, which appears as early as Anglo-Saxon in the form *buterflēge;* *buttercup*, *butter fat*, *butterfish*, *buttermilk*, *butternut*, *butterscotch*, and the more learned *butane*, *butyl*, *butyric*). A Celtic cognate, appearing in a place name, is *Boyne*, from *Boouinda*, while the Indo-Iranian cognate is *gaus*, *go*, "cow", which may possibly appear in the family name of the Buddha, *Gautama* or *Gotama*. *Buccaneer*, once thought to be connected with French *boeuf*, is now generally conceded to come from an American Indian language.

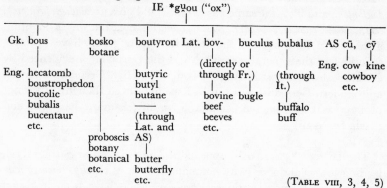

IE *g̑u̯ou ("ox")

Gk. bous	bosko botane	boutyron	Lat. bov-	buculus	bubalus	AS cū, cȳ
Eng. hecatomb boustrophedon bucolic bubalis bucentaur etc.		butyric butyl butane ——— (through Lat. and AS)	(directly or through Fr.) bovine beef beeves etc.	bugle	(through It.)	Eng. cow kine cowboy etc.
	proboscis botany botanical etc.	butter butterfly etc.			buffalo buff	

(TABLE VIII, 3, 4, 5)

In the case of the IE root *trei*, "three", there is a little difficulty in keeping apart Greek and Latin compounds, both of which have *tri-* (so do even Slavic and Indo-Iranian: the Hindu Trinity, composed of Brahma the Creator, Vishnu the Preserver, and Siva the Destroyer, is *Trimurti*, appearing in English, but only as a proper noun). In Anglo-Saxon, the root produces *thrī(e)*, which develops into *three*, with numerous compounds (*threefold*, *threepenny*, *threescore*, *threesome*, etc.); and *thridda*, which gives us *third* (with *third class*, *third degree*, etc.). There is also *thriga*, giving us *thrice*; *thrēotȳne*, which becomes *thirteen*; *thrēotēotha*, which becomes *thirteenth*; *thrētig*, which turns into *thirty*. Greek *treis* appears in a few very learned words, like *treiskaidekaphobia*, "fear of the number thirteen"; while the neuter *tria*, shortened to *tri-*, gives us *triad*, *triclinium*, *tricycle*, *trigonometry*, *trinòmial*, *trilogy*, *triphthong*, *tripod*, *Tripoli* ("three cities"), *triptych*, *tristich*, *tritium*, *Triton*. Latin *tres*, with a neuter form *tria*, appears for the most part in words that have gone through French, like *trefoil*, *treble*, *trellis*, *trey* (*Trecento* is Italian); it appears as *tri-* in *triangle*, *Triassic*, *tricentennial*, *tricolor*, *trident*, *trilateral*, *trilingual*, *trillion*, *trine*, *Trinity*, *triple*, *triplet*, *triplane*, *triplicate*, *trireme*, *trisect*, *triumvirate*, *triune*, *trivial* (*trio* is Italian). *Tri-* becomes *tra-* in *tripalium* (a three-poled instrument of torture) which turns into French *travail* and English *travail* and *travel*. *Ter*, Latin for "thrice", appears in *tercentenary*, *tern*, *ternary*, *tercet* (Italian), and *tertius*, "third" appears in *tertium quid*, *tertiary*, *tertian*, *sesterce*, *sestertius*, *sestertium*, the French *tierce*, and the Italian *terza rima*. Two Latin derivatives of *tres* (the first a little more doubtful than the second) are *tribus*, "tribe", from which come *tribe, tribal, tribesman, tribute, tributary, attribute, contribute, contribution, contributor, distribute, distribution, retribution, tribune, tribunal*; and *testis*, "witness" (originally **ter-stis*, "the third stander, the bystander"). Here the ramifications are: *testament, testamentary, testate, testator, intestate, testes* or *testicles* ("little witnesses"

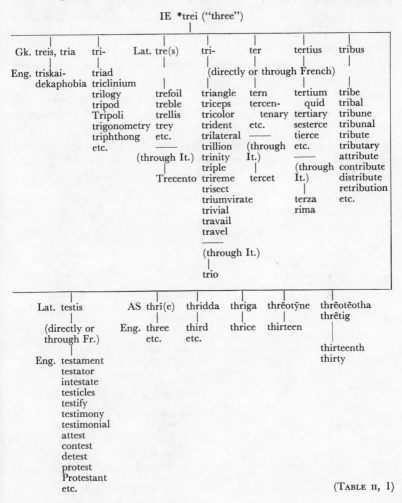

IE *trei ("three")

Gk. treis, tria	tri-	Lat. tre(s)	tri-	ter	tertius	tribus
Eng. triskai-dekaphobia	triad triclinium trilogy tripod Tripoli trigonometry triphthong etc.	trefoil treble trellis trey etc. ——— (through It.) Trecento	(directly or through French) triangle triceps tricolor trident trilateral trillion trinity triple trireme trisect triumvirate trivial travail travel ——— (through It.) trio	tern tercen- tenary etc. ——— (through It.) tercet	tertium quid tertiary sesterce tierce etc. ——— (through It.) terza rima	tribe tribal tribune tribunal tribute tributary attribute contribute distribute retribution etc.

Lat. testis	AS thrī(e)	thridda	thriga	thrēotȳne	thrēotēotha thrētig
(directly or through Fr.)	Eng. three etc.	third etc.	thrice	thirteen	thirteenth thirty
Eng. testament testator intestate testicles testify testimony testimonial attest contest detest protest Protestant etc.					

(TABLE II, 1)

to a man's virility, or perhaps from the custom of swearing by one's most treasured possessions), *testicular, testificate, testify, testimonial, testimony*, and numerous compounds: *attest, attestation, contest, contestant, detest, detestable, incontestable, protest, protestation, Protestant*, etc.

The root **kered*, "heart", gives the Anglo-Saxon *heorte* that develops into *heart*, with *hearty, heartiness, heartily, dishearten, heartbreak, heartland, heartburn, heartfelt, heartless, heart-rending, heartsick*, etc. The Greek *kardia* gives us *cardiac, cardiology, cardiogram, endocardial, pericardium*, and other medical terms. Latin *cor* (root *cord-*) gives us, directly or through French, *core, cordial, cordiality, accord, accordion, concord, concordance, discord, discordant, record, recorder*, and also *recourse, misericord, courage, encourage, discourage*, etc. Most authorities link Latin *credo*, "to believe", with the "heart" root, and here we get *creed* and *credo, credence* and the Italian *credenza* (a cabinet to which you "entrust" possessions), *credentials, credible, incredible, credibility, credulous, incredulity*, the Italian *credit*, with *accredit, discredit, creditor, creditable*, the French *miscreant* and *recreant*. Slavic cognates have *s* where the IE root has **k* (Russian *serdtse*, "heart", *sreda*, "middle, Wednesday, or midweek").

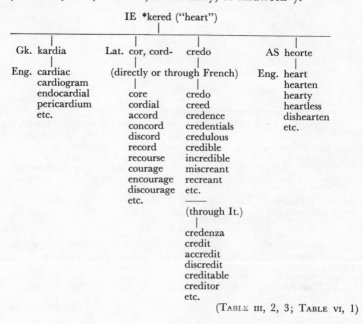

IE *kered ("heart")

Gk. kardia	Lat. cor, cord-	credo	AS heorte
Eng. cardiac	(directly or through French)		Eng. heart
cardiogram			hearten
endocardial	core	credo	hearty
pericardium	cordial	creed	heartless
etc.	accord	credence	dishearten
	concord	credentials	etc.
	discord	credulous	
	record	credible	
	recourse	incredible	
	courage	miscreant	
	encourage	recreant	
	discourage	etc.	
	etc.	———	
		(through It.)	
		credenza	
		credit	
		accredit	
		discredit	
		creditable	
		creditor	
		etc.	

(Table iii, 2, 3; Table vi, 1)

The root *okᵘ, "to see, eye", produces in Anglo-Saxon *ēage*, which becomes *eye*, with compounds like *eyebrow, eyelash, eyetooth, eyeful, eyeglass, eyesight, eyesore, eyestrain, eyewink, eye-witness*, etc. From another Germanic source, Old Norse, *vindauga* (literally "wind-eye") comes to English as *window*. In Greek the root takes two forms, *ops*, "face", with *opsomai*, "I shall see", which come to English in the form of *optic, optical, optician, Cyclops, myopia*, other scientific words in *-opia*, *autopsy, synopsis*, possibly *hydropsy* or *dropsy;* and *ophthalmos*, "eye", which yields *ophthalmic, ophthalmia, ophthalmology, ophthalmologist, ophthalmoscope*, etc. The Latin form is *oculus*, from which come *ocular, oculist, binocular, monocle*, as well as *atrocious* (literally "black-eyed"), with *atrocity*, and *ferocious* ("fierce-eyed") with *ferocity*. Other forms are *ocellate, inoculate* (the original meaning is "to graft, to put into the eye"); also *inveigle*, which comes from the French *aveugler*, "to blind", *aveugle*, "blind" (the latter in turn comes from a Vulgar Latin formation *ab oculo*, "away from the eye", "eyeless"); *antlers*, which are *ante oculares*, "before the eyes". The Latin *oculus*, entering Low German in the form *oegeln*, is passed on to English as *ogle*. Slavic cognates include the word for "window" (Russian *okolo*) and the *ochi* of *Ochi Chornyya* ("Black Eyes").

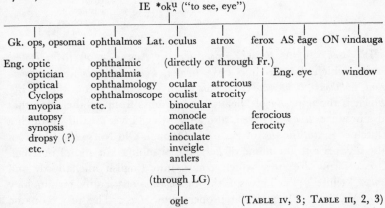

IE *okᵘ ("to see, eye")

Gk. ops, opsomai	ophthalmos	Lat. oculus	atrox	ferox	AS ēage	ON vindauga
Eng. optic	ophthalmic	(directly or through Fr.)				
optician	ophthalmia				Eng. eye	window
optical	ophthalmology	ocular	atrocious			
Cyclops	ophthalmoscope	oculist	atrocity			
myopia	etc.	binocular				
autopsy		monocle		ferocious		
synopsis		ocellate		ferocity		
dropsy (?)		inoculate				
etc.		inveigle				
		antlers				

(through LG)

ogle　　　　(TABLE IV, 3; TABLE III, 2, 3)

IE *kreu*, "blood, bloody, raw meat", produces in Anglo-Saxon *hrēaw*, which becomes *raw* (with *rawness, rawhide, rawboned*, etc.), and *hrēr*, which becomes the *rare* of meat, to be distinguished from *rare* meaning "uncommon", which comes from Latin *rarus*. Old High

German *hrosa* enters into the name of *Mount Rosa* in the Alps, which has nothing to do with roses, but a good deal to do with raw, cold weather. Greek has *kreas*, "meat", which appears in English *pancreas* ("all meat"), *pancreatic, creatine, creosote;* and *kryos*, "cold", which appears in *cryogen, cryolite, cryoscope,* and other scientific terms, as well as *krystallos*, which becomes *crystal*, with *crystallize, crystallization, crystalline,* etc. Latin offers *cruor*, "blood", with *crudus*, "raw", from which we get *crude, crudeness, crudity, recrudescence,* and the French *écru; crudelis*, which leads to *cruel* and *cruelty;* and *crusta*, which produces *crust, crusty, crustacean, crustaceous, encrust.* In this group, the eastern Indo-European languages have *k*, not *s*, corresponding to western *k*, and Sanskrit has *krava* and Russian *krov'* as the word for "blood".

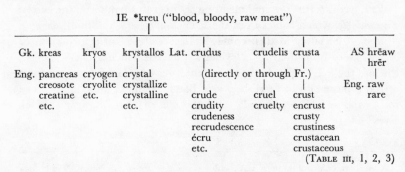

IE *kreu ("blood, bloody, raw meat")

Gk. kreas	kryos	krystallos	Lat. crudus		crudelis	crusta	AS hrēaw hrēr
Eng. pancreas creosote creatine etc.	cryogen cryolite etc.	crystal crystallize crystalline etc.	(directly or through Fr.)				
			crude crudity crudeness recrudescence écru etc.		cruel cruelty	crust encrust crusty crustiness crustacean crustaceous	Eng. raw rare

(TABLE III, 1, 2, 3)

IE *leuk*, "light, to see", produces in Anglo-Saxon *lēoht, lȳhtan, līegetu*, which develop into *light, lighten, lightning, enlighten, enlightenment, lighthouse, light year,* etc. (This "light" is distinct from the "light" which is the opposite of "heavy", and comes from another root that also produces *levity*). There is also a *lēah* which gives *lea* and, through a Dutch cognate, the *-loo* of *Waterloo.* Through Old Norse *logi*, this root also gives rise to the name of *Loki*, the Scandinavian god of mischief. Greek forms are *lynx*, which comes into English unchanged, and *leukos*, "white", which gives us the *leuko-, leuco-* of scientific terminology (*leucocyte, leukemia*), and the proper name *Luke.* The proper name *Roxana* comes from a Persian (Indo-Iranian) form of the root. In Latin, the basic words are *lux*, "light", *luna* (from *louksna*, "the shining one"), "moon", and *lumen* (from *leuks-men*), "light". *Lux* gives rise to *lux, lucerne, lucent, lucid, lucidity, pellucid* (*per-lucid*, "shining through"), *elucidate, elucidation*, proper names like *Lucius, Lucy, Lucille,*

Lucifer ("Light-bearer"). There are also *lucubrate, lucubration* ("to work by artificial light"); possibly *pollex*, from *pollucere* ("to let shine"); possibly *luxus* (with *luxury, luxuriousness, de luxe*); and a *lucus* meaning "grove" which, like *lea*, originally meant an open spot or field where the sun shone, and later came to mean a shady spot reserved for religious rites (interestingly, a Roman etymologist says that *lucus* comes from "*non lucendo*", the fact that it does not shine). *Luna* gives us *lunar, sublunar, lunette, lunacy, lunatic* and *loony*. From *lumen* we get *lumen, luminary, luminous, illuminate, illumination, illuminati*, and *limn*. Another derivative, *luster*, gives *luster, lustrous, illustrious, illustrate, illustration*, etc.

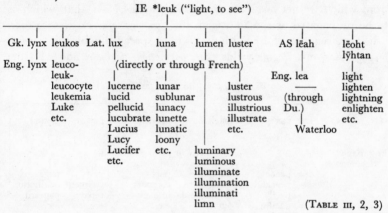

IE *leuk ("light, to see")

Gk. lynx	leukos	Lat. lux	luna	lumen	luster	AS lēah	lēoht lȳhtan
Eng. lynx	leuco-	(directly or through French)					
	leuk-					Eng. lea	light
	leucocyte	lucerne	lunar	luster			lighten
	leukemia	lucid	sublunar	lustrous		——	lightning
	Luke	pellucid	lunacy	illustrious		(through	enlighten
	etc.	lucubrate	lunette	illustrate		Du.)	etc.
		Lucius	lunatic	etc.			
		Lucy	loony			Waterloo	
		Lucifer	etc.				
		etc.		luminary			
				luminous			
				illuminate			
				illumination			
				illuminati			
				limn		(TABLE III, 2, 3)	

The IE root *pāk, *pag*, "to make fast", appears in Greek *hapax legomenon* (what is said only once), derived from the verb *pegnymi*, "to make fast". The Germanic branch has Anglo-Saxon *feng*, giving English *fang* (an archaic verb *fang*, from Anglo-Saxon *fōn*, corresponding to German *fangen*, is no longer used). Latin gives us *pax*, "peace"; *paciscor* (past participle *pactus*), "to agree"; a Vulgar Latin *pacare*, "to appease, pacify, pay off"; the verb *pango*, "to make fast", with a nasal infix and a past participle which is also *pāctus*, but with long *a;* this, in Romance development, merges with the *pactus* of *paciscor*. Other Latin forms from this root are *pagina*, originally "trellis", then "page of writing"; *pagus*, "village"; *palus*, "stake, pole", whence *palatium*, "palace" (probably from *Palatinus*, the Palatine Hill of Rome, so called because once enclosed by a palisade). *Tripalium*, an instrument of torture consisting of three poles, becomes French *travail* and English *travail* and *travel*, with *traveler*. There is the further possibility that *palatum*, "palate", may come from this source, but *pala*, "shovel", seems more likely. *Pax*, directly or through French, gives us *peace, peaceful, peaceable, pacifist, pacify, Pacific, appease, appeasement,* and the religious *pax vobiscum*. The participial *pactus*, from either *paciscor* or *pango*, gives *pact, compact, impact,* and, through Spanish *despacho, dispatch* (but this may also come from the *foot* root of *im-pedicare, dis-ped-icare*). *Pangere*, through its compound *impingere*, gives *impinge* and *impingement*. The root of *pango*, shorn of its nasal infix, produces a noun *propages*, "what is extensively made fast or spread", from which we get *propagate, propagation, propaganda* ("that which is to be propagated or spread", from the *Congregatio de Propaganda Fide*, "the Congregation of the Faith that is to be spread"), with *propagandist, propagandize,* etc. *Pagina* yields *page, pagination, paginate,* and with the

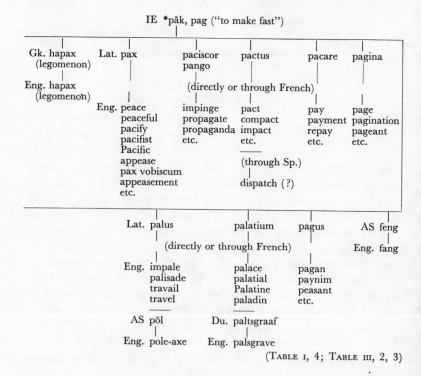

IE *pāk, pag ("to make fast")

Gk. hapax (legomenon)	Lat. pax	paciscor pango	pactus	pacare	pagina
Eng. hapax (legomenon)		(directly or through French)			
	Eng. peace peaceful pacify pacifist Pacific appease pax vobiscum appeasement etc.	impinge propagate propaganda etc.	pact compact impact etc. (through Sp.) dispatch (?)	pay payment repay etc.	page pagination pageant etc.

	Lat. palus		palatium	pagus	AS feng
		(directly or through French)			Eng. fang
	Eng. impale palisade travail travel		palace palatial Palatine paladin	pagan paynim peasant etc.	

	AS pōl	Du. paltsgraaf
	Eng. pole-axe	Eng. palsgrave

(TABLE I, 4; TABLE III, 2, 3)

original meaning of "trellis" developing into "scaffold, stage", also *pageant* and *pageantry*. *Pagus*, ("village") gives *pagan, paganism, paganize, paynim* (the country districts and villages clung longer to the traditional Roman gods and rejected Christianity, which first spread in the larger cities). An adjective derived from *pagus, pagensis*, "pertaining to a village", becomes the French noun *pays*, "village, town, district, country", and on this is formed a new adjective *paysan*, which in English becomes *peasant* and *peasantry*. *Pacare*, through French *payer*, becomes *pay, payment, payable, repay, payee*, etc. *Palus* produces *impale, palisade*, and, through Anglo-Saxon *pōl*, the *pole* of *pole-axe*, while *palatium* and *Palatinus* give us *palace, palatial, Palatine, paladin, Palatinate*, then (through Dutch *paltsgraaf) palsgrave*, "palace count". If *pala* and *palatum* belong here, we have also *palate* and *palette*.

The root **plā-k, *plā-g, *plə-k* means "wide, flat, to broaden". It gives the Greek *pelagos*, "sea", from which we get *pelagic* and *archipelago*, and *Pelasgian*. Germanic forms are represented by Anglo-Saxon *flōc*, "fluke"; Old Norse *flak*, "flake", and *flaga*, which leads to the *flag* of *flagstone;* Norwegian *flo*, leading to *floe*; Middle English *flawe*, "crack", leading to *flaw*. Latin forms involve *placeo*, "to please"; *placidus*, "placid"; *placo*, "to placate"; *plaga*, "beach", which is the forefather of French *plage*, and shows a *g* that conforms to the Greek *g* and the Germanic *k*. Here we get some straight Latin forms, like *placebo*, "I shall please", a remedy that pleases the taker, but has no particular effect; and *placitum*, used as a law term (Old French *plait*) and leading

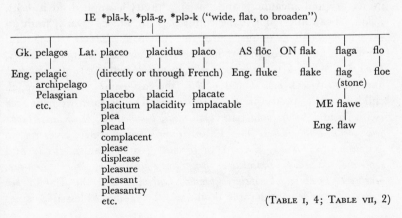

IE **plā-k, *plā-g, *plə-k* ("wide, flat, to broaden")

Gk. pelagos	Lat. placeo	placidus	placo	AS flōc	ON flak	flaga	flo
Eng. pelagic	(directly or through French)			Eng. fluke	flake	flag	floe
archipelago						(stone)	
Pelasgian	placebo	placid	placate				
etc.	placitum	placidity	implacable			ME flawe	
	plea						
	plead					Eng. flaw	
	complacent						
	please						
	displease						
	pleasure						
	pleasant						
	pleasantry						
	etc.						

(TABLE I, 4; TABLE VII, 2)

to *plea, plead. Placo* gives us *placate, implacable. Placidus* gives us *placid, placidity. Placeo*, in varied forms, mostly derived through French, gives us *complacent, complacency, please, displease, pleasure, plaisance, complaisance, pleasant, pleasantry, pleasurable*, etc. A possible link appears with the root **plān*, and if this is so, further extensions would include English *flat, plain, place, piano, piazza*, etc.

The IE root **deu, *dou, *du*, "to honor, honorable", produces in Germanic an Anglo-Saxon *getawian, tōw*, which gives English *taw*, and a *tōl* that results in *tool*. Greek *dynamai, dynamis* give us the *dyna-* root of *dyne, heterodyne, dynamic, dynamite, dynamism, dynamo, electrodynamic, hydrodynamic,* etc. They also provide *dynast, dynasty, dynastic*. In Latin the forms are *duenos* (archaic), with an adverbial *duene* and a secondary *duenelos*, and these, by the archaic Latin change whereby initial **dw* becomes *b*, turn into *bonus*, "good", *bene*, "well", and *bellus*, "beautiful". *Bonus* appears in English in Latin form in *bonus* and *bona fide*, while its derivative *bonitas*, through French *bonté*, becomes English *bounty* (with *bounteous* and *bountiful*). Other ramifications are *boon* (in *boon companion;* the *boon* which is granted comes from an unrelated Scandinavian source); *bonny*; perhaps *bonnet*; *debonnaire* ("of good air"); *boniface; Bonaparte* and *Bonapartist*; also numerous French forms like the reduplicative *bonbon* ("goody goody"), *bon gré mal gré, bon ton, bon vivant, bon voyage, bon marché*. English *Marylebone* represents French *Marie la bonne*, "Mary the good", and *bonne* itself, in the sense of "maid", has entered English. Through Spanish come *bonanza* ("good weather" in its original meaning) and *bonito* ("pretty", applied to a fish). *Bellus*, "beautiful" (not to be confused with *bellum*, "war", from an earlier *duellum*) gives us, through Italian, *belladonna* ("beautiful woman"), and through French, *beauty, beauteous, beautiful, beautify, beautician, beauty salon* (or *beauty parlor*, or even *beauty shop*); also *embellish* and *embellishment, bibelot* and *bauble* (the last comes from a French childish *belbel*, "pretty pretty"). In straight French form we have *beau* (with *bo* and *hobo*), *beau geste, beau idéal, beau monde, beaux arts, beaux yeux, belle, belles lettres*. The Latin adverb *bene*, "well", gives rise to *benediction* or *benison, Benedict* or *Bennett* (with Spanish *Benito* and *sanbenito*), *benedict, Benedictine, benefactor, benefaction, benefit, benefice, beneficent, beneficial, beneficiary, benign, benignity*, and the Italian *ben trovato*. There is considerable doubt whether *beatus*, "blessed", comes from the same root. If it does, we may add *beatitude, beatific, beatify, Beatrice,* etc.

IE *deu, *dou, *du ("to honor, honorable")

Gk. dynamis	Lat. bonus	bene	bellus	AS getawian	tōl
				tōw	
Eng. dynamo	(directly or through French)				
dynamic				Eng. taw	tool
dyne	bonus	benedict	beauty		
dynamite	bona fide	benediction	beautify		
dynasty	bounty	benison	beautician		
etc.	bountiful	Benedictine	beautiful		
	boon	Bennett	embellish		
	bonny	benefactor	bauble		
	boniface	benefit	bibelot		
	Bonaparte	benefice	beau		
	debonnaire	beneficiary	belle		
	bonbon	benevolent	beaux arts		
	bon gré	benign	belles lettres		
	bon mot	benignity	etc.		
	bon vivant	etc.			
	bon voyage	———	(through It.)		
	bon marché	(through It.)			
	Marylebone		belladonna		
	———	ben trovato			
	(through Sp.)				
	bonanza				
	bonito		(TABLE VI, 1; CHAPTER 3, p. 37)		

A root *deik,* with a possible variant *deig,* "to show", produces in Anglo-Saxon *tǣcean,* from which we derive *teach* (with *teacher, teachable,* etc.), along with *tācen,* which gives us *token, betoken.* In Greek the root produces *dike,* "justice", with *dicast,* and the verb *deiknymi,* "to show", with a noun *deixis.* These give us *paradigm, paradigmatic, deictic, apodeictic, paradeictic.* From *apodeixis,* "a showing forth", comes *apodeixa,* "receipt", which Italian turns into *polizza,* and this becomes the *policy* of insurance (but not that of national interest, which comes from the root of *polis,* "city"). In Latin, we have *dico,* "to say", with past participle *dictus,* and secondary formations in *-dicare* (which give us forms in *-dicate*), *-dictio* (leading to our *-diction* and *-dition;* but the latter need to be kept separate from *-dition* forms that come from the root of *do,* "to give"); *-dex* (as in *judex,* "judge, the one who shows or speaks the law", or *vindex,* "avenger"); and *digitus,* "finger" ("the one that shows, points out, indicates"). Latin forms appear straight in *dictum* and *obiter dicta,* while *ditto* and *vendetta* show Italian forms of *dictus* (*ditto*, however, also shows some confusion between Latin *dictus* and Italian *detto*). Other forms involving the participial *dict-* are *diction*, *addict*, *addiction*, *contradict*, *contradictory*, *benedict* (with *Bennett*, and the Spanish *Benito* and *sanbenito*), *benediction*, *benison*, *malediction*, *edict*, *indict*, *indictment*, *indite*, *interdict*, *interdictory*, *predict*, *prediction*, *verdict*, *dictionary*, *jurisdiction*. *Dictare*, which leads to *dictate*, *dictation*, *dictator*, *dictatorial*, *dictatorship*, and the French *dictée* which comes out in English as *ditty*, also leads to Anglo-Saxon *dihtan*, which comes out as *bedight*. The combining form *-dicare* gives us *abdicate*, *abdication*, *dedicate*,

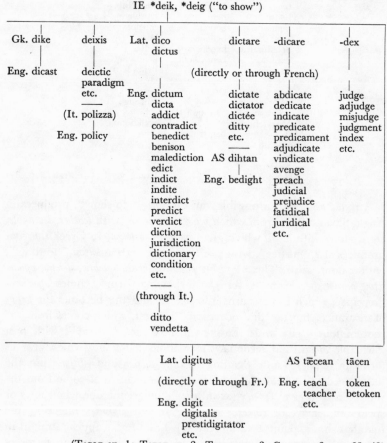

IE *deik, *deig ("to show")

Gk. dike	deixis	Lat. dico dictus	dictare	-dicare	-dex
Eng. dicast	deictic paradigm etc.	(directly or through French)			
		Eng. dictum	dictate	abdicate	judge
		dicta	dictator	dedicate	adjudge
(It. polizza)		addict	dictée	indicate	misjudge
		contradict	ditty	predicate	judgment
Eng. policy		benedict	etc.	predicament	index
		benison		adjudicate	etc.
		malediction AS dihtan		vindicate	
		edict		avenge	
		indict Eng. bedight		preach	
		indite		judicial	
		interdict		prejudice	
		predict		fatidical	
		verdict		juridical	
		diction		etc.	
		jurisdiction			
		dictionary			
		condition			
		etc.			

(through It.)

ditto
vendetta

Lat. digitus		AS tǣcean	tācen
(directly or through Fr.)		Eng. teach	token
Eng. digit		teacher etc.	betoken
digitalis			
prestidigitator			
etc.			

(TABLE VI, 1; TABLE III, 2; TABLE VII, 2, CHAPTER 3, pp. 35, 42) *dedication, indicate, indication, indicator, fatidical, predicate, predicament, adjudicate, vindicate, revindicate.* But *vindicare*, through Old French *vengiier*, also gives us *avenge, avenger, revenge, vengeful,* while *praedicare* becomes *prechier* (modern French *prêcher*) and English *preach,* with *preacher, preachment.* Combinations with *jus,* "law", give us *judicial, judicable, prejudice, prejudicial, juridical,* while French development appears in *judge, adjudge, misjudge, judgment. Index* (plural *indices*) appears in Latin form. The *-ditio* which is a weakening of *-dictio* gives us *condition, conditional, recondition. Digitus* gives *digit, digital, digitalis, prestidigitator,* etc.

The root **bhā,* "to speak", produces in Greek a verb *phemi* which, in compounds that pass into Latin and, usually, French, gives us *blaspheme* and *blasphemous* in a more learned version, *blame* and *blameless* in a more popular one, as well as *euphemy, euphemism, prophet, prophetess, prophecy, prophesy, prophetic,* and *aphasia.* The noun *phone,* "sound", derived from the same Greek root, enters Latin in one of its compounds, *antiphonon,* which in Anglo-Saxon becomes *antefen,* and in later English, *anthem.* More learned treatment produces *antiphon* and *antiphony,* while other compounds give us *phonic, phonetic, phonetician, phonology, phoneme* and *phonemic, telephone, phonograph, apophony, metaphony, symphony, symphonic, euphony, euphonic, diphthong, monophthong, triphthong,* etc. A Germanic cognate appears in Anglo-Saxon *bannan,* "to summon by proclamation". This gives us *ban, banns, banish, banishment, banal* (with *banality; banal* was in origin an adjective applied to feudal service, rendered in response to a proclamation, but often performed in perfunctory fashion, as though unimportant). In many of these later developments, Anglo-Saxon *bannan* gets crossed with Old French forms derived from the Old High German of the Franks, but going back to the same original Germanic source. The Old High German form appears in French *banlieue;* one development is Old French *abandoner,* from the Latin preposition *ad* combined with the Germanic *bandon,* "jurisdiction", with the original meaning of "to give up legally"; this comes into English as *abandon.* Another form built on the Germanic root, but coming originally through Italian, is *bandit,* with *banditism, banditry,* etc. (*banditti* shows, from the Italian standpoint, an erroneous doubling of *t*). *Contraband.* "against the law", may have reached us from Italian or from Spanish. The Latin descendant of the root is *for*, "to speak", with infinitive *fari* and past participle *fatus*, and numerous secondary formations: *facundus*, "endowed with the gift of speech"; *fabula*, "fable"; *fateor*, "to avow"; *fatum*, "fate"; *fama*, "fame"; *fascinus*, "fascination". The root of *for* produces *nefarious*, "unspeakable"; *infant*, "not speaking", with *infancy*, the Spanish *Infante* and *Infanta*, *infanticide*, *infantile*, the French *enfant gâté* and *enfant terrible;* also *infantry* and *infantryman* (from Italian or Spanish; the semantic progression is from child to boy to young

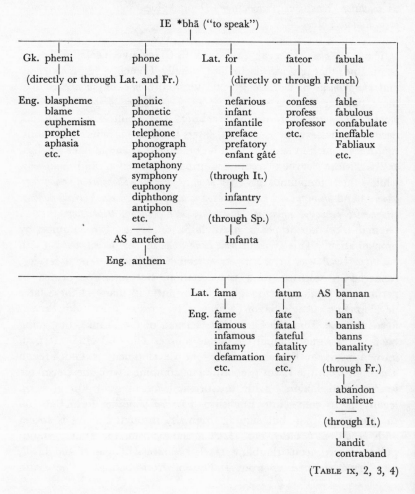

IE *bhā ("to speak")

Gk. phemi	phone	Lat. for	fateor	fabula
(directly or through Lat. and Fr.)		(directly or through French)		
Eng. blaspheme	phonic	nefarious	confess	fable
blame	phonetic	infant	profess	fabulous
euphemism	phoneme	infantile	professor	confabulate
prophet	telephone	preface	etc.	ineffable
aphasia	phonograph	prefatory		Fabliaux
etc.	apophony	enfant gâté		etc.
	metaphony	——		
	symphony	(through It.)		
	euphony			
	diphthong	infantry		
	antiphon	——		
	etc.	(through Sp.)		
	——			
AS antefen		Infanta		
Eng. anthem				

Lat. fama	fatum	AS bannan
Eng. fame	fate	ban
famous	fatal	banish
infamous	fateful	banns
infamy	fatality	banality
defamation	fairy	——
etc.	etc.	(through Fr.)
		abandon
		banlieue
		——
		(through It.)
		bandit
		contraband

(TABLE IX, 2, 3, 4)

man to enlisted young man or foot soldier); also *preface* and *prefatory*. *Facundus*, "one endowed with the gift of gab" gives *facundity*, an obsolete word meaning "eloquence". From *fabula* come *fable, fabulous, ineffable, confabulate, confabulation*, the Spanish *hablar* ("to speak"; the older form was *fablar*), the Portuguese *falar*, the Old French *Fabliaux*. Two compounds of *fateor* (*confiteor* and *profiteor*) give us *confess, confession, profess, profession, professor, professorial*. *Fatum* ("that which is spoken") gives *fate, fatal, fatalism, fatality, fateful, fated*, and, through Old French *feerie*, derived from Vulgar Latin *fateria*, "enchantment", *fairy*. *Fama* gives *fame, famous, infamy, infamous, defame, defamation*. The doubt involved in *fascinus* (*fascinate, fascination*) is that it may come from the root of *fasces*, "bundle", which produces *fascist* and *fascism*. There is also the question whether *fatuus*, which gives us *fatuous* and *infatuation*, may belong here, or with the root of *vapidus*.

Another highly productive root is that of *(s)*pend*, *(s)*pond*, "to draw, spin, stretch" (though in Greek and Latin it acquires a religious significance, "to pour out a libation"). The Germanic branch shows Anglo-Saxon *spannan*, leading to *span* (with *outspan, inspan*, etc.); *spinnan*, "to spin", with *spinel* (*spindle, spinster, spindly*); *spithre* (*spider*, "the one who spins"). The Greek forms are *spān* or *spaein*, "to draw, cause convulsions", which gives us *spasm, spasmodic, spastic;* and *sponde*, "libation", which gives us *spondee* and *spondaic*. Latin has various and varying roots: *spont-*, represented by (*sua*) *sponte*, "of one's own free will"; *spond-*, appearing in *spondeo*, past participle *sponsus*, "to promise, pledge"; *pend-*, with *pendeo* and its past participle *pensus*, "to hang"; and *pond-*, shown by *pondus*, "weight". *Sponte* gives us *spontaneous* and *spontaneity*. *Spondeo*, in its various compounds, directly or through French, gives *sponsor, spouse, espouse, espousal, despondent, despondency* (here the story is curious: a father, giving away or "desponding" his daughter to her future husband, feels depressed, "despondent"; a less picturesque account is that you "de-spond", or swear off, hope); *respond, responsive, responsible, irresponsibility, response, correspond, correspondent, correspondence*, etc. *Pendeo*, "to hang", in its *pend-* root gives us *pend, impend, suspend, suspenders, append, appendage, appendix, appendicitis, appendectomy, expend, expenditure, stipend, propend, compendium, compendious, spend, spendthrift, spender, depend, dependent, independence, dispend, perpendicular, pendant, pending, pendicle, pendulous,* *pendulum, pendule, penchant, penthouse,* the *painter* or fastening rope of a boat, etc. The participial root *pens-* gives *pensile, pensive, le Penseur, pansy* (French *pensée*, "thought", the flower being the thought-violet); Spanish *peso, peseta*, from the idea of weight, derived from that of "hanging in the balance"); *suspense, expense, expensive, propensity,*

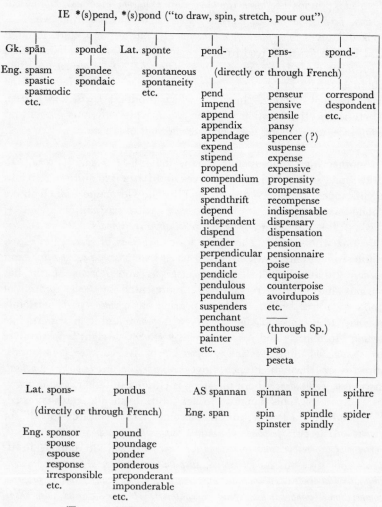

IE *(s)pend, *(s)pond ("to draw, spin, stretch, pour out")

Gk. spān	sponde	Lat. sponte	pend-	pens-	spond-
Eng. spasm	spondee	spontaneous		(directly or through French)	
spastic	spondaic	spontaneity			
spasmodic		etc.	pend	penseur	correspond
etc.			impend	pensive	despondent
			append	pensile	etc.
			appendix	pansy	
			appendage	spencer (?)	
			expend	suspense	
			stipend	expense	
			propend	expensive	
			compendium	propensity	
			spend	compensate	
			spendthrift	recompense	
			depend	indispensable	
			independent	dispensary	
			dispend	dispensation	
			spender	pension	
			perpendicular	pensionnaire	
			pendant	poise	
			pendicle	equipoise	
			pendulous	counterpoise	
			pendulum	avoirdupois	
			suspenders	etc.	
			penchant	———	
			penthouse	(through Sp.)	
			painter		
			etc.	peso	
				peseta	

Lat. spons-	pondus	AS spannan	spinnan	spinel	spithre
(directly or through French)	(directly or through French)	Eng. span	spin	spindle	spider
Eng. sponsor	pound		spinster	spindly	
spouse	poundage				
espouse	ponder				
response	ponderous				
irresponsible	preponderant				
etc.	imponderable				
	etc.				

(TABLE I, 4; TABLE VI; for *-nd-* to *-nn-* in AS, see CHAPTER 3, p. 33) *recompense*, *compensate*, *compensation*, *dispense*, *indispensable*, *dispensary*, *dispensation*, possibly *Spencer* and *spencer; pension*, *pensioner*, the French *pension* and *pensionnaire*. From a more popular and advanced French development, we have *poise*, *equipoise*, *counterpoise*, *avoirdupois*. *Pondus*, "weight", gives us, in various incarnations, *pound* and *poundage*, *ponder*, *imponderable*, *preponderant*, *ponderous*, etc.

An IE root **bhel*, "blade, bloom, to sprout", appears in Greek *phyllon*, "leaf", from which come such scientific terms as *chlorophyll*, *phylliform*, and *phylloxera* (the last is the vine disease that almost wiped out the European wine grape, rescued in the nick of time by the grafting of the American Concord variety, immune to the disease). In Latin, we have on the one hand *folium*, with a plural *folia*, from which come *foliage*, *foliaceous*, and *foil* (in the sense of *tinfoil*), along with botanical terms like *trifolium*, *folium*, *foliolate*, and the *folio* used in bookbinding, as well as the French *feuilleton* (it may be remarked that the Romance words for "leaf" are derived from the Latin plural *folia* (French *feuille*, Spanish *hoja*, Italian *foglia*, which become feminine singulars, while in Italian the Latin singular *folium* remains as *foglio*, "sheet of paper"). Latin also has the verb *floresco*, "to bloom", which, through French, gives us *flourish*, and the noun *flos* (root *flor-*), "flower", from which come *floral*, *flora*, *florid*, *Florida* (this is a Spanish adjectival form meaning "flowery"), *Florence*, *florin* (the Florentine coin), *florescent*, *efflorescent*, *defloration*, *florist*, *floriculture*, etc. French development gives us *flower* (with *flowery*, *flowerpot*, etc.), and also *flour* ("the flower of the wheat"); *flirt* (from *fleurette*, "little flower", used in such expressions as *conter des fleurettes*, "to tell little flowery tales, sweet nothings"). There are also *fleuret* and *fleur-de-lys*, in straight French form; *Fiorello* (Italian for "little flower"); and a special development of the feminine name *Florence* to *Flossie*, then to *floosie*. On the Germanic side, we have Anglo-Saxon *blæd*, which becomes *blade*, *blædre* to *bladder*, *blōwan* to *blow* (only in the sense of flowers: *full-blown*); *blēgen* to the *-blain* of *chilblain*; a hypothetical **blōtian* to *bloat*. Anglo-Saxon *blōd*, *blēd*, *blēdan* give us *blood*, *bleed*, with such formations as *bloody*, *blood-curdling*, *bloodhound*, *bloodshot*, *bloodthirsty*, *bleeding heart*, etc. *Blēdsian*, "to consecrate by sprinkling with blood", becomes *bless*, with *blessing*, *blessed* or *blest*, *blessedness*, etc. Lastly, there are the two *blooms* of English, the metallurgical one, which comes from Anglo-Saxon *blōstma*, *blōma*, and the botanical one, from Old Norse *blomi;* while Anglo-Saxon *blōstmian* is responsible for *blossom.*

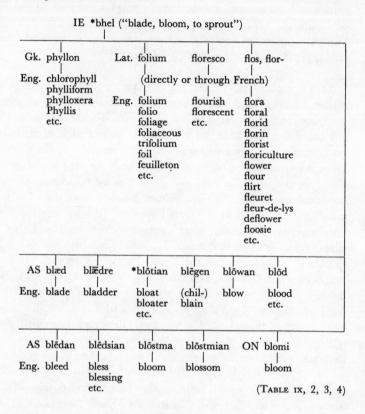

IE *bhel ("blade, bloom, to sprout")

Gk. phyllon	Lat. folium	floresco	flos, flor-
Eng. chlorophyll	(directly or through French)		
phylliform			
phylloxera	Eng. folium	flourish	flora
Phyllis	folio	florescent	floral
etc.	foliage	etc.	florid
	foliaceous		florin
	trifolium		florist
	foil		floriculture
	feuilleton		flower
	etc.		flour
			flirt
			fleuret
			fleur-de-lys
			deflower
			floosie
			etc.

AS blæd	blǣdre	*blōtian	blēgen	blōwan	blōd
Eng. blade	bladder	bloat	(chil-)	blow	blood
		bloater	blain		etc.
		etc.			

AS blēdan	blēdsian	blōstma	blōstmian	ON blomi
Eng. bleed	bless	bloom	blossom	bloom
	blessing			
	etc.			

(TABLE IX, 2, 3, 4)

The IE root *ger,* "to grow old, mature", keeps its original semantics in Greek, where *geron,* "old man", gives us *gerousia,* the Athenian senate, and such medical terms as *gerontology* and *geriatrics.* In Germanic, there is a shift to the idea of a man mature enough to be free, with the result that Old Norse *karl,* "freeman", gives us the *house-carl* of the days of King Harold, while the same word in Anglo-Saxon, *ceorl,* becomes *churl,* with *churlish.* Used as a proper name, *Karl* is appropriated by Vulgar Latin and turned into *Carolus* and later into *Charles,* giving us such proper nouns and adjectives as *Charlemagne (Carolus Magnus,* "Charles the Great"), *Carolingian* or *Carlovingian, Carlist, Carolina,*

Carol, Charlotte, etc., as well as the colloquial *charley horse*. Since Charlemagne, bearer of the name, spread its fame to the east, the word was borrowed by Slavic and Hungarian in the forms *korol'*, *król, király*, etc., and given in those languages the meaning of "king", thus offering a remarkable example of semantic differentiation, with a lowering of concept at one end that results in "churl", an enhancement at the other end that results in "king". Applied to the vegetable world, with the meaning of "mature", the root also produces Anglo-Saxon *corn* and *cyrnel*, leading to English *corn, kernel* (with *cornflower, cornbread, corncob, corntassel*, and even the ultra-modern *corny*. There are also Anglo-Saxon *cyrin, ciern*, which produce English *churn*. The Latin descendant, with the same meaning as *corn*, is *granum*, which ultimately produces in English *grain, ingrained, filigrain* and *filigree, pomegranate, granule, granular, granulated, grenade* and *grenadier, granary* and *grange, garner* and *garnet*, all having some connection with *grain*, as well as the Italian-derived *granite*. *Gravy* is also held by some to come from French *grané*, "grained", but this is not altogether certain.

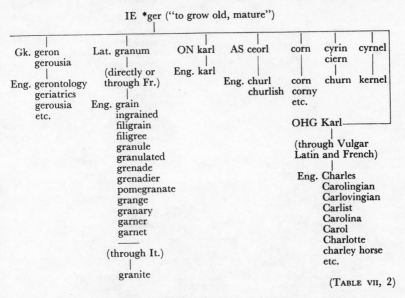

IE *ger ("to grow old, mature")

Gk. geron gerousia	Lat. granum	ON karl	AS ceorl	corn	cyrin ciern	cyrnel
Eng. gerontology geriatrics gerousia etc.	(directly or through Fr.) Eng. grain ingrained filigrain filigree granule granulated grenade grenadier pomegranate grange granary garner garnet ——— (through It.) granite	Eng. karl	Eng. churl churlish	corn corny etc.	churn	kernel

OHG Karl

(through Vulgar Latin and French)

Eng. Charles
Carolingian
Carlovingian
Carlist
Carolina
Carol
Charlotte
charley horse
etc.

(TABLE VII, 2)

The IE root *ped*, *pod*, "foot", gives us Anglo-Saxon *fōt*, leading to *foot* (with *football, footprint, footstep, footpath, foothold, foothill, footing*,

footman, *footpad*, *afoot*, *underfoot*, and disguised forms like *fetlock*);
Anglo-Saxon *feotor*, which becomes *fetter; fetian*, "to go on a foot

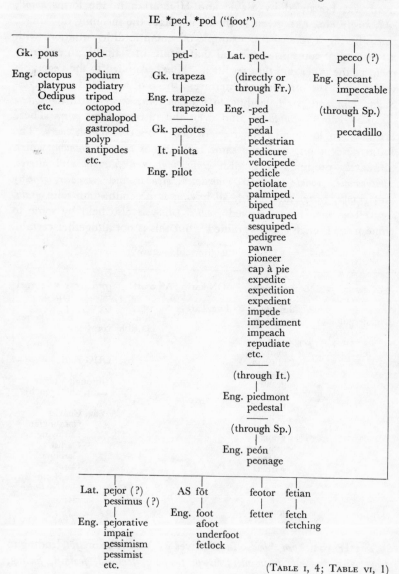

IE *ped, *pod ("foot")

Gk. pous	pod-	ped-	Lat. ped-	pecco (?)
Eng. octopus	podium	Gk. trapeza	(directly or	Eng. peccant
platypus	podiatry		through Fr.)	impeccable
Oedipus	tripod	Eng. trapeze		
etc.	octopod	trapezoid	Eng. -ped	(through Sp.)
	cephalopod		ped-	
	gastropod	Gk. pedotes	pedal	peccadillo
	polyp		pedestrian	
	antipodes	It. pilota	pedicure	
	etc.		velocipede	
		Eng. pilot	pedicle	
			petiolate	
			palmiped	
			biped	
			quadruped	
			sesquiped-	
			pedigree	
			pawn	
			pioneer	
			cap à pie	
			expedite	
			expedition	
			expedient	
			impede	
			impediment	
			impeach	
			repudiate	
			etc.	

(through It.)

Eng. piedmont
pedestal

(through Sp.)

Eng. peón
peonage

Lat. pejor (?)	AS fōt	feotor	fetian
pessimus (?)			
	Eng. foot	fetter	fetch
Eng. pejorative	afoot		fetching
impair	underfoot		
pessimism	fetlock		
pessimist			
etc.			

(TABLE I, 4; TABLE VI, 1)

journey", which turns into *fetch*, with *fetching*. Greek *pous, pod-*, produces forms in *-pod, -pode, -poda*, and also forms in *-pus: octopus, platypus, Oedipus, podium, tripod, podiatry, podiatrist, octopod, cephalopod, gastropod, polyp* (*poly-pod*, "many-footed"), *antipodes;* and, in disguised form, *trapeze* and *trapezoid* (originally *tetra-ped-*, "four-footed"). There is also a Greek *pedotes*, which gets into Italian in the form *pedota, pidota, pilota*, and eventually gives us *pilot*. Latin forms, from *pes, ped-*, "foot", include *pedal, pedestrian, pedicure, velocipede, pedicle, petiolate, palmiped, biped, quadruped, sesquipedalian* ("a foot and a half long"), the Italian *pedestal*, the French *pied de grue*, "crane's foot", which turns into *pedigree* (the genealogical lines being likened to the diverging toes of a crane). The *ped-* that means "foot" must be carefully distinguished from the *ped-* that comes from Greek *pais, paid-* and means "child" (*pediatrician, pedagogue*, etc.). There are semi-disguised forms of *ped-* in the Spanish-derived *peón* and *peonage*, equivalent to the *pawn* of chess (*pedonem*, "foot-man, foot soldier, man on foot", as distinguished from the member of the upper classes, who rides), and the French-derived *pioneer*. *Piedmont* is the Italian *pie di monte*, "foot of the mountain, foothill". *Cap à pie* is straight French for "head to foot". Compounds include *expedient, expediency, expedite, expedition, expeditionary, expeditious, impede, impediment, impedimenta* (this is straight Latin, and was used in Roman army circles for "baggage, that which got underfoot when you wanted to march or fight"). Latin *impedio*, "to impede, hinder, get between the feet of", led to a Vulgar Latin formation *impedicare*, which in French became *empêcher* and in English *impeach*, with *impeachment* ("to hinder, prevent one from performing his appointed functions') There are also *repudiate* and *repudiation*. Forms that are somewhat dubiously linked with the *foot* root are Latin *peccare*, "to sin" (with *peccant, impeccable*, the Spanish-derived *pecadillo*, "trifling sin", misspelt, probably by Latin or Italian influence, as *peccadillo*); *pejor*, "worse", leading to *pejorative, impair, impairment*, etc.: *pessimus*, "worst", leading to *pessimism, pessimist*, etc.

The IE root **pet*, "to fly, fall", produces an Anglo-Saxon *fether*, which ultimately becomes *feather* (with *feathery, featherbed, featherweight*, etc.). In Greek, we have *pipto*, "to fall", from which come *ptosis*, a scientific term for a falling of the eyelid, and *ptoma*, "corpse, fallen body", from which we derive *ptomaine;* also *potamos*, "river, falling body of water", which appears in *hippopotamus* ("river-horse") and *Mesopotamia* (the land "between the rivers", Tigris and Euphrates). There is also in Greek the form *pteryx*, "wing", from which we get *diptera*, *coleoptera*, *hymenoptera*, *lepidoptera*, and other classes of insects described by their wings, as well as *pterodactyl*. Latin forms include *penna* and *pinna* (the latter apparently a dialectal form), derived from an original **petsna*, and from these come *pen* (with *penknife*, *penmanship*, *pennant*, etc.); *pinna*, *pinnate*, *pinniped*, *pinion*, *pinnacle*, and, through

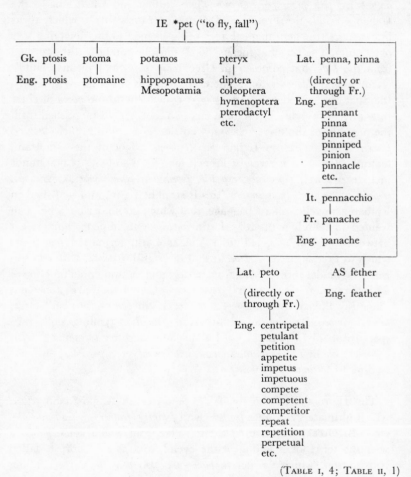

(TABLE I, 4; TABLE II, 1)

Italian *pennacchio*, the French *panache*. Another Latin form is *peto*, "to seek, fall upon, attack"; here compound forms give us *centripetal*, *petulant*, *petition*, *appetite*, *appetizing*, *appetizer*, *impetus*, *impetuous*, *compete*, *competence*, *competitor*, *repeat*, *repetition*, *repetitious*, *perpetual*, *perpetuity*, *perpetuate*, etc.

IE *pəter*, "father", produces Anglo-Saxon *fader*, which becomes *father*, with *fatherhood*, *fatherly*, *father-in-law*, *godfather*, *grandfather*, etc. The High German variant *Vater* gives us *Vaterland*. Greek *pater* gives

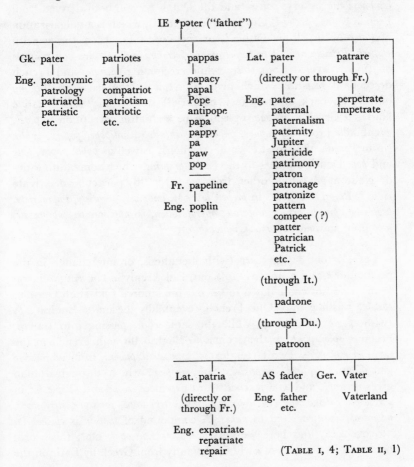

IE *pəter ("father")

Gk. pater	patriotes	pappas	Lat. pater	patrare
Eng. patronymic	patriot	papacy	(directly or through Fr.)	
patrology	compatriot	papal		
patriarch	patriotism	Pope	Eng. pater	perpetrate
patristic	patriotic	antipope	paternal	impetrate
etc.	etc.	papa	paternalism	
		pappy	paternity	
		pa	Jupiter	
		paw	patricide	
		pop	patrimony	
			patron	
	Fr. papeline	patronage	
		patronize	
	Eng. poplin	pattern	
		compeer (?)	
		patter	
		patrician	
		Patrick	
		etc.	

(through It.)

padrone

(through Du.)

patroon

Lat. patria	AS fader	Ger. Vater
(directly or through Fr.)	Eng. father	Vaterland
Eng. expatriate repatriate repair	etc.	

(TABLE I, 4; TABLE II, 1)

forms like *patronymic*, *patrology*, *patriarch*, while *patriotes* supplies *patriotic*, *patriotism*, *patriot*, *compatriot*. Latin *pater*, coinciding in form with the Greek, produces *paternal*, *paternalism*, *paternity*, *patristic* (this, however, may equally well come from the Greek), *Jupiter* (*Deus Pater*, "God the Father"); straight Latin forms like *pater familias* and *pater patriae;* *patricide* or *parricide*, *patrimony; patron*, *patroness*, *patronize*, *patronage*, and the Italian *padrone;* the Spanish and Italian *padre*, the British *pater*, the French *père;* possibly *compeer*, where *par* and *pater* seem to merge (French *compère* and Italian *compare* may favor the former, Spanish *compadre* the latter); *pattern* and the Dutch *patroon*, both derived from French *patron; patter* ("glib or rapid speech"), which is a vulgarization of *Pater Noster*, "Our Father", or the Lord's Prayer; *patrician*, with *Patrick*, *Patricia* and *Pat; perpetrate*, *perpetrator*, *impetrate* are compounds of *patrare*, derived from *pater;* while *expatriate*, *repatriate*, and French descendant *repairier* (which gives us *repair* in the sense of "betake oneself, go back to one's own country") stem from *patria*, "native land". A Greek form *pappas*, said to be a childish corruption of *pater*, eventually produces *papacy*, *papal*, *papish*, *Pope*, *antipope*, *popery*, *poplin* (from *Papelin*, the papal town of Avignon), as well as *papa*, *pappy*, *paw* and *pop*. Doubt attaches to the Latin *proprius*, which some authorities derive from *pro-patrius*, others from *pro-privus*, "by particular or private right". *Proprius* appears in *proper*, *property*, *improper*, *propriety*, *impropriety*, *proprietor*, *proprietary*, *appropriate*, *appropriation*, *misappropriate*, *expropriate*, *propitious*, *proximity*, *approach*, *reproach*, etc.

The IE root *spek*, *skep* (with metathesis, or interchange in the position of *k* and *p*) means "to scout, look keenly". The Anglo-Saxon forms have not come down to us, but the kindred Old High German *spehōn*, passing into Old French, eventually becomes English *spy* (with *spyglass*) and *espy*, while the same root, passing into Italian, becomes *spione*, which then comes to English through French in the form of *espionage*. Two Greek forms appear, *skeptomai*, from which we get *skeptic*, *skeptical*, *skepticism;* and *skopein*, which through Italian gives us *scope*, and as a learned word produces *-scope* and *-scopic*, as in *gyroscope*, *kaleidoscopic*, *telescope*, *horoscope*, *stethoscope*, *periscope*, *stereoscope*, *microscope* (abbreviated to *mike*). A compound of *skopein* is *episkopein*, "to oversee", and here we get *episcopate*, *Episcopal*, etc.; this word, borrowed in the days of early Christianity from Greek by Latin in the form *episcopus*, produced the Anglo-Saxon *biscop* which later became *bishop* (with *bishopric, archbishop*, etc.). Latin forms include *species*, with its adjective *specialis;* the noun *speculum*, "mirror"; and the verb *specio* with past participle *spectus* and numerous compounds (*aspicio, conspicio, respicio, despicio, circumspicio*, etc.). Other verbal formations are built on the participial root, giving forms like *exspecto*. From *species* and *specialis* we get *species* and *specie, special* and *especial, specious, specify* and *specification, specialty* or *speciality, specialist, specialization, specimen, spice, spicy, spicery*. *Specu-* gives us *speculum, specular, speculate*,

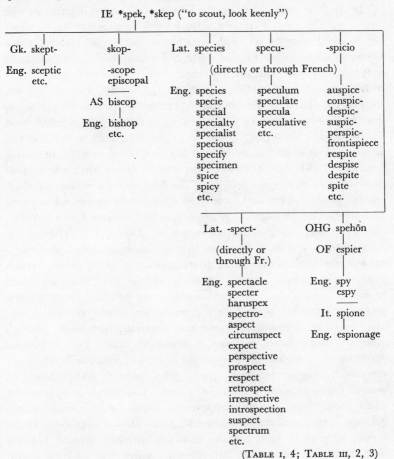

IE *spek, *skep ("to scout, look keenly")

Gk. skept-	skop-	Lat. species	specu-	-spicio
Eng. sceptic etc.	-scope episcopal	(directly or through French)		
	—— AS biscop	Eng. species	speculum	auspice
	Eng. bishop etc.	specie	speculate	conspic-
		special	specula	despic-
		specialty	speculative	suspic-
		specialist	etc.	perspic-
		specious		frontispiece
		specify		respite
		specimen		despise
		spice		despite
		spicy		spite
		etc.		etc.

Lat. -spect-	OHG spehōn
(directly or through Fr.)	OF espier
Eng. spectacle	Eng. spy
specter	espy
haruspex	
spectro-	It. spione
aspect	
circumspect	Eng. espionage
expect	
perspective	
prospect	
respect	
retrospect	
irrespective	
introspection	
suspect	
spectrum	
etc.	

(TABLE I, 4; TABLE III, 2, 3)

speculation, speculator, speculative. Spic- gives us *auspice, auspicious, conspicuous, despicable, perspicuous, perspicuity, perspicacity, suspicious, frontispiece, respite, despise, despite* and the cut-down *spite, spiteful, spitefulness. Spect-* and *specto* give *spectacle, spectacular, specter, spectral, spectrum, spectroscope, haruspex, aspect, circumspect, circumspection, expect, expectant, expectation, expectancy, perspective, prospect, prospector, prospective, prospectus, respect, respectful, respectable, respectability, irrespective, retrospect, introspection, suspect,* etc.

The IE root **gen,* "to beget", is one of the most fruitful in our language. On the Germanic side, it produces Anglo-Saxon *cynn, cennan,* which give us *kin* (with *kinship, kinsman, kinsfolk, akin*); Anglo-Saxon *gecynd,* leading to *kind, unkind, kindness, kindly;* Anglo-Saxon *cyning* (this is *cynn* with an *-ing* which is a patronymic suffix: "kinborn"), which becomes *king,* with *kingly, kingship, kinglet, kingdom, kingfish,* etc. There is the possibility, but by no means the certainty, that Anglo-Saxon *cniht* may also belong to this group, in which case we would also have *knight, knighthood, knightly,* etc., as well as the German *Knecht* and *Landsknecht.* German *Kind,* which definitely belongs to this family, gives us *kindergarten.* In Greek, the verb *gignomai* produces two stems, *gen-* and *gon-.* The first appears in *gene, genealogy, genesis, genetic, palingenesis, heterogenous* and *heterogeneous, homogenous* and *homogeneous, homogenize, genotype, genocide* (a Greek-Latin hybrid), *epigene, oxygen, hydrogen, eugenic, exogenous, Eugene,* etc. The second helps to form *gonococcus, gonorrhea, theogony, cosmogony, gonad,* and many other compounds. Latin *genus, gener-* appears in *genus, genera,* French *genre, gender, engender, genitive,* possibly *genuine* (but this may come from the root of *knee,* or that of *cheek;* see pp. 105, 155); *progeny, progenitor, congenital, genito-urinary, primogeniture, generic, generate, generation, degenerate, degeneration, degenerative, regenerate, regeneration, generous, generosity, miscegenation, ingenuous, ingenious, ingenuity,* French *ingénue, engine, engineer, engineering, gin* (in the sense of "machine"), *congenial, congeniality, congener, indigenous, genius, genial, geniality, general, generalize, generality, generalization,* Italian *generalissimo.* Latin *gens, gent-,* from the same root, "race, nation", appears in *gentle, genteel, Gentile, jaunty, gentility, gentry, gentleman, gentlewoman, gendarme.* Latin *germen,* "germ, seed", appears in *germ, germane, germinate, germinal,* possibly *German.* The **gen* root appears in Latin *gn-ascor, nascor,* "to be born", with

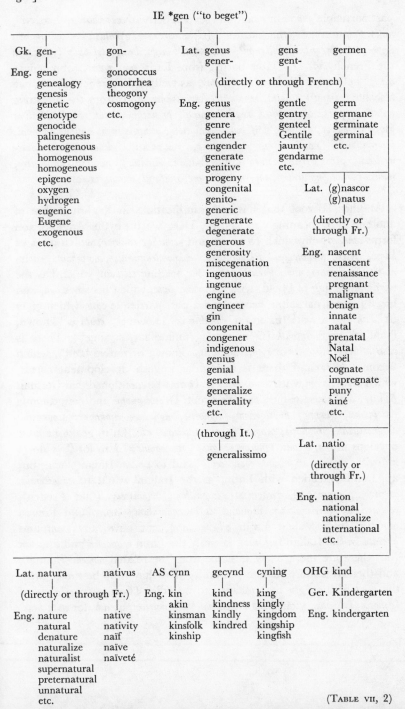

IE *gen ("to beget")

Gk.	gen-	gon-	Lat.	genus	gens	germen
				gener-	gent-	

Eng. gene
　genealogy
　genesis
　genetic
　genotype
　genocide
　palingenesis
　heterogenous
　homogenous
　homogeneous
　epigene
　oxygen
　hydrogen
　eugenic
　Eugene
　exogenous
　etc.

gonococcus
gonorrhea
theogony
cosmogony
etc.

(directly or through French)

Eng. genus
　genera
　genre
　gender
　engender
　generate
　genitive
　progeny
　congenital
　genito-
　generic
　regenerate
　degenerate
　generous
　generosity
　miscegenation
　ingenuous
　ingenue
　engine
　engineer
　gin
　congenital
　congener
　indigenous
　genius
　genial
　general
　generalize
　generality
　etc.

gentle
gentry
genteel
Gentile
jaunty
gendarme
etc.

germ
germane
germinate
germinal
etc.

Lat. (g)nascor
　　(g)natus

(directly or
through Fr.)

Eng. nascent
　renascent
　renaissance
　pregnant
　malignant
　benign
　innate
　natal
　prenatal
　Natal
　Noël
　cognate
　impregnate
　puny
　aîné
　etc.

(through It.)

generalissimo

Lat. natio

(directly or
through Fr.)

Eng. nation
　national
　nationalize
　international
　etc.

Lat. natura	nativus	AS cynn	gecynd	cyning	OHG kind
(directly or through Fr.)		Eng. kin	kind	king	Ger. Kindergarten
Eng. nature	native	akin	kindness	kingly	
natural	nativity	kinsman	kindly	kingdom	Eng. kindergarten
denature	naïf	kinsfolk	kindred	kingship	
naturalize	naïve	kinship		kingfish	
naturalist	naïveté				
supernatural					
preternatural					
unnatural					
etc.					

(TABLE VII, 2)

past participle *gnatus* or *natus*, and several derivatives: *nativus*, "native", *natio*, "nation", *natura*, "nature". (*G*)*nascor* and (*g*)*natus* give us *cognate*, *impregnate*, *pregnant*, *malignant*, *benignant*, *benign*, *benignity*, *puny* (which is the French *puis né*, "later born", from Latin *post natus*), opposed to *aîné*, "before born", from *ante natus;* as well as the French *né, née;* we also have *innate*, *nascent*, *renascent*, *Renaissance*, and, from the adjective *natalis*, "pertaining to a birth", *natal*, *prenatal*, *Natal*, *Noel*. *Nativus* gives us *native*, *nativity*, *naïf*, *naïve*, *naïveté*. *Natio* gives us *nation*, *national*, *international*, *nationalism*, *nationalize*, *nationality*, *denationalize*, *antinational*, etc. From *natura* come *nature*, *denature*, *natural*, *naturalize*, *naturalization*, *naturalist*, *supernatural*, *preternatural*, *unnatural*, etc.

Another IE root that has vast ramifications in English is that of another **gen* meaning "to know". Here we have the Anglo-Saxon forms *cennan* from which come *ken* and *kenning; cnāwan*, which gives us *know*, with *knowledge*, *acknowledge*, *acknowledgment*, *know-how*, *know-nothing*, *unknown*, *unbeknownst*, etc.; *cēne*, leading to *keen*, which has the earlier meaning of "bold, wise"; *cunnan*, *cann*, which becomes *can*, and has a present participle *cunning* and a past participle *cūth*, which gives us *couth* and *uncouth* (in origin, *cunning* is "knowing", *couth* is "known, familiar", and *uncouth* is "unknown, unfamiliar, strange"). There is also a derivative form *cȳth*, meaning "known or native land", which becomes *kith;* and there is a Middle English development *connan*, which gives us *con*, with *conning-tower*. It may be mentioned that German *Kunst*, "art", also comes from this root. Greek *gnome* and *gignosko* give us *gnome*, *gnomic*, *physiognomy; gnostic*, *agnostic*, *diagnose*, *diagnostic*, *diagnostician*, *prognosis*, *prognostic*, *prognosticate*, etc. Latin *gnosco* or *nosco* develops into *ignorant*, *ignorance*, *ignore*, *ignoramus* (Latin for "we don't know"); *cognize*, *cognition*, *cognoscenti* (said to be an Italian form, but apparently blended with Latin, as the Italian would be *conoscenti*), *cognizant*, *cognizance*, *recognize*, *recognition*, *connoisseur* (Old French), *reconnaissance*, *reconnoiter*, *acquaint* and *acquaintance* (from Old French *acointier*, from Vulgar Latin *ad-cognitare*), cut down to *quaint* and *quaintness*, the Italian *incognito*, possibly the Latin *cognomen* and *agnomen* (but these are more likely to come from the related *nomen*, "name", and there is a more remote possibility that they may be linked with the root of the **gen* that means "to beget"). The past participle of (*g*)*nosco*, (*g*)*notus*, yields *note* (with *notebook*, *noteworthy*, *n.b.* for *nota bene*, "note well", *notice, notify, notification, noticeable, notion, notional, denote, denotation, prenotion, notable, notability, notabilia, notary, notarial, notarize, notate, notation, annotate, annotation, connote, connotation, notorious, notoriety,* etc. (*G*)*nobilis,* literally "knowable", gives *noble, nobility, nobleman, noblewoman, ennoble, ignoble, nobilitate, noblesse oblige,* and, if the tale is true (it is more likely to be pure folk etymology), *snob,* from an abbreviation *s. nob.,* for *sine nobilitate,* "without nobility", said to have been entered after the names of people without titles. Two ramifications of the Latin *know* root are *norma,* "carpenter's square", which gives us *norm, normal, normalcy, normalize, normality, anormal, abnormal, normative, enormous, enormity,* etc.; and *narro,* "to narrate, make known", from which come *narrative, narrator, narration,* etc. Slavic cognates, with *z* for western *g,* include Russian *znat'*, "to know", and *znamya,* "banner".

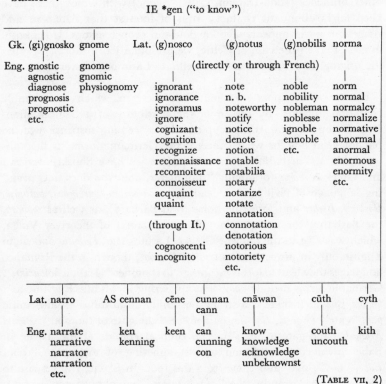

IE *gen ("to know")

Gk. (gi)gnosko	gnome	Lat. (g)nosco	(g)notus	(g)nobilis	norma
Eng. gnostic	gnome	(directly or through French)			
agnostic	gnomic			noble	norm
diagnose	physiognomy	ignorant	note	nobility	normal
prognosis		ignorance	n. b.	nobleman	normalcy
prognostic		ignoramus	noteworthy	noblesse	normalize
etc.		ignore	notify	ignoble	normative
		cognizant	notice	ennoble	abnormal
		cognition	denote	etc.	anormal
		recognize	notion		enormous
		reconnaissance	notable		enormity
		reconnoiter	notabilia		etc.
		connoisseur	notary		
		acquaint	notarize		
		quaint	notate		
			annotation		
		(through It.)	connotation		
			denotation		
		cognoscenti	notorious		
		incognito	notoriety		
			etc.		

Lat. narro	AS cennan	cēne	cunnan	cnāwan	cūth	cyth
			cann			
Eng. narrate	ken	keen	can	know	couth	kith
narrative	kenning		cunning	knowledge	uncouth	
narrator			con	acknowledge		
narration				unbeknownst		
etc.						

(TABLE VII, 2)

CHAPTER 7

Families of Four and Five Branches

These are relatively scarce, but there are enough to offer a good sampling. For the most part, they are made up of the familiar three (Greek, Latin, Germanic), with the addition of one or two of the other branches (Indo-Iranian, Celtic, Slavic) with which there have been fairly abundant contacts. It is of interest that Albanian and Armenian never appear, save for doubtful proper names. It is also of interest that in the case of Celtic, we are often left in doubt whether the original borrowing was from Celtic to Latin or vice-versa.

One root of apparently four branches, in which considerable confusion appears, by reason of the possibility of a Semitic (non-Indo-European) influence, coupled with a seeming suspension of the phonological law for what concerns the Germanic forms, is the call-word *baba, "to babble, stammer". Here we have Sanskrit barbaras and Greek barbaros (originally "stammerer, one who does not speak" the language of civilization), leading to barbarian, barbarous, barbaric, Barbary, Berber and barb (the horse from Barbary), as well as rhubarb, the barbarous or foreign plant from the banks of the river Volga, which was Rha to the ancient Greeks. Latin balbus, balbutio appear in English only in proper names (Balbo, Balboa), though in the Romance languages they lead to forms meaning "to stammer" (Italian balbuziare). Germanic forms include baby, first appearing in Middle English; and babble, in which there is a strong possibility of an influx from Semitic bab, "gate" (Bab-el, Bab-ilu, or Babylon, "the gate of the god"; Bab el Mandeb, "the gate of tears"). The Biblical episode of the Tower of Babel involved a confusion and stammering of tongues. German Bube, "boy", may also come from this root. In Slavic, it gives rise to the word for "grandmother" (a "stammering old woman"), baba, with a diminutive *babushka;* the latter is appropriated by English in the sense of "headkerchief, that which the little old Russian grandmother wears". Another form said to stem from this root is the Italian *babbo,* "daddy".

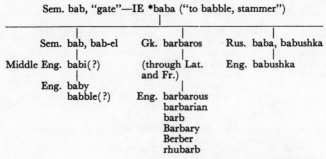

Sem. bab, "gate"—IE *baba ("to babble, stammer")

Sem. bab, bab-el	Gk. barbaros	Rus. baba, babushka
Middle Eng. babi(?)	(through Lat. and Fr.)	Eng. babushka
Eng. baby babble(?)	Eng. barbarous barbarian barb Barbary Berber rhubarb	

(TABLE V, 1—inoperative by reason of nature of word or Semitic influx)

One interesting group in which Indo-Iranian joins the customary three of the western world is *penkᵘe,* the IE root for "five". Here both Latin and Germanic show assimilation, Germanic of the progressive variety, with the Germanic *f* of the initial syllable bringing on another *f* in place of the IE *kᵘ, which should have given *hw* or *wh* in Germanic; while Latin has retrogressive assimilation, with the *kᵘ of the second syllable turning the initial *p* into another *kᵘ (other Italic dialects, such as Oscan, show the expected *p* in both places; Oscan has *pompe* corresponding to Latin *quinque*). From Indo-Iranian come the Sanskrit *Pancatantra* ("five books") of the sacred Hindu writings; *Punjab* (Sanskrit and Hindustani *panjāb,* "five rivers"), with *Punjabi,* and the drink *punch,* which is Sanskrit and Hindi *pañca,* "five", because originally made with five ingredients. Greek *pente* yields such compounds as *pentagon, pentathlon, pentameter, Pentateuch, Pentecost.* Latin *quinque* gives us *quinquagenarian, Quinquagesima, quinquennium (Cinquecento* is from Italian, and *Cinque Ports* from French); *quinctus* or *quintus,* "fifth", gives *quintuple, quintuplet, quint, quintessence, Quentin;* and *quini,* "by fives", gives rise to *keno. Pompeii* and *Pontius* may show the Oscan form *pompe.* In Anglo-Saxon we have *fíf,* which becomes *five* (with *fiver,* etc.); *fífta,* which yields *fifth* (with *fifth wheel, fifth column,* etc.); *fíftig* and *fíftýne,* which become *fifty* and *fifteen.*

Finger (with *finger nail*, *finger wave*, etc.), which has the same form in Anglo-Saxon, probably comes from the *five* root, though some authorities prefer to connect it with the root of *fang*.

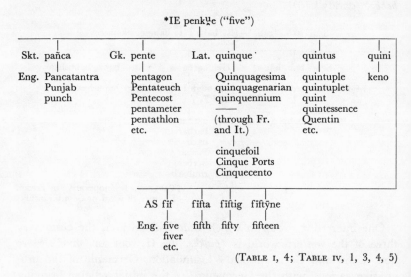

*IE penk^ue ("five")

Skt. pañca	Gk. pente	Lat. quinque	quintus	quini
Eng. Pancatantra	pentagon	Quinquagesima	quintuple	keno
Punjab	Pentateuch	quinquagenarian	quintuplet	
punch	Pentecost	quinquennium	quint	
	pentameter	———	quintessence	
	pentathlon	(through Fr.	Quentin	
	etc.	and It.)	etc.	
		cinquefoil		
		Cinque Ports		
		Cinquecento		

AS fíf	fífta	fíftig	fíftȳne
Eng. five	fifth	fifty	fifteen
fiver			
etc.			

(TABLE I, 4; TABLE IV, 1, 3, 4, 5)

Another four-branch root that includes Indo-Iranian in addition to the familiar Greek, Latin, and Germanic is that of IE *mūs*, "mouse, rat". Here Anglo-Saxon *mūs* provides us with *mouse* and *mousy*, while an imagery that extends also to Greek, likening a rippling muscle to a scurrying mouse, appears in Latin *musculus*, "little mouse" (*muscle*, *muscular*, *musculous*, *intramuscular*, etc.). From Anglo-Saxon *musle*, derived from Latin *musculus*, we get *mussel*. In cases other than the nominative, the Latin root is *mur-*, by reason of the fact that Latin turns *s* between vowels to *r*. Hence, we have *marmot* and *marmoset*, through French, from a Latin *murem montanum*, "mountain mouse". The Greek *mys*, *myo-* gives us scientific forms in *myo-* (*myotic*, *myotomy*, *myocarditis*, *myology*, etc.), and *myosotis*, which is "mouse-ear". Lastly, there are two separate Indo-Iranian developments that reach us. One is Sanskrit *muska*, or Old Persian *mushk*, which becomes Greek *moskos*, Latin *muscus* and English *musk* (*muskmelon*, *musk-ox*, *muskrat*, etc.), with the possibility that this may extend to *muscatel* (the alternative theory is that *muscat* may come from the city of Masqat in

Mesopotamia, where muscatel grapes are alleged to have first been grown). The other is Sanskrit *musa-angusa*, "mouse-mongoose", which in Mahratti, a modern language of India, becomes *mungūs*, and ultimately reaches us as *mongoose*, the little ferret-like animal that destroys cobras.

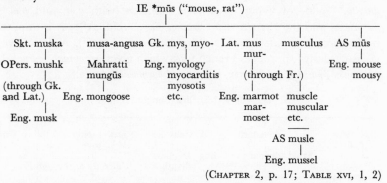

IE *mūs ("mouse, rat")

Skt. muska	musa-angusa	Gk. mys, myo-	Lat. mus	musculus	AS mūs
OPers. mushk	Mahratti	Eng. myology	mur-		Eng. mouse
(through Gk.	mungūs	myocarditis	(through Fr.)		mousy
and Lat.)		myosotis			
	Eng. mongoose	etc.	Eng. marmot	muscle	
Eng. musk			mar-	muscular	
			moset	etc.	

AS musle
|
Eng. mussel

(CHAPTER 2, p. 17; TABLE XVI, 1, 2)

The IE root *dei*, appearing also as *deyə*, *dī*, *diā*, means "bright, to shine". In Anglo-Saxon, it produces the name of the god *Tīg* or *Tīw* (the Norse *Tȳr*), of which the genitive case, *Tīwes*, appears in *Tīwesdæg*, which becomes *Tuesday*. In Indo-Iranian, we have Sanskrit *deva*, "god" and *devī*, "goddess", as well as Hindustani *deodar*, from Sanskrit *devadaru*, "god's tree". Greek *Zeus*, with its genitive *Dios*, gives us *Dioscuri* (Zeus' sons) and *dianthus* (Zeus' flower). In Latin we have *Jup(p)iter* (*Deus Pater*, "god the father"), with its other case forms in *Jov-*, from which come *Jove, jovial, joviality;* a further extension of this palatalized form appears in *Julius*, from which come such names as *Julian, Julia, Juliet*, the month of *July*, the soup named *julienne*. The unpalatalized form appears in *deus*, "god" (*deus ex machina*), from which come *deify, deification, deity, joss* (which is a Portuguese-Chinese development of *deus*), French *Dieu* and *adieu*, Spanish *Dios* and *adiós* ("to God"). There are also the name *Diana* (originally *Diviana*), and *divus, divinus*, from which come the Italian *diva* and the English *divine, divinity, divination*. In addition, there is the Latin *dies*, "day" (despite the similarity of appearance and meaning, the two words are unrelated; English *day* comes from the root of *dawn;* to be related, the English form should have *t*, not *d*). *Dies* gives rise to Italian *dì*, the French *-di* of *lundi, mardi*, the Spanish *día;* it appears in Latin form in *per diem* and *sine die;* in *triduum, diary, diarist, diurnal, dial* and *dialing, dismal,* (Old French *dis mal,* from Latin *dies mali,* "day of evil"); in ˙*hodiernal* (Latin *hodie,* "this day, today"); *diet* (only in the sense of "governmental body", which meets daily, or requires a day's journey to reach; the food *diet* comes from Greek *daiaita,* "mode of living"); *quotidian, meridian* (with *a.m.* and *p.m.*), *meridional* and the French *midi* (*medium diem,* "midday"); it is implied in *dominical* (from *dies dominica,* "the day of the Lord"). A derivative, *diurnus,* "daily", produces French *jour,* which gives us *journal, journalist, journalism, journey, journeyman, adjourn, adjournment, sojourn.*

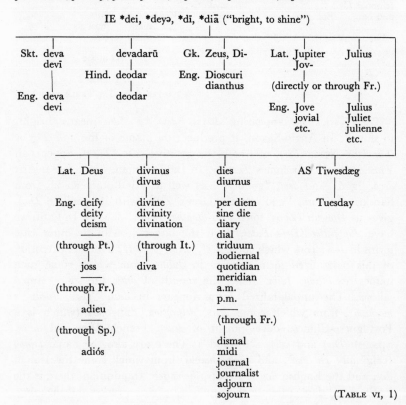

IE *dei, *deyə, *dī, *diā ("bright, to shine")

Skt.	deva devī		devadarū	Gk.	Zeus, Di-	Lat.	Jupiter Jov-	Julius
		Hind.	deodar	Eng.	Dioscuri dianthus			
							(directly or through Fr.)	
Eng.	deva devī		deodar			Eng.	Jove jovial etc.	Julius Juliet julienne etc.

Lat.	Deus	divinus divus	dies diurnus	AS	Tiwesdæg
Eng.	deify deity deism	divine divinity divination	˙per diem sine die diary dial		Tuesday
	(through Pt.)	(through It.)	triduum hodiernal quotidian meridian a.m. p.m.		
	joss	diva			
	(through Fr.)		(through Fr.)		
	adieu		dismal midi journal journalist adjourn sojourn		
	(through Sp.)				
	adiós				

(TABLE VI, 1)

The IE root *yu-go-m,* "yoke", appears in Anglo-Saxon as *geoc, geocian,* giving rise to *yoke,* noun and verb, and possibly *yokel.* In

Sanskrit it appears in *Yoga* and *Yogin,* "Yogi" (from *Yuga,* "the four ages of the world"). Greek forms include *zeugma* (from the root of *zeugnymi,* "to unite"), which appears in English, and *zygon,* which gives rise to *zygo-* compounds (*zygote, zygospore, syzygy,* etc.). In Latin, we have the verb *jungo,* with past participle *junctus,* developing into French *joindre, joint;* the verb *juvo,* with past participle *jutus,* which, in the compound form *ad-jutare,* develops into Old French *aidier* (modern French *aider*); the nouns *jugum,* "yoke", and *jumentum,* "beast of burden"; the adjective *jucundus* (originally "helpful", then, possibly with an assist from *joco,* "to play", "jocund, jolly"); and the adverb-preposition *juxta,* "near, adjoining". These give rise to numerous English forms: *juncture, junction, conjunction, conjuncture, conjunctive, conjunctivitis, disjunctive, injunction, subjunctive; conjugate, conjugal, conjugation, subjugate; join, joiner, joint, adjoin, disjoin, subjoin, enjoin, rejoin, rejoinder;* the Spanish *junta; adjuvant, adjutant, coadjutor, aid, aide; jugular, jumentous; jocund, jocundity,* the Italian *Gioconda; juxtapose, juxtaposition, joust, jostle;* and, possibly, *adjust, adjustment* (though here the possibility that the root may be that of *justus,* "just", is strong).

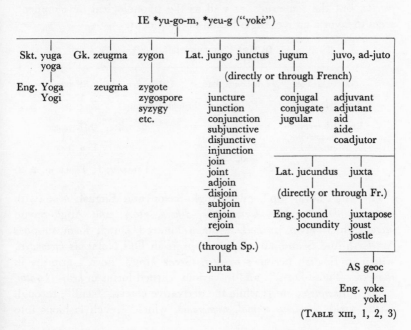

IE *yu-go-m, *yeu-g ("yoke")

Skt. yuga yoga	Gk. zeugma	zygon	Lat. jungo junctus	jugum	juvo, ad-juto
			(directly or through French)		
Eng. Yoga Yogi	zeugma	zygote zygospore syzygy etc.	juncture junction conjunction subjunctive disjunctive injunction join joint adjoin disjoin subjoin enjoin rejoin	conjugal conjugate jugular	adjuvant adjutant aid aide coadjutor

Lat. jucundus   juxta

(directly or through Fr.)

Eng. jocund   juxtapose
jocundity   joust
jostle

(through Sp.)

junta

AS geoc

Eng. yoke
yokel

(TABLE XIII, 1, 2, 3)

A root in which four branches possibly appear (the fourth, Celtic, presents some doubtful features) is IE *bak*, "support staff, rod". This in Greek produces *bakterion*, "staff, rod", from which come, in Latin form, *bacterium* and its plural *bacteria*, with *bacterial, bacteriology, bacteriophage*, etc. (the germ, under the microscope, looks like a little rod). The same transfer of meaning appears in Latin *baculum, bacillus*, from *baca* or *bacca*, "rod, staff". Latin *bacca* becomes confused with Celtic *bach*, meaning "young, young man", so that *baccalaris* becomes *bachelier* in French and *bachelor* in English; but there is more than a suspicion that the Celtic form may have been previously borrowed from Latin *baca*. A further confusion appears in the meaning of the ending -*laris* with *laureus*, "laurel", and this leads to *baccalaureate. Baca* or *bacca* further develops into French *baie*, which appears in English as *bay* (leaf). There are further possible but doubtful extensions in *Bacchus*, with *Bacchanal, Bacchanalian, Bacchic*, etc., and in French *débacle*. Anglo-Saxon *pægel, pægl*, "gage-rod", gives rise to *peg* and *pail* (the latter in origin a wine-measure); some authorities suppose that the Anglo-Saxon form may have been borrowed from Latin *pagella* or *patella*, but the semantics, as well as the phonological development, seem to favor a native Anglo-Saxon development.

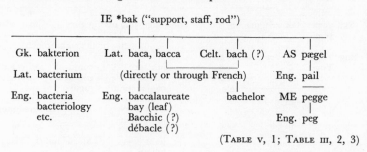

IE *bak ("support, staff, rod")

Gk. bakterion	Lat. baca, bacca	Celt. bach (?)	AS pægel
Lat. bacterium	(directly or through French)		Eng. pail
Eng. bacteria bacteriology etc.	Eng. baccalaureate bay (leaf) Bacchic (?) débacle (?)	bachelor	ME pegge Eng. peg

(TABLE V, 1; TABLE III, 2, 3)

IE *ker*, "horn, top", gives Anglo-Saxon and English *horn* (with *horny, hornbill, hornpipe, hornswoggle, dehorn*, etc.); and Anglo-Saxon *heorot*, which gives us *hart*, while a kindred Dutch form supplies *hartebeest*, and Scandinavian *hrān* appears in Old Norse as *hreinndȳri*, which in English becomes *reindeer*. Greek *keras*, "horn", appears in *rhinoceros* ("nose-horn"), and in various learned forms in *kera-* (*keratin, keratoid, trikeratops*, etc.); while the derivative *kranion*, "skull", through Latin, yields *cranium, cranial, hemicrania*, which French fashions into *migraine* and English further contorts into *megrim*. The *horn* root in Celtic form appears in the name of *Cornwall*, with *Cornish* and the common noun *Cornish hen*; it may also appear in *cerevisia*, the word that gives us Old French *cervoise* and Spanish *cerveza*, "beer", if we accept the hypothesis that the original meaning is "deer-colored", and that the word does not come from the name of Ceres, goddess of the harvest. Latin forms include *cornu*, from which we get *corn* (in the sense of a horny excrescence, usually on the foot), *cornea, cornucopia, cornet, tricorn, Capricorn, unicorn*, etc., while from a derivative *corneria*, French *cornière*, comes *corner*, with *cornerstone*, etc.; *cervus*, "deer", which gives French *cerf* and English *cervine*; *cervix*, which gives *cervix* and *cervical*; *cerebrum*, which yields *cerebrum, cerebral, cerebrate, cerebellum*, etc. A Slavic cognate appears in Russian *korova*, "cow", but does not get into English.

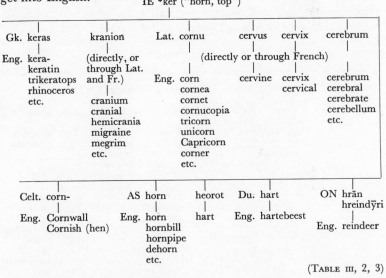

IE *ker ("horn, top")

Gk. keras	kranion	Lat. cornu	cervus	cervix	cerebrum
Eng. kera- keratin trikeratops rhinoceros etc.	(directly, or through Lat. and Fr.) cranium cranial hemicrania migraine megrim etc.	(directly or through French) Eng. corn cornea cornet cornucopia tricorn unicorn Capricorn corner etc.	cervine	cervix cervical	cerebrum cerebral cerebrate cerebellum etc.

Celt. corn-	AS horn	heorot	Du. hart	ON hrān hreindȳri
Eng. Cornwall Cornish (hen)	Eng. horn hornbill hornpipe dehorn etc.	hart	Eng. hartebeest	Eng. reindeer

(TABLE III, 2, 3)

A doubtful four-branch family (the doubt attaches to the Celtic branch) is IE *$g^{u}_{\sim}er$, "hard". This in Sanskrit produces *guruh*, "heavy", which comes into English as *guru*, "teacher, one who is heavy or influential by reason of his learning". The Greek *barys*, "heavy", gives us *barytone, isobar, barium, barometer, barograph*; while *hybris*, "wild boar", analyzed as "on-heavy, heavy upon" gives us *hybrid* and *hybridism* (the wild boar is the descendant of a wild pig and a tame sow). Latin *gravis* gives us *grave* (in the "serious", not in the "burial-place" sense; the latter comes through Germanic, from a different root); *gravity, gravitate, gravitation, aggravate, aggravation,* as well as the French-derived *grief, grieve, grievous, grievance,* etc. The apparently Oscan *brutus* (there is also a possibility that Latin may have borrowed this form from Celtic *bruth,* "weight") gives us *brute, brutal, brutality, brutalize, brutish,* and the French *brut,* applied to champagne. A possible Celtic form appears in Old Irish *brīg,* "strength", which may be the source of Italian forms that give us English *brigand, brigade, brigadier, brigandage, brigantine* or *brig* (but it is more likely that the Celtic *brig* forms come from the root of **bheregh,* "high, lofty", related to German *Berg,* "mountain" and to English *borough* and *barrow*). The Germanic cognate, which does not develop in Anglo-Saxon, appears in Old High German *krēg* and modern German *Krieg,* from which English borrows such compounds as *Blitzkrieg* and *Kriegspiel.*

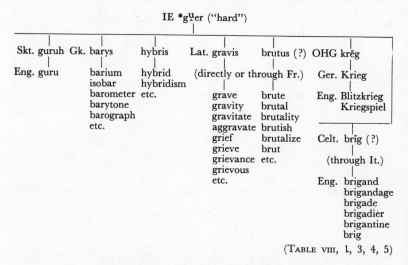

IE *gʷer ("hard")

Skt. guruh	Gk. barys	hybris	Lat. gravis	brutus (?)	OHG krēg
Eng. guru	barium	hybrid	(directly or through Fr.)		Ger. Krieg
	isobar	hybridism			
	barometer	etc.	grave	brute	Eng. Blitzkrieg
	barytone		gravity	brutal	Kriegspiel
	barograph		gravitate	brutality	
	etc.		aggravate	brutish	
			grief	brutalize	Celt. brīg (?)
			grieve	brut	
			grievance	etc.	(through It.)
			grievous		
			etc.		Eng. brigand
					brigandage
					brigade
					brigadier
					brigantine
					brig

(TABLE VIII, 1, 3, 4, 5)

The IE root **kar,* or, with reduplication, **karkar,* "hard", produces in Greek *karkinos,* "crab. tumor", from which we get *carcinoma* and *carcinogen.* There is also *kratos,* "power", which appears in the suffixes *-crat, -cracy* (*democracy, autocrat, plutocrat, aristocracy, bureaucracy, theocracy,* even *mobocracy*) as well as in *pancratium.* There is also a possibility that *krateros*, "crater", may come from this source. Slightly less doubtful are the Celtic *crag* and *cairn* (the former is Irish *carrac*, *craig*, or Welsh *carreg*, *craig;* the latter is an inflectional form of *carn*). From Latin *cancer*, "crab", come *Cancer*, *cancer*, *cancerous*, the French-derived *chancre*, *chancroid*, the Norman-Picard *canker*. The diminutive *cancelli*, "little crabs", applied to lattice-work, gives rise to *cancel* and *cancellation* (an erasure of something written by drawing crosswise lines across the script), and, supposedly because of the lattice-like grill or crossbars, to *chancel*, then *chancellor*, *chancellery*, *chancery*. Another Latin form is *carcer*, "prison" (crossbars blocking the exit), and this appears in *incarcerate*, *incarceration*, and the place name *Chartres*, formerly *Carceres*, "Prisons". Still another form is *carina*, "keel", which gives us *careen*. On the Germanic side, Anglo-Saxon *heard* produces *hard*, with *hardly*, *hardness*, *harden*, etc.; *hardy* and *hardihood* come from the cognate Old High German *hartjan*, which appears in French *hardi;* the same form appears in the *-ard*, *-art* of *Reynard* (*Reginhart*), *coward*, *braggart*, *drunkard*, *standard*, *poniard*, *Richard*, *Leonard*, *Spaniard*. A Scandinavian form gives rise to Middle English *harsk*, English *harsh*, with *harshen*, *harshness*.

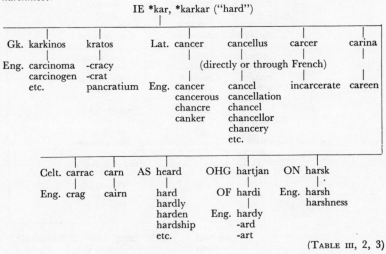

IE *kar, *karkar ("hard")

Gk.	karkinos	kratos	Lat.	cancer	cancellus	carcer	carina
Eng.	carcinoma carcinogen etc.	-cracy -crat pancratium		(directly or through French)			
			Eng.	cancer cancerous chancre canker	cancel cancellation chancel chancellor chancery etc.	incarcerate	careen

Celt.	carrac	carn	AS heard	OHG hartjan	ON harsk
Eng.	crag	cairn	hard hardly harden hardship etc.	OF hardi Eng. hardy -ard -art	Eng. harsh harshness

(TABLE III, 2, 3)

The IE root *ker*(s), "cart, wagon", produces in Anglo-Saxon *hros*, *hors* (though some authorities deny this), which becomes *horse*, with such derivatives as *unhorse, horsy, horseback, horseman, horse chestnut, horse marine, horseradish, horsepower, horse sense, horseshoe, horsewhip;* the same root in Old High German produces in Romance a word for "nag" which eventually appears in *Rocinante,* Don Quixote's steed. From Scandinavian comes *hrossvalr* ("horse-whale"), which passes into Dutch, is reversed, and passed on to English as *walrus.* In Greek, the root appears in the name of *Epicurus* ("one who hastens to help"), and gives *Epicurean, Epicureanism,* etc. The Latin form is *curro,* past participle *cursus,* "to run", from which come numerous English forms: *current, currency,* probably *curule, cursory, course, courser, cursive, recur, recurrent, incur, incursion, concur, concurrent, discourse, discursive, precursor,*

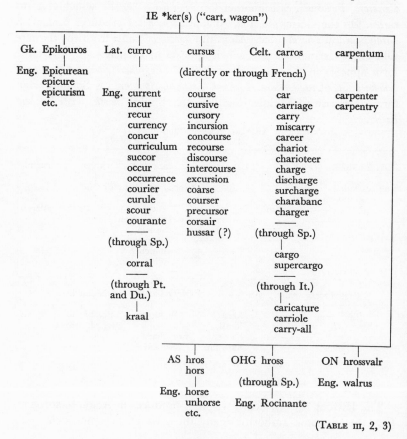

IE *ker(s) ("cart, wagon")

Gk. Epikouros	Lat. curro	cursus	Celt. carros	carpentum
Eng. Epicurean epicure epicurism etc.		(directly or through French)		
	Eng. current	course	car	carpenter
	incur	cursive	carriage	carpentry
	recur	cursory	carry	
	currency	incursion	miscarry	
	concur	concourse	career	
	curriculum	recourse	chariot	
	succor	discourse	charioteer	
	occur	intercourse	charge	
	occurrence	excursion	discharge	
	courier	coarse	surcharge	
	curule	courser	charabanc	
	scour	precursor	charger	
	courante	corsair	———	
	———	hussar (?)	(through Sp.)	
	(through Sp.)			
	corral		cargo	
			supercargo	
	(through Pt. and Du.)		(through It.)	
	kraal		caricature	
			carriole	
			carry-all	

AS hros hors	OHG hross	ON hrossvalr
Eng. horse	(through Sp.)	Eng. walrus
unhorse etc.	Eng. Rocinante	

(TABLE III, 2, 3)

excursion, occur, occurrence, succor, concourse, recourse, intercourse, the Latin curriculum (vitae), the Italian courier, the French courante, the Portuguese corral and the Dutch kraal derived from it; also corsair and possibly the Hungarian-derived hussar, if it comes, like corsair, from the Greek koursorios; but it may also come from Hungarian húsz, "twenty"; coarse, scour; possibly scurrilous from scurra, "buffoon", but this is doubtful. In Celtic, there is the Gaulish carros, which comes into Latin as carrus and in French becomes char, but in Norman-Picard car. Here we get car, carload, career (Latin carraria, "highway" for conveyances), carriage, carry, miscarry, the Italian-derived carriole and the carry-all derived from it by popular etymology, the Italian caroche, caricature, caricaturist. Standard French forms give us char-à-bancs or charabanc, chariot and charioteer, charge, charger, discharge, surcharge, while Spanish contributes cargo and supercargo. A Gaulish two-wheeled vehicle, carpentum, gives rise to carpenter.

The IE root *gal, "to call, shout", shows development into at least three, and perhaps four branches that contribute to English vocabulary. In Anglo-Saxon, it produces the verb callian, which becomes call (with calling, callable, recall, overcall, etc.); also clacu, the ancestor of clack (the French claque comes from the same formative root, but through Old High German); clatrian and clatrung, which give us clatter; and clæppan, which blends with Old Norse klapp to give us clap. Old

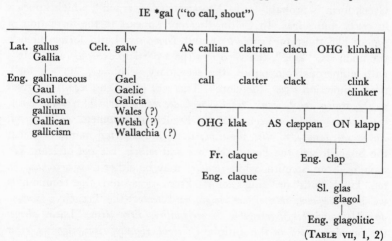

IE *gal ("to call, shout")

Lat. gallus	Celt. galw	AS callian	clatrian	clacu	OHG klinkan
Gallia					
Eng. gallinaceous	Gael	call	clatter	clack	clink
Gaul	Gaelic				clinker
Gaulish	Galicia				
gallium	Wales (?)	OHG klak	AS clæppan	ON klapp	
Gallican	Welsh (?)				
gallicism	Wallachia (?)	Fr. claque	Eng. clap		
		Eng. claque			
			Sl. glas		
			glagol		
			Eng. glagolitic		

(TABLE VII, 1, 2)

High German *klinkan* or Dutch *klinken* gives us *clink* and *clinker*, possibly also *clank* (Old High German *klagōn* appears in the related German *klagen*). Latin *gallus*, "cock, rooster", may or may not be a borrowing from Celtic; it produces *gallinaceous*, and possibly the Latin name of Gaul, *Gallia*, from which came the name of the chemical element *gallium*, along with *Gallican* and *gallicism*. The Celtic form is *galw*, and from this may come the Latin *gallus* and *Gallia;* in addition, it gives us *Gael* and *Gaelic*, *Galicia* in Spain, and may have something to do with the formation of *Wales*, *Welsh* and *Wallachian*, though these forms are more likely to arise from a Germanic source. In Slavic, the word for "voice", *golos* or *glas*, is related to *glagol*, "word", from which comes *glagolitic*, the name of the alphabet used by the Slavs before the adoption of Cyrillic. It may be noted that in this form the eastern Indo-European languages have the same *g* as the western, instead of the sibilant *z* which is their more usual development.

The root **reg*, "straight, king", produces in Sanskrit the forms that appear in *rājan*, *rājñī*, which give us *rajah*, *ranee* (or *rani*), *maharajah*, *maharani*, as well as in *raj*, "government", *svaraj*, "self-government", *Rajasthan* and *Rajasthani* (from a combination meaning "king's palace"), *Rajputana* and *Rajput* (*rājaputra*, "king's son"). There is also from the Indo-Iranian branch the Romany Gypsy *rye*, which acquires in the slang of the English gypsies the meaning of "gentleman". A connected Greek form is probably *orego*, "to stretch for, reach", which appears in *orectic* and *origan*. In Celtic, the root appears in the formation of names like those of *Vercingetorix* and *Dumnorix*. Latin forms include the noun *rex*, "king", the verb *rego* (past participles *rectus*), "to rule", with numerous compounds, the secondary verb *rogo*, "to ask for", the conjunction *ergo*, "therefore". The root of *rex* and *rego*, *reg-*, gives us *rex*, *regina*, *regal*, *regale*, *regalia*, *regicide*, *regime*, *regimen*, *regent*, *regency*, *regiment*, *regimentation*, *regimental;* in French development we have *roi*, *Roy*, *royal*, *royalty*, *royalist*, *royalism;* there are assorted names of coins: the Spanish *real*, the Portuguese *reis* and *milreis*, the *rial* of Iran. We have *rey* from Spanish, while *corduroy* may be either *corde* or *couleur· du roi*, "king's cloth" or "king's color". From *regnare* and other compounds we have *regnum*, *interregnum*, *reign*, and *realm* (the French *royaume*); *dirigible*, *corrigible*, *incorrigible*, *incorrigibility*, *dirge* (from Latin *dirige*, the opening word of the antiphon); *rigid*, *rigidity*, *rigor*, *rigorous*, *rigor*

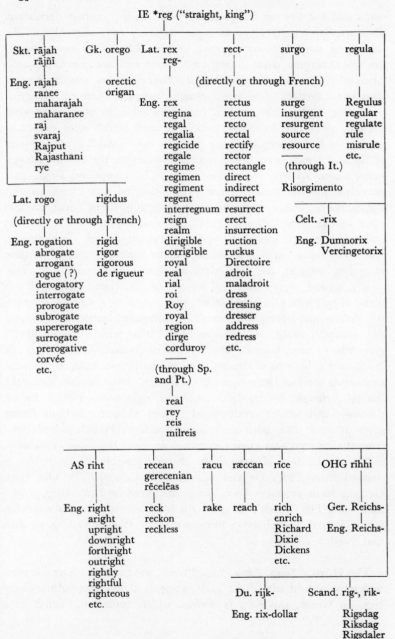

IE *reg ("straight, king")

| Skt. rājah | Gk. orego | Lat. rex | rect- | surgo | regula |
| rājñī | | reg- | | | |

Eng. rajah	orectic		(directly or through French)		
ranee	origan				
maharajah		Eng. rex	rectus	surge	Regulus
maharanee		regina	rectum	insurgent	regular
raj		regal	recto	resurgent	regulate
svaraj		regalia	rectal	source	rule
Rajput		regicide	rectify	resource	misrule
Rajasthani		regale	rector	——	etc.
rye		regime	rectangle	(through It.)	
		regimen	direct		
		regiment	indirect	Risorgimento	
Lat. rogo	rigidus	regent	correct		
		interregnum	resurrect		
(directly or through French)		reign	erect	Celt. -rix	
		realm	insurrection		
Eng. rogation	rigid	dirigible	ruction	Eng. Dumnorix	
abrogate	rigor	corrigible	ruckus	Vercingetorix	
arrogant	rigorous	royal	Directoire		
rogue (?)	de rigueur	real	adroit		
derogatory		rial	maladroit		
interrogate		roi	dress		
prorogate		Roy	dressing		
subrogate		royal	dresser		
supererogate		region	address		
surrogate		dirge	redress		
prerogative		corduroy	etc.		
corvée					
etc.		(through Sp.			
		and Pt.)			
		real			
		rey			
		reis			
		milreis			

AS riht	recean	racu	ræccan	rīce	OHG rīhhi
	gerecenian				
	rēcelēas				

Eng. right	reck	rake	reach	rich	Ger. Reichs-
aright	reckon			enrich	
upright	reckless			Richard	Eng. Reichs-
downright				Dixie	
forthright				Dickens	
outright				etc.	
rightly					
rightful					
righteous		Du. rijk-		Scand. rig-, rik-
etc.				
		Eng. rix-dollar		Rigsdag
				Riksdag
				Rigsdaler

(TABLE VII, 1, 2; Latin *rect-* (instead of **regt-*) and AS *riht* (instead of **rikt*) are due to the assimilative pull of the *t*. The change from **gt* to **kt* occurred in Indo-European.)

mortis and the French *de rigueur* are from *rigidus*, another derivative. The derivative *regio* gives us *region, regional, regionalism*. From the participial stem *rect-* come *rectus, rectum, recto, rectal, rector, rectory, rectangle, rectangular, rectitude, rectify, rectification, rectilinear*, etc. Compound forms of *rect-* include *direct, indirect, direction, directional, directive, director, directorate, directory, Directoire; correct, correction, corrective, resurrect, resurrection, erect, erection, erectile, insurrection* (this, in one special connection, gives rise to *ruction*, which in turn blends with *rumpus* to produce *ruckus*). There are, from *surgo*, "to rise" (which is a compound of *sub* and *rego*), *surge, resurge, resurgent, insurgent*, the Italian *Risorgimento, source, resource, resourcefulness*, etc. The compound *dirigo*, past participle *directus*, produces the French-derived *dress*, with *dressing, address, redress, dresser*, while *directus*, turning into French *droit*, gives us *adroit* and *maladroit*. *Regula*, "rule", gives us *Regulus, regulate, regular, irregular, regularity, regulation, regulator*, and, in French development, *rule, ruler, ruling, misrule*. From *rogo* come *rogation, rogatory, abrogate, abrogation, arrogant, arrogance* (with a possible development in *rogue, roguery, roguish, rogue's gallery*, if we accept the theory that *rogue* is a blend of *rogo* with Old Norse *hrōhr*); also *arrogation, derogatory, interrogation, interrogative, interrogatory, prorogation, subrogation, prerogative, supererogation, surrogate, surrogation*. Latin *corrogata*, "that which is demanded", gives rise to French *corvée*. On the Germanic side, Anglo-Saxon *riht* (with an *h* explained as coming from the participial root, in the same manner as the *c* of Latin *rectus*) gives us *right, aright, upright, downright, outright, forthright, rightly, rightful, righteous, righteousness, rightist*. *Recean, gerecenian* and *rēcelēas* produce *reck, reckon, reckoning, reckless*. *Ræccan* gives us *reach*. *Rīce*, with some assistance from French *riche* derived from the kindred Old High German *rīhhi*, gives *rich, enrich, enrichment, Richard* (with *Dick, Dixon, Dixie, Dickens*, possibly *Nixon*, if this is derived from *Dick's son* and not from *Nick's son*). The Old High German form produces *Reich, Reichsmark, Reichsbank, Reichstag, Reichswehr*, etc. The Dutch *rijk* gives *rijksdaler* which becomes *rix-dollar*, while kindred Scandinavian forms appear in Danish *Rigsdag, rigsdaler* and Swedish *Riksdag*.

The IE root **deru, *doru, *dru*, "tree", produces the Sanskrit *dāru*, which, combined with *deva*, "god", appears in the name of the *deodar* tree. In Greek, the form is *dendron*, which comes to English as a combining form (*rhododendron*, "rose-tree", etc.); in another form, *drys*, it appears in *drupe*, as well as in *Dryad* and *Hamadryad;* *Doric* probably also comes from this root. While there is some doubt concerning the Celtic *Druid*, *Druidism*, it appears likely that it comes from the root of Old Irish *drūi* (Gaulish *dru-talos*, "high-brow", is another form in which the Celtic "tall tree" root probably appears). Latin forms are mainly connected with *durus*, "hard", a quality of the tree. Here we have *durum wheat*, *duration*, *durable*, *durability*, *dour*, *duress*, *endure*, *endurance*, *perdure*, *obdurate*, etc. Since *Dante's* name is in full form *Durante*, "enduring", *Dantesque* also comes from this source. In Anglo-Saxon, *trēow* gives us both *tree* and *true* (with *truism*, *truly*, *untrue*); *trēowth* gives *truth;* *teoru* gives *tar*. Derivative forms include *untruth*, *truce* (the Middle English form of this is *trewes*); *trow*, from *trēowian;* *tray*, from *trīg;* *trim*, from *trum;* *trough*, from *trog, troh*. *Troth*, *betroth*, *betrothal*, are derivative forms of *truth*. The Scandinavian branch of

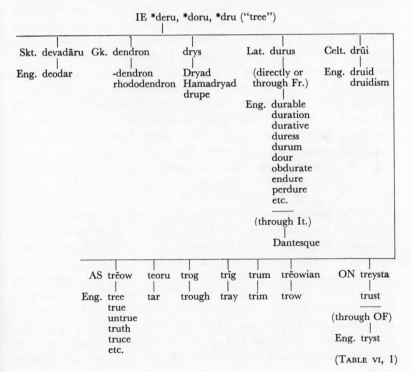

IE *deru, *doru, *dru ("tree")

Skt. devadāru	Gk. dendron	drys	Lat. durus	Celt. drūi
Eng. deodar	-dendron	Dryad	(directly or	Eng. druid
	rhododendron	Hamadryad	through Fr.)	druidism
		drupe		
			Eng. durable	
			duration	
			durative	
			duress	
			durum	
			dour	
			obdurate	
			endure	
			perdure	
			etc.	
			(through It.)	
			Dantesque	

	AS trēow	teoru	trog	trīg	trum	trēowian		ON treysta
	Eng. tree	tar	trough	tray	trim	trow		trust
	true							
	untrue							(through OF)
	truth							
	truce							Eng. tryst
	etc.							

(TABLE VI, 1)

Germanic furnishes *tryst* (Old Norse *treysta*) through Old French, where the meaning is "spot where hunter lies in wait for game". *Treysta* also supplies English directly with *trust* (*trustee, trusteeship, trusty, trustful, trustworthy, entrust, distrust, mistrust*). Among Slavic forms, which do not find their way into English, are Russian *derevo*, "tree", and *zdrav, zdorov*, "health" (the common Russian greeting *zdravstvuyte* literally means "be healthy").

One Indo-European root in which no fewer than five branches collaborate to form English cognates is **aw, *awed, *awer*, "wet, to flow". Greek *hydor*, "water", gives us our very numerous *hydr-, hydro-* compounds (*hydrant, Hydra, hydraulic, hydrochloric, hydrogen, hydrometer, hydrargyron* ("water-silver", or the element mercury, whose symbol is *Hg*), *hydrophobia, hydroplane, hydroxide, hydroponic, dehydrate, clepsydra* ("steal-water", or "water clock"), *dropsy* (from *hydrops*, "water-eye"). Latin forms appear in *unda*, "wave", with *undine* or *Ondine, ondograph, undulant, undulate, undulatory, inundate, inundation, abound, abundance, redound, redundant, superabundant, surround, surroundings, sound* (in the sense of to take depth measurements; French *sonder* from Latin *subundare*, "to go under water"); also in *uter*, "wine-skin", with *utriform* and *utricle* (with an original *dr* turning to *tr* for obscure reasons, perhaps under the influence of *uterus*, "womb"). Some doubt attaches to *urina*, from which come *urine, urinal, urinate, uric, ureter, diuretic*, etc. Germanic forms include Anglo-Saxon *wæter*, becoming *water*, with numerous compounds and derivatives (*watery, waterless, watercress, water-line, watermark, watermelon, waterproof, waterfall, waterlog, watershed*, etc.). The same Low Germanic root, going through Dutch, gives us *Waterloo*. Anglo-Saxon *wascan* produces *wash, washer, wishy-washy, washboard, washerwoman*, etc. Anglo-Saxon *wæt* becomes *wet*, with *wet blanket, wet nurse*, etc. Anglo-Saxon *winter* gives *winter, wintry, wintergreen*. Anglo-Saxon *otor* produces *otter*. Old High German *ūrohso*, borrowed by Latin in the form *urus*, reaches us in that form, as well as in the more native form *aurochs*. Old Irish *uisce*, later *uisge-beatha*, "water of life", produces *whiskey*, while the *av*-root of Celtic, appearing in place names like *Avon*, also gets into the form *ausarios* which develops into French and English *osier*. The Slavic form, *voda*, "water", becomes *vodka*, "little water", used even by Americans. Among the very numerous place names attributed to this root are the Latin *Aventine*, the ancient *Edessa* and *Metaurus*, and the French *Eure*. There are even claims for Greek *kentauros*, leading to *centaur* and *Centaurus*, and for *thesauros*, becoming *thesaurus* and *treasure*, but they are too uncertain to warrant inclusion.

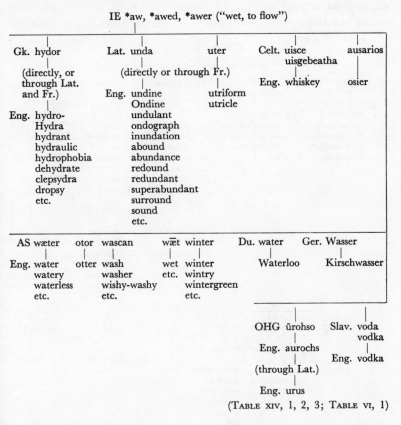

IE *aw, *awed, *awer ("wet, to flow")

Gk. hydor	Lat. unda	uter	Celt. uisce	ausarios
(directly, or through Lat. and Fr.)	(directly or through Fr.)		uisgebeatha	
			Eng. whiskey	osier
Eng. hydro-	Eng. undine	utriform		
Hydra	Ondine	utricle		
hydrant	undulant			
hydraulic	ondograph			
hydrophobia	inundation			
dehydrate	abound			
clepsydra	abundance			
dropsy	redound			
etc.	redundant			
	superabundant			
	surround			
	sound			
	etc.			

AS wæter	otor	wascan	wǣt	winter	Du. water	Ger. Wasser
Eng. water	otter	wash	wet	winter	Waterloo	Kirschwasser
watery		washer	etc.	wintry		
waterless		wishy-washy		wintergreen		
etc.		etc.		etc.		

OHG ūrohso	Slav. voda
	vodka
Eng. aurochs	
	Eng. vodka
(through Lat.)	
Eng. urus	

(TABLE XIV, 1, 2, 3; TABLE VI, 1)

Another family in which five Indo-European branches appear in English is that of *meg(h)*, "big". Here Sanskrit *mahāt*, "great", appears in *Mahabharata*, *mahatma* ("great soul"), *maharajah* and *maharanee* ("great king", "great queen"), *Maharashtra* or *Mahratti* ("great kingdom"). Greek *megas*, *megalos* appear in *megaphone*, *megatherium*, *megasaur*, *megalomaniac*, and numerous scientific words, including the jocular *megabuck*. Latin formations are numerous: the goddess *Maia*,

after whom is named the month of *May* (with *Mayfair*, *Maypole*, etc.);
magnus, "great", which appears in *magnum*, *magnum opus*, *Magna
Charta*, *magna cum laude*, and in compounds like *magnanimous*, *magna-
nimity*, *magnitude*, *magnificence*, *magnificent* (and the Italian *magnifico*),
magniloquent, *magnify*, *magnate*; its comparative *major*, from which come
on the one hand *major*, *majority*, *majorette*, on the other, *mayor*, *mayoralty*,

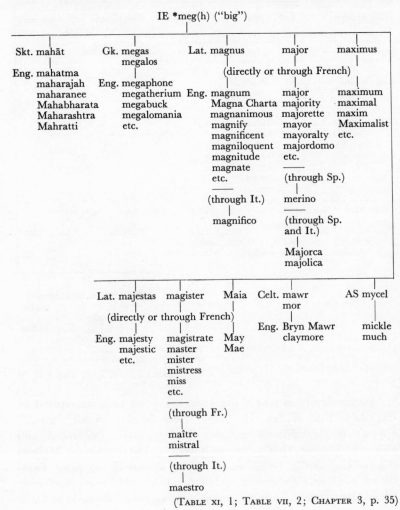

IE *meg(h) ("big")

| Skt. mahāt | Gk. megas megalos | Lat. magnus | major | maximus |

Eng. mahatma
maharajah
maharanee
Mahabharata
Maharashtra
Mahratti

Eng. megaphone
megatherium
megabuck
megalomania
etc.

(directly or through French)

Eng. magnum
Magna Charta
magnanimous
magnify
magnificent
magniloquent
magnitude
magnate
etc.

major
majority
majorette
mayor
mayoralty
majordomo
etc.

maximum
maximal
maxim
Maximalist
etc.

(through It.)

magnifico

(through Sp.)

merino

(through Sp.
and It.)

Majorca
majolica

| Lat. majestas | magister | Maia | Celt. mawr mor | AS mycel |

(directly or through French)

Eng. majesty
majestic
etc.

magistrate
master
mister
mistress
miss
etc.

May
Mae

Eng. Bryn Mawr
claymore

mickle
much

(through Fr.)

maître
mistral

(through It.)

maestro

(TABLE XI, 1; TABLE VII, 2; CHAPTER 3, p. 35)

mayoress, with a Vulgar Latin compound, *major-domo*; the name of the island of *Mallorca*, which gives rise to the Italian *majolica*; and a variety of sheep called *majorinus*, which in Spanish becomes *merino;* the superlative form *maximus*, from which come *maximum*, *maxim*, *maximal*, *Maximalist;* *majestas*, which gives us *majesty*, *majestic; magister*, originally "helmsman", from which come *master* (with *masterful*, *masterly*, *mastery*, *masterpiece*, etc.), *mister* (with *mistress*, Mrs., *miss* and *missy*); the French *maître*, the Italian *maestro*, and also *magistrate*, *magistracy*, *magisterial*, and the French *mistral* (once *magistralis*). There is a Celtic cognate, *mawr* (Welsh) or *mor* (Irish), "large, great", which appears in *Bryn Mawr* ("Big Hill") and in *claymore*, from *claidheamh mor*, "big sword" (but see p. 76). Lastly, in Germanic, we have Anglo-Saxon *mycel* from which come both *mickle* and *much*, with *muchness*.

The root **w(e)di*, "to see", first appears in Sanskrit *vēdas*, *veda*, "knowledge, sacred lore", from which come *Vedas*, *Vedic*, *Rig-Veda*, *Vedantas*, *Vedantic*. There is a possibility that it may appear in Celtic *Druid*, if the word is analyzed as *dru uid*, "strong knowledge" (the **dru* root, meaning "tree", may also have the meaning of "strong, strength"). In Greek, where an original *w*, indicated in some Greek dialects by the digamma, usually disappears, we have *eidomai*, "to see", from an earlier **widomai*, and *ideia* from **widesa*. *Ideia* produces *idea*, *ideal*, *idealism*, *idealistic*, *ideogram*, *ideology*, etc. *Eidolon*, "shape", from the same root, gives us *idol*, *idolize*, *idolatry*, *idolater*. *Eidyllion*, "short lyric poem", gives *idyll*, *idyllic*. *Kaleidoscope* combines the roots of *kalos*, "beautiful", *eidolon*, "shape", and *skopein*, "to look". This root also appears in the *-oid*, *-ode* suffix that means "similar to", "of the same appearance as" (*typhoid*, *rhomboid*, *trapezoid*, *geode*, etc.). An original *vistor*, *histor*, "knowing", gives rise to *historia*, which gives us *history*, *historical*, *historicity*, *historiography*, *prehistoric*, *prehistory; history* is cut down to *story*, and the later meaning of what the British spell *storey* comes from tiers of painted windows, which tell a story, but at the same time mark a vertical division in a house or building. In Anglo-Saxon, *wītan*, *wita*, *witt* provide us with *wit* (*witticism*, *witty*, *witness*, *witless*); *wot* (originally *wāt*, the first singular present of *wītan*, "I know"); *wist*, the past tense; and with the Anglo-Saxon council *witanagemot*, a gathering of collective knowledge, which might be

paraphrased as "brain-trust". *Twit* is *aetwītan*, "to reproach". *Wis(e)*
gives us *wise, wisdom, wisecrack, wiseguy, wiseacre,* and the *wise* of *wondrous
wise,* as well as the *-wise* suffix of *lengthwise, crosswise,* which becomes
highly disguised in *rightwise,* later *righteous* (with *righteousness*). *Wizard*
and *wizardry* also come from *wīs(e)*. The same root in Old High
German *wīsa, wīsan* is carried by the Franks into Old French and

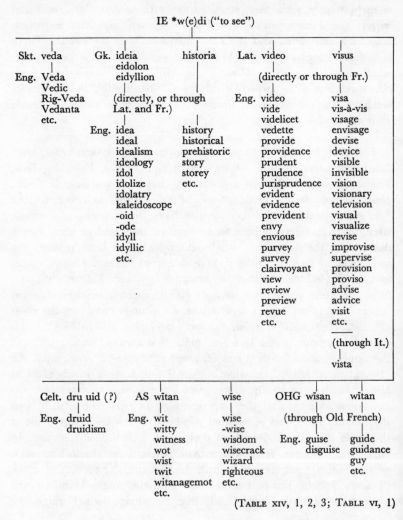

IE *w(e)di ("to see")

Skt. veda	Gk. ideia		historia	Lat. video		visus
	eidolon					
Eng. Veda	eidyllion			(directly or through Fr.)		
Vedic						
Rig-Veda	(directly, or through			Eng. video		visa
Vedanta	Lat. and Fr.)			vide		vis-à-vis
etc.				videlicet		visage
	Eng. idea	history		vedette		envisage
	ideal	historical		provide		devise
	idealism	prehistoric		providence		device
	ideology	story		prudent		visible
	idol	storey		prudence		invisible
	idolize	etc.		jurisprudence		vision
	idolatry			evident		visionary
	kaleidoscope			evidence		television
	-oid			prevident		visual
	-ode			envy		visualize
	idyll			envious		revise
	idyllic			purvey		improvise
	etc.			survey		supervise
				clairvoyant		provision
				view		proviso
				review		advise
				preview		advice
				revue		visit
				etc.		etc.
						———
						(through It.)
						vista

Celt. dru uid (?)	AS wītan	wīse	OHG wīsan	wītan
Eng. druid	Eng. wit	wise	(through Old French)	
druidism	witty	-wise		
	witness	wisdom	Eng. guise	guide
	wot	wisecrack	disguise	guidance
	wist	wizard		guy
	twit	righteous		etc.
	witanagemot	etc.		
	etc.			

(TABLE XIV, 1, 2, 3; TABLE VI, 1)

produces *guise* and *disguise*, while an earlier form *wītan* eventually gives us *guide*, *guidance*, the *guy* of *guy-rope*, *Guy Fawkes*, and the American slang *guy*, *wiseguy* (the last form is curious, because in it the word is repeated, first in Anglo-Saxon, then in Old High German form). The basic Latin form is *video*, past participle *visus*, "to see". Here we have a series of direct borrowings of Latin forms, including the *video* of TV, the directions *vide* and *videlicet* (or *viz.*), the *visa* on a passport. Other foreign forms include Italian *vista* and French *vis-à-vis* and *vedette* or *vidette*. Compounds, most of which appear in Latin itself, are numerous. Among them are: *provide*, *provident*, *providence*, *evident*, *evidential*, *evidence*, *prevident*, *invidious;* contracted forms of *provident* give *prudent*, *prudence*, *prudential*, *imprudent*, *jurisprudence*, etc.; French developments of *invidia* give *envy*, *envious*, *enviable*. *Purvey*, *purveyor*, *survey*, *surveyor* come from the older French *veir*, while *clairvoyant*, *clairvoyance* come from the later *voir*. Forms built on the participial root of *visus* include *visage*, *envisage*, *devise*, *visible*, *invisible*, *visibility*, *vision*, *visionary*, *television*, *visual*, *visualize*, *revise*, *revision*, *revisionism*, *improvise*, *improviser*, *supervise*, *supervisor*, *prevision*, *provision*, *provisional*, *proviso*, *advise*, *advice*, *advisable*, *advisability*, *devise*, *device*. From the participial root comes also *visit* ("to go and see"), with *visitor*, *visitation*, *visitant*. The French participle of *voir*, *vu*, gives us *view*, *review*, *revue*, *preview*, *viewer*, *view halloo*, *interview*, *purview*.

The IE root **pel*, **pelə*, **ple*, "to fill", has secondary meanings, "to pour in, flow, flutter, filled-up rampart", leading to the idea of "city, crowd, mass, much, many". In Sanskrit it gives rise to the *pūr*, "city", that appears in place names like *Cawnpore*, *Singapore*, and to *jodhpurs*, taken from the name of an Indian city. In Celtic we have the *Llan-* that appears as a prefix in many Welsh place names (*Llandudno*, *Llandaff*, etc.), and there is the possibility that it may appear in the Celtic (Welsh) *lann*, "enclosure", that gives us *lawn*, though the root of *land* is also possible. Greek developments include *pimplemi* and *pletho*, "to fill", *pleres*, *pleos*, "full"; *poly-*, "much", with comparative *pleios* and superlative *pleistos; polemos*, "war"; and *polis*, "city". The *pletho* root gives us *plethora*, *plethoric*, *Pleiades* ("star cluster"), and the French literary *Plëiade*. *Pleos* appears in *pleonasm*, *pleonastic*. *Poly-* appears in the plural *hoi polloi*, "the many", and in numerous compounds (*polytechnic*, *polyglot*, *polyphonic*, *polygon*, *polygamy*, *Polynesia*, *polychrome*, *polypus* or *polyp, polytheism, polyclinic, polysyllabic* are only a few). The comparative *pleios* appears in *Pliocene* ("more recent"), and the superlative *pleistos* in *Pleistocene* ("most recent"). *Polemos*, "war", appears in *polemics, polemicist. Polis*, "city", gives us the *-polis* of *Minneapolis Gallipolis, Tripoli, Naples (Neapolis,* "Newtown"), possibly *Istanbul* (if it is derived from *eis ten polin,* "into the city"), *necropolis, acropolis, cosmopolitan, metropolitan; policy, polity, police, policeman, politics, political, politician,* the Spanish *político,* the Russian *Politburo.* It is possible that through the verb *psallo,* "to pull", we also have *psalm, psalmist, psalmody, psalter, psaltery* from this root. Latin forms include *plenus,* "full", and *pleo,* "to fill", with past participle *pletus.* The first gives us *plenary, plenum, plenipotentiary, plenitude* and *plenty* (with *plentiful, plenteous*), *replenish,* the French *plein air.* The verb *pleo* gives us *implement, implementation, complement, complementary, supplement, supplementary, supplemental. Compliment* and *complimentary* belong to this root, but come through Spanish *cumplir. Supply, supplier* are from French; *comply, compliance, compliant* from Italian. The participial root, *plet-*, gives us *implete, impletion, replete, repletion, complete, completion, incomplete, expletive, deplete, depletion.* Latin also offers *manipulus,* "handful", from which come *maniple, manipulate, manipulator, manipulation. Plus,* "more", from the same root, yields *plus, surplus,* the Italian musical *più, plural, plurality, plurilateral, pluperfect,* etc. In addition, Latin has *plebs,* "crowd, mob, common people" and *populus,* "people". The first gives us *plebe, plebeian, plebiscite,* while the second yields *populace, popular, popularity, populate, population, populous, Populist, depopulate,* the French *peuple* and the Spanish *pueblo.* The adjective *publicus* gives rise to *public, publication, publicist, publicize, publicity, publish, publisher,* and *res publica,* "the public thing, the state," gives us *republic, republican.* If we accept the "flutter" meaning for this root, *palpo,* "to feel, touch," gives us *palpate, palpation, impalpable, palpitate, palpitation, palpebral* ("of the eyelid"), *palpitant,* while the derivative *papilio,* "butterfly", gives us *papillon* and *pavilion,* and *palma* gives us *palm, palmistry, palmist, palmer* and *palmetto* (from the Spanish *palmito*). Germanic forms include Anglo-Saxon *full* and *fyllan,* from which come *full, fulness, fulsome, fulfill, fill, filler, refill, fullback, fullblooded,* etc. There is also *fælan,* from which come *feel, feelings, unfeeling,* etc. *Floterian* gives us *flutter,* and the same root in Old High German *fledarmūs* gives rise to the name of the opera *Fledermaus.* Anglo-Saxon *folc* gives us *folk, folkways, folklore, folkmoot,* *folksy*, while the German equivalent *Volk* appears in *Herrenvolk*, *Volkswagen*, *Volkslied*, etc.

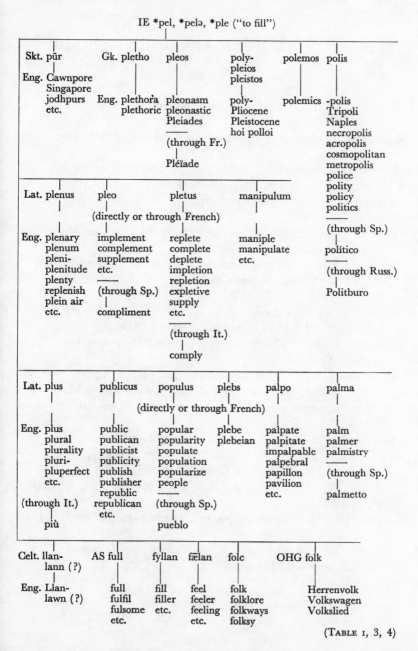

IE *pel, *pelə, *ple ("to fill")

Skt. pŭr	Gk. pletho	pleos	poly- pleios	polemos	polis
Eng. Cawnpore			pleistos		
Singapore					
jodhpurs	Eng. plethora	pleonasm	poly-	polemics	-polis
etc.	plethoric	pleonastic	Pliocene		Tripoli
		Pleiades	Pleistocene		Naples
			hoi polloi		necropolis
		(through Fr.)			acropolis
					cosmopolitan
		Pléïade			metropolis
					police
					polity
					policy
					politics

Lat. plenus	pleo	pletus	manipulum		(through Sp.)
	(directly or through French)				político
Eng. plenary	implement	replete	maniple		
plenum	complement	complete	manipulate		(through Russ.)
pleni-	supplement	deplete	etc.		
plenitude	etc.	impletion			Politburo
plenty		repletion			
replenish	(through Sp.)	expletive			
plein air		supply			
etc.	compliment	etc.			
		(through It.)			
		comply			

Lat. plus	publicus	populus	plebs	palpo	palma
		(directly or through French)			
Eng. plus	public	popular	plebe	palpate	palm
plural	publican	popularity	plebeian	palpitate	palmer
plurality	publicist	populate		impalpable	palmistry
pluri-	publicity	population		palpebral	
pluperfect	publish	popularize		papillon	(through Sp.)
etc.	publisher	people		pavilion	
	republic			etc.	palmetto
(through It.)	republican	(through Sp.)			
	etc.				
più		pueblo			

Celt. llan- lann (?)	AS full	fyllan	fǽlan	folc	OHG folk
Eng. Llan- lawn (?)	full	fill	feel	folk	Herrenvolk
	fulfil	filler	feeler	folklore	Volkswagen
	fulsome	etc.	feeling	folkways	Volkslied
	etc.		etc.	folksy	

(Table i, 3, 4)

List of Works Most Frequently Consulted

BATTISTI, C., and ALESSIO, G., *Dizionario etimologico italiano*, Barbera, Firenze, 1950–1957.

BAUGH, A. C., *History of the English Language*, Appleton-Century, New York, 1935.

BLOCH, O., and VON WARTBURG, W., *Dictionnaire étymologique de la langue française*, Presses Universitaires de France, Paris, 1950.

BOISACQ, E., *Dictionnaire étymologique de la langue grecque*, Winter, Heidelberg, 1950.

BRÜCH, J., *Der Einfluss der germanischen Sprachen auf das Vulgärlatein*, Winter, Heidelberg, 1913.

BUCK, C. D., *A Grammar of Oscan and Umbrian*, Ginn, Boston, 1928.

CARR, C. T., *German Influence on the English Vocabulary*, Society for Pure English, Tract XLII, Clarendon, Oxford, 1934.

CLARK, G. N., *Dutch Influence on the English Vocabulary*, Society for Pure English, Tract XLIV, Clarendon, Oxford, 1934.

CONWAY, R. S., *The Italic Dialects*, Harvard University Press, Cambridge, Mass., 1897.

CONWAY, R. S., WHATMOUGH, J., and JOHNSON, S. E., *The Prae-Italic Dialects of Italy*, Harvard University Press, Cambridge, Mass., 1933.

DAUZAT, A., *Dictionnaire étymologique de la langue française*, Larousse, Paris, 1957.

DOTTIN, G., *La Langue gauloise*, Klincksieck, Paris, 1920.

DUCANGE, C. DE F., *Glossarium Mediae et Infimae Latinitatis*, Akademische Druck- und Verlagsanstalt, Graz, 1954–1955.

ERNOUT, A., *Les Eleménts dialectaux du vocabulaire latin*, Champion, Paris, 1909.

ERNOUT, A., *Les Eléments étrusques du vocabulaire latin*, Champion, Paris, 1930.

ERNOUT, A., and MEILLET, A., *Dictionnaire étymologique de la langue latine*, Klincksieck, Paris, 1951.

FEIST, S., *Vergleichendes Wörterbuch der gotischen Sprache*, Brill, Leiden, 1939.

FÖRSTEMANN, E., *Althochdeutsches Namenbuch*, Hanstein, Bonn, 1900.

GODEFROY, F., *Dictionnaire de l'ancienne langue française*, Vieweg, Paris, 1880–1902.

GRAY, L. H., *Foundations of Language*, Macmillan, New York, 1939.

HOLDER, A., *Altkeltischer Sprachschatz*, Teubner, Leipzig, 1896.

KÖRTING, G., *Lateinisches-romanisches Wörterbuch*, Schöningh, Paderborn, 1907.

LIDDELL, H. G., and SCOTT, R., *Greek-English Lexicon*, Clarendon, Oxford, 1925–1940.

LOKOTSCH, K., *Etymologisches Wörterbuch der europäischen Wörter orientalischer Ursprungs*, Winter, Heidelberg, 1927.

MATHEWS, M. M., *Dictionary of Americanisms*, University of Chicago Press, Chicago, 1951.

MEILLET, A., *Introduction à l'étude comparative des langues indo-européennes*, Hachette, Paris, 1949.

MEYER-LÜBKE, W., *Romanisches etymologisches Wörterbuch*, Winter, Heidelberg, 1935.

MIGLIORINI, B., and DURO, A., *Prontuario etimologico della lingua italiana*, Paravia, Torino, 1941.

MIKLOSIĆ, F., *Etymologisches Wörterbuch der slawischen Sprachen*, Braumüller, Wien, 1886.

New English Dictionary on Historical Principles, Oxford University Press, Oxford, 1884–1928.

PALMER, L. R., *The Latin Language*, Macmillan, New York, 1954.

PARTRIDGE, E., *Origins: a Short Etymological Dictionary of Modern English*, Macmillan, New York, 1958.

PATRICK, G. Z., *Roots of the Russian Language*, Pitman, New York and Chicago, 1938.

POKORNY, J., *Indogermanisches etymologisches Wörterbuch*, Francke, Bern, 1951–1959.

PRATI, A., *Vocabolario etimologico italiano*, Garzanti, Torino, 1951.

REAL ACADEMIA ESPAÑOLA, *Diccionario de la lengua castellana*, Hernando, Madrid, 1914.

ROBERTSON, S., *Development of Modern English*, Prentice-Hall, New York, 1938.

SCHÖNFELD, M., *Wörterbuch der altgermanischen Personen- und Völkersnamen*, Winter, Heidelberg, 1911.

SHIPLEY, J., *Dictionary of Word Origins*, Philosophical Library, New York, 1945.

Shorter Oxford English Dictionary, Oxford University Press, Oxford, 1955.

STAPPERS, H., *Dictionnaire synoptique de la langue française*, Larousse, Paris, 9th ed.

WALTEMATH, W., *Die fränkische Elemente in der französischen Sprache*, Schöningh, Paderborn, 1885.

Webster's New Collegiate Dictionary, Merriam, Springfield, 1951.

Webster's New World Dictionary, World, Cleveland and New York, 1959.

Webster's Third New International Dictionary, *unabridged*, Merriam, Springfield, Mass., 1961.

WEEKLEY, E., *Concise Etymological Dictionary*, Dutton, New York, 1952.

WRIGHT, J., *Grammar of the Gothic Language*, Clarendon, Oxford, 1954.

WUST, W., *Vergleichendes und etymologisches Wörterbuch des Altindoarischen*, Winter, Heidelberg, 1935.

Topical index

Word index

This word index includes all words, from whatever language, that appear in the text, save that we often omit obvious derivatives (such as *acknowledgment* from *acknowledge*, *agnosticism* from *agnostic*, *ambrosial* from *ambrosia*, *anticipation* from *anticipate*).

The reader is reminded that forms preceded by an asterisk (such as **dha*) are hypothetical reconstructions, usually, but not invariably, of Indo-European roots.

Abbreviations used in this word index are listed below. For reasons of space, periods are omitted, and abbreviations are run together. Thus, *carton* (FE) indicates that the word appears in both French and English; *cabriolet* (FPrE) indicates that the word appears in French, Provençal and English; *campus* (LE) indicates that the word appears in both Latin and English.

ABBREVIATIONS

Alb—Albanian	Hind—Hindustani	OPers—Old Persian
AN—Anglo-Norman	Hot—Hottentot	Osc—Oscan
Arab—Arabic	Icel—Icelandic	OSp—Old Spanish
Arc—Archaic	Ir—Irish	Pers—Persian
Arm—Armenian	It—Italian	Pol—Polish
AS—Anglo-Saxon	Jap—Japanese	Pr—Provençal
Av—Avestan	L—Latin	Pt—Portuguese
Celt—Celtic	LG—Low German	Rum—Rumanian
Chin—Chinese	Lith—Lithuanian	Rus—Russian
Cz—Czech	Mahr—Mahratti	SAf—South African
Dan—Danish	Mal—Malay	SC—Serbo-Croatian
Dor—Doric	ME—Middle English	Scan—Scandinavian
Du—Dutch	MHG—Middle High	Scot—Scottish English
E—English	German	Sem—Semitic
F—French	MLG—Middle Low	Sk—Sanskrit
Fal—Faliscan	German	Sl—Slavic
G—German	NF—Northern French	Sp—Spanish
Gaul—Gaulish	(Norman-Picard-	Sum—Sumerian
Gic—Germanic	Walloon)	Swed—Swedish
Gk—Greek	Nor—Norwegian	Tokh—Tokharian
Goth—Gothic	OF—Old French	Umb—Umbrian
Gyp—Gypsy (Romany)	OHG—Old High German	VL—Vulgar Latin
Heb—Hebrew	OIr—Old Irish	Wal—Walloon
HG—High German	OIt—Old Italian	We—Welsh
	ON—Old Norse	

Note—For purposes of alphabetization, the phonetic symbol *ə* is placed with *e*, *ð* with *d*, *ʮ* with *u*.

240

A

Aachen 114f
aard (Du) 105
aardvark (DuE) 105
aardvolk (DuE) 105
abandon 191f
abandoner (OF) 191f
abase 49f
abate 150f
abatis (FE) 150f
abattoir (FE) 150f
abdicate 190
abduct 132
ability 144
abjure 56
ablative 94f
-able 144
able-bodied 144
ablution 121
abnormal 206f
ab oculo (VL) 183
abolish 125
A-bomb 92
abound 224f
abrasion-ive 122f
abrogate 221f
abs- (L) 101
abscond 101
abstract 133
abstruse 111
abundant-ce 224f
abut 150f
abyss-mal 49f
abyssos-us (GkL) 49f
acanthus (LE) 37
a cappella (ItE) 137
accelerate 138
accendo (LIt) 61
accent-uate 126f
accentum (L) 126f
accept-ance 135f
acclaim-amation 139
accommodate-ion 163f
accompany-ist 141
accomplice 166f
accord-ance 182
accredit 182
ach (G) 25
ache (OHG) 114f
achever (F) 136f

achieve 136f
acknowledge 206f
acointier (OF) 206f
acquaint-ance 206f
acropolis 230f
actus (L) 156
ad (L) 139, 191
adcognitare (VL) 206f
add-end-um 101
addict-ion 190
addition-al 101
additive 101
address 221f
adduce 132
Adelphi 84f
adelphos (Gk) 84f, 146f
adhibeo (L) 143f
adhibit 144
adieu (F) 211f
adiós (Sp) 211f
adjoin 213
adjourn 212
adjudge 190f
adjudicate 190f
adjure 56
adjust 56, 213
adjutant 213
adjutare (VL) 213
adjuvant 213
admonish 12
adolescent 125
adroit 221f
adult-erate-ery 125
adverb-ial 160
advice 228f
advise-r 228f
advocate 93
aeon (LE) 154f
aera (L) 113
aeronaut 177
aes (L) 113
aestimari-tus (L) 92, 113
aetas (L) 154f
aeternus (L) 154f
ætwītan (AS) 228
aevum (L) 154f
*aew 154f
affiliate-ion 64f
affinity 128
afoot 198
-age (FE) 41

age-less 154f
āgen (AS) 35
agenda (LE) 38
agent provocateur (FE) 93
aggravate-ion 216
aggregate 155f
agnis (Sk) 53
agnomen (L) 164f, 206f
agnostic 206f
ago (L) 155f
agora (GkE) 155f
agoraphobia (GkE) 155f
ahead 136f
ahwa (Goth) 114
aid-e 213
aider (F) 213
aidier (OF) 213
aihwa (Goth) 88
ail-ment 125
ainé (F) 205f
aio (Gk) 89f
aion (Gk) 154f
airdrome 81f
aisthanesthai (Gk) 89f
aisthetes (Gk) 89f
aiws (Goth) 154f
Aix 114f
akanthos (Gk) 37
akin 204f
*akwa 114f
al- (Arab) 150
*al 55, 125
Albert 15, 47f
Albrecht 47f
Albuquerque 149f
alcázar (SpE) 62f
alcorque (Sp) 149f
alderman 125
alibi (LE) 38
alimentary 125
alimony 125
allegory-ical 155f
aller (F) 55
alley 55
allocate 43
allocation (F) 43
alloco (L) 43
allopath 73
allot-ment 139f
allow 43
allure (FE) 55

astrum (L) 158f
Atalanta 94f
athair (Ir) 21
-aticum (L) 41
Atlantic-s 94f
Atlas 94f
atmosphere 153
atom-ic-ize 92
atrocious-ity 183
atrox (L) 183
atta (Goth) 78
attain 68
attainder 68
attaint 68
attas (Sk) 78
attempt 60f
attest-ation 181f
attract-ion-ive 133
attribute 181
auctio (L) 117
auction-eer 117
auctor (L) 117
auctoricare (VL) 117
audible 89f
audience 89f
audio (LE) 89f
audition 89f
auditor-ium 89f
auf Wiedersehen (G) 79
Auge (G) 23
augeo (L) 117
augment-ation 117
augur-y 117
augurium (L) 117
august 117
August-an-ine-inian 117
augustus (L) 117
aunclum (VL) 40
aural 30f
aureate 169f
Aurelia 169f
aureola (LE) 169f
aureomycin 169f
auricular 30f
auriferous 169f
auris (L) 30f
aurum (L) 40, 169f
aurochs 224f
Aurora (Borealis) 169f
aurous 169f
ausaria (VL) 114f

ausarios (Celt) 224f
auso (Goth) 30f
auspicious 203f
Aussie 170
Auster 169f
austere-ity 170
Austin 117
austral 170
Australasia 170
Australia 170
Austria 170
author-ess-ship 117
authority-arian 117
authorize 117
autochthonous 170f
autocrat-cy 216f
autonomy-ous 167f
autopsy 183
autumn 117
auxiliary 117
auxilium (L) 117
av (Celt) 114
avenge-r 190f
Aventine 224f
aver 54
avere (It) 143
Avesta 89f
aveugle-r (F) 183
Avistāk (Pers) 90
āvišya (Pers) 90
avocation 93
avoid-ance 129
avoir (F) 143
avoirdupois 193f
Avon 224f
avow-al 93
avuncular 106
avunculus (L) 40, 106
avus (L) 106
*aw 89f
*aw 224ff
*aw (AS) 117, 170
āwa (AS) 154f
away 142f
*awed 224f
*aweg 117
*awĕi 89f
*awer 224f
*(aw)es 169f
*awos 106
ay(e) 154f

*ayos 112f
*ayu 154f
-azum (Osc) 30f, 37

B

bab (Sem) 208f
baba (Sl) 208f
*baba 208f
babble 208f
babbo (It) 209
Bab-el 208f
Bab el Mandeb 208f
babi (ME) 208f
Bab-ilu 208f
babushka (RusE) 209
baby 208f
Babylon 208f
bac(c)a (L) 214
baccalaris (L) 214
baccalaureate 214
Bacchanal-ian 214
Bacchus-ic 214
bach (Celt) 214
bachelier (F) 214
bachelor 214
bacillus (LE) 214
bacterial-ology-phage 214
bacterium-a (LE) 214
baculum (L) 214
bad 10
bagnio 52f
baie (F) 214
baírths (Goth) 47f
*bak 214
baksheesh (PersE) 71
bakterion (Gk) 214
balaneion (Gk) 53
Balbo 208f
Balboa 208f
balbus (L) 208f
balbutio (L) 208f
balbuziare (It) 208f
balca (AS) 154
balk 154
ballet (FE) 43
ballista (L) 52f
ballistics 52f
ballo (Gk) 52f
balneology 52f
ban 191f
bana (Gk) 78

*bhēdh 108
*bheid 108f
*bhel 45, 154, 195f
*bhendh 72f
*bhereg 216
*bherəg 47f
*bhlag 55f
*bhlag(men) 70f
*bhlē 109
*bhlek 167
*bhlendh 71
bhrāta-r (Sk) 26, 146f
*bhrāter 146f
*bhrēg 47f
*bhrēi 118
bibber 59f
bibelot (FE) 188f
bibo (L) 59f
bibulous 59f
biceps 137
bident 169
bierce (AS) 48
big 10
Big Bertha 47f
biginti (VL) 38
bilateral 60
bilingual 112
bind-er-y 72f
bindan (AS) 72f
binnacle 144
binocular 183
binomial 167f
biology 26
bios (Gk) 26
biped 198f
birch 5, 48
bird 9
bireme 106
Birmingham 147
bis coctum (L) 96
biscop (AS) 34, 36, 203
biscuit (FE) 96
bishop-ric 34, 36, 203
bisque (FE) 96
bit 108f
bita (AS) 108f
bitácula (Pt) 144
bītan (AS) 108f
bite-r 108f
bitel (AS) 108f
bitter 10, 108f

bitula (AS) 108f
Bjerk, Björk 47
bladder 195f
blade 195f
blæd (AS) 195f
blǣdre (AS) 195f
blætan (AS) 109
blagodaryu (Rus) 101
-blain 195f
blame-less 191f
blare 109
blaspheme-ous 191f
blather 109
blathra (Scan) 109
bleat 109
blēd-an (AS) 195f
blēdsian (AS) 195f
bleed-ing 195f
blēgen (AS) 35, 195f
blend 71
bless-ing-ed-ness 195f
blest 195f
blind 71
Blitz-krieg (GE) 216
bloat-er 195f
bloc (FE) 154
block-ade-buster-head-
    house 154
blōd (AS) 195f
bloh (OHG) 154
blōma (AS) 195f
blomi (ON) 195f
blond 71
blood-thirsty-y 195f
bloom 195f
blossom 195f
blōstma (AS) 195f
blōstmian (AS) 195f
*blōtian (AS) 195f
blow 195f
blōwan (AS) 195f
blunder 71
bo 188f
boat 108f
bocse (AS) 36
boeuf (F) 179f
bofi (ON) 147
Bog (SlRus) 71
bogaty (SlRus) 71
boire (F) 59
bois (F) 179f

bole (Gk) 52f
bolograph-meter 52f
bolr (ON) 154
bolwerk (LG) 83f
bon (F) 188f; (FE) gré mal
    gré 75, 188f; marché
    188f; ton 188f; vivant
    188f; voyage 188f
bona fide (LE) 188f
bonanza (SpE) 188f
Bonaparte-ist 188f
bonbon (FE) 188f
bond-age-sman 72f
bonda (AS) 72f
bōndi (ON) 72f
boniface 188f
bonitas (L) 188f
bonito (SpE) 188f
bonne (FE) 188f
bonnet 188f
bonny 188f
bonté (F) 188f
bonus (LE) 37, 188f
boom 13
boon (companion) 188f
Boouinda 179f
boroda (Rus) 2, 107
Borodino 107
borough 216
bos (L) 179f
boscage 179f
boscus (L) 179f
bosko (Gk) 179f
bosky 179f
boss 150f
botane (Gk) 179f
botany-ical 179f
boukolikos (Gk) 179f
boulevard (FE) 83f
bounty-eous-ful 188f
bous (Gk) 179f
boustrophedon (GkE) 179f
bout (F) 150
boutade (F) 150f
boutelier (F) 43
boutyron (Gk) 36, 179f
bov- (L) 179f
bovine 179f
box 36
boy 147
Bovne 179f

bradhnah (Sk) 71
braggart 217
Brahma-n-ism 70f
brahman (Sk) 70f
Brahmaputra 65
Brahmin 70f
brat-r (Sl) 26
bráthair (Ir) 26
breathe 9
-brecht (G) 47f
br'er 146f
brethren 146f
bridegroom 171
bridge 34
brīg (OIr) 216
brig-antine 216
brigade-ier 216
brigand-age 216
bright 10, 15, 34, 47f
brine 118
brisance (FE) 118
briser (F) 118
britva (Rus) 118
brother-hood-ly 9, 19, 26, 146f
brothōr (AS) 146f
brotos (Gk) 157f
brown 10
Brož 157f
Bruder (G) 19, 26
brunette (FE) 43
brut (FE) 216
brute-al-ity-ize 216
bruth (Celt) 216
bruth-faths (Goth) 97
brutish 216
brutus (LOsc) 216
brycg (AS) 34
brydguma (AS) 171
brȳne (AS) 118
Bryn Mawr 76, 226f
bubalis 179f
bubalus (L) 26, 179f
Bube (G) 147, 208
buccaneer 180
bucentaur 179f
bucolic 179f
buculus (L) 179f
bufalo (It) 179f
bufalus (L) 26, 179f
buff 179f

buffalo 26, 179f
buffet 59
buffoon 43
bugle-r 179f
bulrush 154
bulwark 83f
Bund 72f
Bund-esrat (GE) 72f
bundel (Du) 72f
bundle 72f
buobo (OHG) 147
bureau-crat-cy 217f
burn 9
bus 66f
but (F) 150
butane 179f
butere (AS) 36
buterflēge (AS) 179f
butt (ASE) 150
butter-cup-fly-milk 36, 43, 179f
buttock 150
button 150f
buttress 150f
buttuc (AS) 150
butyl 179f
butyric 179f
butyrum (L) 36, 179f
buvette (F) 59
buxus (L) 36
bylgan (AS) 35, 45
byword 160

C

cab-by 40, 59
caballarius (L) 41
caballero (Sp) 41
caballo (Sp) 33
caballus (L) 88
cabildo (SpE) 137
cabra (PrSp) 40
cabrilla (SpE) 58
cabriole (FE) 58
cabriolet (FPrE) 40, 58
cachier (NF) 41
cad-dy 137
cadet 137
cæppe (AS) 136f
cage (FE) 42
cairn 217

caisson 135f
caitiff 41, 43, 135f
calan (AS) 130
caldaria (L) 57
calefacio (L) 57
calefaction 57
Calendae (L) 138f
calendar 138f
Calends 138f
caleo (L) 57
calf 35, 84f
calid 57
*calidare (VL) 57
calidus (L) 57
caliginous 57
caligo (L) 57
call-able-ing 10, 219f
callian (AS) 219f
calo (L) 138f
calorie-meter 57
calve 84f
cam(b) (Celt) 63f
cambial-ist 63f
cambiare (L) 41
cambio (ItE) 63f
cambium (LE) 63f
camera (GkLItE) 36, 74, 141
camisade 74
camisia (GaulL) 41, 74
camisole 74
camomile 170f
camp-ing, 41, 63f
campagna (It) 63f
campaign 63f
Campania 63f
campo(santo) (It) 63f
campus (LE) 63f
can 206f
canaglia (It) 157
canaille (FE) 157
(Islas) Canarias 157
canary 157
cancel-lation 217
cancelli (L) 217
cancer-ous 217
candel (AS) 61f
candela (LIt) 61f
candelabrum-a (LE) 61f, 121
candeo (L) 61f

courteous 131
courtesan 131
courtesy 131
courtier 131
courtly 131
cousin (FE) 107
cousiner (F) 107
couth 206f
couvre-chef (F) 136f
cow-boy-hide-slip 179f
coward-ice 105, 217
coy 43
crab-by 82f
-cracy 216f
crag 217
craig (IrWe) 217
cram 156
crama (Gaul) 85f
crammian (AS) 156
cramp 156
cranium (LE) 10, 37,
  214f
craps 82f
-crat 216f
crater 216f
crawfish 82f
crayfish 82f
cream-y-ery 37, 86
creatine 184
crebba (AS) 82f
credence 182
credentials 182
credenza (ItE) 182
credible-ibility 182
credit-able 182
creditor 182
credo (LE) 182
credulous-ity 182
creed 182
cremate-ion-orium 118f
crème (F) 37, 85f
cremo (L) 118f
creosote 184
creta (L) 85f
cretin-ism 85f
crimp 156
crisma (AS) 85f
criss-cross 85f
Crist-mas-nian-en-endōm
  (AS) 85f
Crna Gora (SC) 69

crosswise 228
crude-ity-ness 184
crudelis (L) 184
crudus (L) 184
cruel-ty 184
cruor (L) 184
crust-y 184
crusta (L) 184
crustacean-eous 184
cryogen-lite-scope 184
crystal-line-lize 184
cū (AS) 179f
cuando (Sp) 161
cue 40
cuig (Ir) 149
cuisine (FE) 96
culina (L) 96
culinary 96
cumedo (VL) 169
cummerbund 72f
cumplir (Sp) 230f
cunae (L) 147f
cunnan (AS) 206f
cunning 206f
-cup-y 135f
current-cy 218
cursive 218
cursory 218
cursus (L) 218
curtain 131
curtsy 131
curule 218
cut 10f
cūth (AS) 206f
cwen-e (AS) 34, 78
cwic (AS) 26
cȳ (AS) 179f
cybernetics 37
cycene (AS) 96
Cyclops 183
cylen (AS) 96
cynegetics 157
cynic-al-ism 157
cyning (AS) 204f
cynn (AS) 35, 204f
cynocephalous 157
cynosure 157
cyrin (AS) 197

cyrnel (AS) 197
cȳth (AS) 206f

D

Dachshund (GE) 157
*dacruma (L) 112
daddy-o 78
Daedalos-us-ian (GkLE)
  89
dæg (AS) 35
daga (ON) 8
dahśina (Sk) 100
daiaita (Gk) 212
dainty 99f
dais (FE) 43
*dakru 111f
Dalmatia-n-ic 64
Dalphinus 84f
-dam (L) 161
*dams-potis 96f
dana (Sl) 101
dandelion 43, 169
Dante-sque 223
dark 10
dāru (Sk) 222f
daśa (Sk) 179
dasask (ON) 109f
dasathr (ON) 109f
dasen (ME) 109f
dastard-ly 109f
data (LE) 100f
date-less 100f
dative 100f
datus (L) 100f
*dau, *dəu 56
daughter 44f
Dauphin 84f
daupjan (Goth) 47
dawn 211
day 2, 8, 35, 211
daze 109f
dazzle 109f
*de 160f
-de- (L) 161
de- 161
dé (F) 100f
*də 100f
dēad (AS) 110
dead-en 110
dean-ery 178

dessert (FE) 43
desyat' (Rus) 179
detain 67f
detect-ion-ive 173
detest-able-ation 181f
detract-ion-or 133
detto (It) 190
*deu 188f
*dəu 56
*deuk 131f
deus (L) 8, 211f
   ex machina (LE) 211f
Deus Pater (L) 201f, 211f
Deuteronomy 167f
deva-ī (Sk) 211f, 222f
devadaru (Sk) 211f, 222f
devastate-ion 129
deviate-ion-ist 142f
device 228f
devil 52f
devious 142f
devise 228f
-dex (L) 189f
dexter-ity-ous 99f
dextrine-ose 99f
*deyə 211f
deyja (ON) 110
*dhagh 8
dhānās (Sk) 9
*dhē 77f, 109f
*dhegh 8
*dhē(i) 44, 64f
*dheigu 127f
*dherāg 132f
*dheu 110
*dheub 47
*dhonas 9
*dhug(h)əter 45
*dhumb 47
*dhwěr 116
-di (F) 2, 8, 211f
dì (It) 211f
*dī, *dīa 211f
día (Sp) 2, 8, 211f
dia- (GkE) 52f
diaballo (Gk) 52f
diablerie (F) 52f
diabolic 52f
Diabolique (F) 52f
diabolos-us (GkL) 52f
diagnose-tic-ian 206f

diagonal 155
dial-ing 212
diameter-tric-al-ly 163f
Diana 211f
dianthus 211f
diaphanous 80f
diarrhea 79f
diary-ist 212
diathermy-ic 156
dīc (AS) 128
-dicare (L) 189f
dicast 189f
-dicate 189f
dice 100f
dichotomy 92
Dick-ens 220f
dicker 178
dico (L) 56, 189f
dictate-ion 190
dictator-ial-ship 190
dictée (F) 190
dictio (L) 189f
-diction 189f
diction-ary 189f
dictum (LE) 189f
dictus (L) 189f
didactic 99f
didaskein (Gk) 99f
didomi (Gk) 100f
die 9, 110
die (pl. dice) 110
dīefan (AS) 47
dīepan (AS) 47
dies (L) 2, 8, 211f mali,
   dominica 211f
diet 212
Dieu (F) 211f
dig 128
Digger 128
digit-al-is 190f
digitus (L) 189f
dignify 99f
dignitas (L) 99f
dignity-ary 99f
dignus (L) 99f
diguer (F) 128
dihtan (AS) 190
dijk (Du) 128
dike 128
dike (Gk) 189f
dilate-ion 60

dilatory 94f
dilute-ion 121
dime 178
dimension-al 163f
dimple 2, 47
dinar 178f
dîner (F) 43
*dingua (L) 112
dinner 43
diocese-an 93f
Dios (GkSp) 211f
Dioscuri (Gk) 211f
dip-per 2, 47
diphthong 191f
diplo- 166f
diplodocus 166f
diploid 166f
diplomat-cy 166f
diptera (GkE) 200
direct-ion-al 221f
directive 221f
Directoire 221f
director-ate-y 221f
directus (L) 221f
dirge 221f
dirige (L) 221f
dirigible 221f
dirigo (L) 221f
disable 144
disaster-ous 158f
disc 43
discharge 218f
disciple 99f
discipline-ary 99f
discipul (AS) 99f
disclaim-er 139
disclose-ure 139
disco (L) 99f
discord-ant 182
discourage-ment 182
discourse-ive 218
discredit 182
discus (LE) 42
disdain-ful 99f
disenchant-ment 126f
disfigure 128
disgrace-ful 75f
disguise 228f
disgust 112
dish 42
dishearten 182

enclose-ure 139f
encode 115
encourage-ment 182
encrust 184
ende (OSp) 161
endeavor 143f
endecasyllabic 178
endleofan (AS) 162
endo- 161
endocardial 182
endocrinology 161
endow-ment 100f
endue 132
endure-ance 9, 223
energy-etic 83f
enfant gâté, terrible (FE) 129, 191
enfilade 128
engage 17, 46
engagement (FE) 46
engager (F) 46
engender 204f
engine-er-ing 204f
England-ish 151f
Engle-isc (AS) 151f
enjoin 213
enlighten-ment 184f
ennoble 206f
*en(o)mn 164f
enormous-ly-ity 207
enrich-ment 221f
ensconce 101
entier (F) 68
entire 67f
entrain 133
entreat-y 133
entrust 223f
enumerate 168
envisage 228f
envois (OF) 93, 142f
envoy 39, 142f
envoyer (F) 93
envy-able-ous 54, 228f
eo- 169f
eocene-lith-ic 169f
eoh (AS) 88
eohippus 88, 169f
eon 154f
eos (Gk) 169f
épée (FE) 40f
epic 92f

Epicurus-ean-ism 218
epigene 204f
epigram 82f
epigraph 82f
Epiphania-y (GkE) 80f
episcopal-ian 202f
episcopus (L) 34, 36, 203
episkopein (Gk) 202f
episkopos (Gk) 34, 36
epitome 92
epoch 50f
eponym 164f
épopée (FE) 92f
epopoiia (Gk) 92f
epos (GkE) 92f
epos (Gaul) 88
equestrian-ienne 88
equilateral 60
equine 88
equinox-ctial 103f
equipoise 194f
equitation 88
Equites (LE) 88
equivocal-ation 93
equus (L) 88
erase-r 122f
Erbe (G) 74
*erǝ 106
erect-ion-ile 221f
erg 83f
ergo (L) 220f
ergon 83f
-ero (Sp) 41
erode-sion 122f
Erzgebirge 113
escapade 137
escape 137
escarole 169
eschamper (OF) 63f
esclave (F) 77
escluse (OF) 140
escole (OF) 36, 51
Esme 92, 113
esmer (OF) 113
esophagus 71
esquisse (FE) 51
espada (SpE) 40
especial 203f
espionage 32, 203f
espose (OF) 38
espouse-al 193f

esprit (FE) 41
espy 203f
essen (G) 168
esteem 92, 113
esthete-ic-s 89f
estimate-ion-ble 92, 113
estimer (F) 113
esus (L) 169
état (F) 41
eternal-ity 154f
eternus (L) 154f
etico (It) 51
étude (FE) 13f
*eu 129
eugenic 204f
eune (Gk) 50f
eunuch 50f
euphemy-ism 191f
euphony-ic 191f
Eure 225
evacuate-ion 129
evade-sion 9
evanesce 129
evanesce 129
evident-ce 228f
évier (F) 114f
evoke 93
ewer 114f
exalt-ation 125
exasperate-ion 153f
except-ion 135f
exchange 63f
exclaim-ation-atory 139
exclude-sion 140
exclusa (L) 140
excursion 218f
exert-ion 105
exhibeo (L) 143f
exhibit-ion-ist 144
exhume 171
existimo (L) 113
exogenous 204f
expatriate 201f
expect-ation-ant-ancy 203f
expedient-cy 198f
expedite-ion-ary-ous 198f
expend-iture 193f
expense-ive 193f
expletive 230f
explicate-ion 166f
explicit 166f
exploit-ation 166f

fijo de algo (OSp) 64f
filament 128
file 128
filial 64f
filigree-ain 128, 197
filius-a (L) 44, 64f
fill-er 230f
fille (de chambre, de joie;
     FE) 64f
filly 65
fils (F) 64f
filum (L) 128
final-ity 128
finance-ial-ier 128
findo (L) 109
fine-ry-sse 128
finger 209f
fingo (L) 128
finial 128
finicky 128
finir (F) 42
finis (L) 128
finish 42, 128
finite 128
Fiorello 195f
fir 149
fire 9, 54
fisc-ian (AS) 32, 34, 102
fish 5, 9, 32, 34, 102
fissile 109
fission-able 109
fissus (L) 109
Fitz- 64f
fiu (OHG) 119
five 149, 209f
fix-ation 128
fixus (L) 128
flag(stone) 35, 187
flaga (ON) 35, 187
flagellant-ate 55
flagellum (L) 55
flagon 167
flagrant 55
flagro (L) 55
flail 55
flak (ON) 187
flamen (LE) 70f
Flaminius-a 70f
Flammenwerfer (GE) 172
flask 167
flat 10, 187f

flaw 35, 187
flawe (ME) 187
flax-en 166f
fleax (AS) 166f
flebilis (L) 39, 109
flecto (L) 167
fledarmūs (OHG) 230f
Fledermaus (G) 230f
fleet 123
fleo (L) 109
flēogan (AS) 35, 123
fleoge (AS) 123
flēot (AS) 123
flēotan (AS) 123
flēte (AS) 123
fleur-et (FE) 40, 195f
fleur de lys (FE) 40,
     195f
fleurette (F) 195f
flight 34, 123
flirt 195f
flo (Nor) 187
float 123
flōc (AS) 187
floe 187
flog 55
floosie 195f
flora-l (LE) 195f
Florence 195f
florescent 195f
floresco (L) 195f
floriculture 195f
florid 195f
Florida 195f
florin 195f
florist 195f
flos (L) 37, 40, 195f
Flossie 195f
flotaison (F) 123
flotation 123
floterian (AS) 123, 230f
floti (ON) 123
flotian (AS) 123
flotilla (SpE) 123
flotsam 123
flotte (F) 123
flour (OFE) 40, 195f
flourish 195f
flow 10, 123
flōwan (AS) 123
flower-y 40, 195f

flugol (AS) 123
fluke 187
flutter 123, 230f
fly 35, 123
flyht (AS) 34, 123
foal 65
foam-y 102f
foda (AS) 140f
fodder 140
fodio (L) 108
foglia-o (It) 195f
foi (F) 39
foible (OFE) 39, 109
foie (F) 49
foil 195f
folc (AS) 230f
fold-er 166f
foliage-ceous 195f
folio (LE) 195f
foliolate 195f
folium-a (L) 195f
folk (OHG) 230f
folk-lore-ways-sy-moot
     230f
foment 8
fōn (AS) 185
food-stuffs 140f
foot 5, 9, 24, 186, 197f
for (L) 192
forceps 135f
foreign-er 116
foremost 76
forensic 116
fores (L) 116
forest-er-ry 116
forfait-ure 116
forfeit (F) 116
forge (FE) 43
forgive-ness 144
foris (L) 116
forthright 221f
forty 178
forum (LE) 116
fossa (LE) 108
fossil-ize 108
fossus (L) 108
foster 140f
fōstor (AS) 140f
fōt (AS) 197f
fōthor (AS) 140f
(petits) fours (FE) 156

*ger, *gere 155f
geræde (AS) 75
*gerebh 82f
gerecenian (AS) 221f
German-y 204f
germander 170f
germane 204f
Germani (L) 156
germen (L) 204f
germinal-ate 204f
geriatrics 196f
geron (Gk) 196f
gerontology 196f
gerousia (GkE) 196f
Gesicht (G) 79
gesiht (AS) 34, 79
gesnott (AS) 177
gestern (G) 27
getæl (AS) 47
getawian (AS) 188f
gethryscan (AS) 111
*geus 110f
gewiht (AS) 143
*ghabh 143ff
*ghdhem 170f
*ghdyes 103
*ghem 170f
*ghērd 130f
*ghosti-pots 97
*ghostis 32, 116f
*ghrēi 85f
*ghyes 103
giefan (AS) 144f
giefu (AS) 144f
gieldan (AS) 35
giest (AS) 32, 116f
gift 144f
gignomai (Gk) 78, 204f
(gi)gnosko (Gk) 206f
gin 204f
gioster(dæg) (AS) 103
gird-le 35, 130f
girth 130f
girthi (ON) 130f
give-away 144f
glacé-e (FE) 130
glacial-er-is 130
glacies (L) 130
glagol (Sl) 219f
glagolitic 219f
glamor-ous-ize 82f

glas (Sl) 219f
glimmer 10
gnagan (AS) 34
gnæt (AS) 34
(g)nascor (L) 204f
gnat 34
(g)natus (L) 204f
gnaw 34
(g)nobilis (L) 206f
gnome (GkE) 206f
gnomic 206f
(g)nosco (L) 24, 206f
gnosko (Gk) 206f
gnostic 206f
(g)notus (L) 206f
go 9
go (Sk) 179f
godfather 201
gold 5
gold-digger 128
golos (Rus) 219f
-gon, -gonal 155
gon- (GkE) 204f
gonad 204f
gondolier 41
gonia (Gk) 155
goniometry 155
gonococcus-rrhea 204f
good 10
goose 5, 19, 27
Gorky 156
gorod (Rus) 131
gospod' (Rus) 117
gospodar (Rus) 117
gospodin' (Rus) 117
Gotama 179f
gourmand-et (FE) 171
gouverner (F) 36
govern-ment 37
grace-ful-less 75f
gracias (Sp) 75f
gracioso (Sp) 75f
gracious 75f
grad (Sl) 131
graft 82
grain 197
gram 82f
gramarye (Scot) 82f
gramma (Gk) 82f
grammar-ian-tical 82f
gramophone 82f

granary 197
grandfather 201
grané (F) 197
grange 197
granite 197
granular-ted 197
granum (L) 197
graph-ic-ite-ology 82f
graphein (Gk) 82f
graphion (Gk) 82
grasp 10
grateful 75f
gratia (L) 75f
gratify-ication 75f
gratis 75f
gratitude 75f
gratuitous 75f
gratus (L) 75f
grave-ity-itation 216
gravis (L) 216
gravy 197
green 10
Greenwich 93f
gregarious 155f
grex (L) 155f
grenade-ier 197
grief (FE) 216
grieve-ance-ous 216
grim 85f
grīma (AS) 85f
grimace 85f
grimazo (Sp) 85f
grime 85f
grind 85f
grīndan (AS) 85f
grip 10
grislic (AS) 85f
grisly 85f
grist 85f
grommeler (F) 85f
groom 171
grow 9
grumble 85f
grumpy 85f
guaitier (OF) 42
guard 42
guardian 42
guastier (OF) 129
guberno (L) 36
*guel 52f
*guelbh 84

Herbert 47f
here 10
heri (L) 27, 103
heritogo (OHG) 132
herizogo (OHG) 132
herpein (Gk) 86
herpetology-ist 86
Herrenvolk (GE) 230f
Herz (G) 19, 24
Herzog (G) 132
hesi (ArcL) 103
hesternal 103
hesternus (L) 103
heterodox-y 99f
heterodyne 188f
heterogenous-eous 204f
heure (F) 36
hew-er 10, 116
hex (GkE) 28
hexagon-al 28, 155, 159f
hexameter-pod-gram 159f
hexane-hedron 159f
hexarch-y 159f
hexyl 159f
Hg 224f
-hibeo (L) 143f
-hibilis (L) 143f
hidalgo (SpE) 65f
hidor (Gk) 153
hidrosis 153
hierophant 80f
hígado (Sp) 49
high 10, 34, 125
hilum (L) 128
hipparch 88
Hippocrates-ic 88
hippodrome 81f, 88
hippogryph 88
hippopotamus 88, 200
histor- (GkE) 227f
historia (GkL) 227f
historiograph 36, 227f
history-ic-al-icity 36, 227f
hit 10
Hitlerjugend (GE) 126
hlēotan (AS) 34, 139f
hlot (AS) 139f
hlōt (OHG) 139f
Hlothaçhar 77
Hlothwīg 77
hlōwan (AS) 34, 138f

hlūd (AS) 77
hlūt (AS) 34, 139f
hlūtha (OHG) 77
hlyst-an (AS) 34, 77
hobo 188f
hoch (G) 125
hodgepodge 59
hodie (L) 212
hodiernal 212
hoi polloi (GkE) 229ff
hoja (Sp) 195
hold-er 138
holo- (GkE) 98
holocaust-graph 98
homage 171
hombre (SpE) 171
home-ly 147
homeopath 73
hominaticum (VL) 171
hominoid-cide-al 171
homme (d'esprit; FE)
    171
homo (sapiens; LE) 171
homogenous-eous-ize 204f
homonym 164f
homunculus (L) 171
honneur (F) 40
honor (L) 40
honor-our 40
hoodwink 137
hooked 10
hope 10
hora (L) 36
horn-y-bill-pipe-swoggle
    214f
horoscope 202f
hors (AS) 217f
hors de combat (FE) 116
hors d'oeuvre (FE) 40, 67,
    115
horse-y 5, 9, 217f
Hortense 130f
horticulture 130f
hortus (L) 130f
hospes (L) 97, 117
hospice 117
hospitable 97, 117
hospital-ity 43, 97, 116f
hospitalis (L) 43
hospodar (Rum)117
host 10, 32, 116f

hostage 117
hostel-ry 43, 97, 117
hostess 117
hostile-ity 10, 32, 116f
*hosti-pots 116
hostis (L) 32, 116f
hostler 117
hot 10
hotchpotch 59
hotel 43, 97, 117f
hound 157
hour 36
houre (OF) 36
hrān (Scan) 214f
hrēaw (AS) 34, 183f
hreinndȳri (ON) 214f
hrēr (AS) 34, 183f
hrōr (ON) 221f
hros (AS) 217f
hrosa (OHG) 184
hrossvalr (ON) 218
huître (F) 95
human-kind-ism-ist-
    itarian-ize 171
humane 171
humanus (L) 171
humble-pie 171
humid-ity-ify-or 171
humilis (L) 171
humility-ate-ion 171
humus (LE) 171
hund (AS) 157
Hund (G) 157
hundred 22, 178f
hussar 218f
húsz (Hung) 218f
hvirfla (ON) 172
hwerf (AS) 172
hwil (AS) 34
hybrid-ism 215f
hybris (Gk) 215f
hydor (Gk) 24, 153, 224f
Hydra 224f
hydrant 2, 11, 224f
hydrodynamic 188f, 224f
hydrogen 204f, 224f
hydro-meter-phobia-
    plane-ponic-xide 224f
hydrops (Gk) 224f
hydropsy 183, 224f
hyes (Gk) 27

matriarch-cide-mony 162f
matriculate-ion 162f
matrix 162f
matro- 162f
matron-ly 162f
matrona (L) 162f
Matrona 162f
matronymic 162f
matter 162f
mature-ity 57
maturus (L) 57
Matuta 57
matutinal 57
Maundy 65f
mawr (We) 76, 226f
maxim-al-ist-um 226f
maximus (L) 226f
may 35, 148
May-fair-pole 226
māyā (Sk) 148
mayor-al-alty-ess 226f
*mē 76
meahte (AS) 34, 148
meal-y-time 163f
measure-able-ment-less
    163f
mechanic-ical-ician-ist-ize
    148
mederi (L) 164
medic-al-ine-ate-ation 164
medieval 154f
meditate 164
Mediterranean 120
medium diem (L) 212
mega-cycle 76, 225f
megabuck 225f
megalomania 225f
megalos (Gk) 225f
megaphone-therium-saur
    225f
megas (Gk) 76, 225f
*meg(h) 225ff
megrim 90f, 215
mehr (G) 76
meist (G) 76
mekhane (Gk) 36, 148
memory 158
*men 68f
*mǝn 65f
menace 68f
*mē-nōt 163f

mensa (L) 38, 164
mensis (L) 33, 163f
menstrual-ate-ion 163f
Mensur (G) 163f
mensura (L) 163f
mensuration 163f
mental 57, 69
mentum (L) 69
*mer 157f
mer (F) 39
mere 121f
meridian-onal 212
merino (SpE) 226f
merisc (AS) 121f
mermaid-man 121f
mes (Sp) 33
mesa (SpE) 3, 38, 164f
mese (It) 33
mesis (VL) 163f
Mesopotamia 200
message (FE) 41
Messer(e) (It) 124
Messieurs (F) 124
mesura (VL) 163f
metabolism 52f
metacarpal 172
metal 9
metaphony 191f
Metaurus 225
meter (Gk) 162f
meter 163f
metior (L) 163f
metonymy 164f
metre 163f
metric-al 163f
metro-nome-nymic 162f
Métro (F) 162f
metron (Gk) 163f
metropolis-itan 11, 162f,
    230f
mickle 226f
micrometer 163f
Micronesia 177
microscope 202f
Middle Ages 154f
midge-t 34
midi (FE) 212
midnight 103f
might-y 34, 148
migraine (FE) 90f, 215
mike 202f

millimeter 163f
milreis (Pt) 220f
minatory 68f
mind 57
mine-r-ing 69
Minenwerfer (GE) 69, 172
mineral 69
Minneapolis 230f
minor (LE) 68f
minster 11
mint 11f
-mir 76
misappropriate 201f
miscarry-iage 218f
miscegenation 204f
mischief-vous 136f
miscreant 182
misdemeanor 68f
misericord 182
misjudge 190f
misnomer 164f
misogynist 78
misrule 223f
miss-y 226f
missaticum (L) 41
mister 76, 226f
Mistral (FE) 226f
mistress 226f
mistrust 223f
mobocracy 217f
moch' (Rus) 148
mode 164
model 164
moderate-ion-or 164
modern 164
modest-y 164
modify-ication 164
moðir (ON) 162f
mōdor (AS) 162f
modus (L) 164
moeras (Du) 122
mogu (Rus) 148
mois (F) 33
mold 164
mōna (AS) 163f
mōnandæg (AS) 163f
mōnath (AS) 163f
Monday 163f
moneo (L) 12
moneta (L) 12
monetary 12

money 12
mongoose 211
monitor 12
monneie (OF) 12
monocle 183
monophthong 191f
mons (L) 68f
Monseigneur (F) 124
Monsieur (F) 124
Monsignor (ItE) 124
montagne (F) 69
Montana 69
Montenegro 69
Monterey 69
Montevideo 69
month-ly 163f
montimbanco (It) 69
Montreal 69
mood-y 164
moon-beam-light-stone 9, 163f
moor 121f
mor (Ir) 226f
mōr (AS) 121f
morass 122
morbid 158
more-over 76
morganatic 145
morgen (AS) 35
morgengeba (OHG) 145
morgue 158
*mori 121f
moribund 158
morine (F) 158
morrow 35
mors (L) 158
mortal-ity 158
mortgage 158
morth (AS) 158
morthor (AS) 158
mortician 158
mortify-ication 158
mortmain 158
mortuary 158
moskos (Gk) 210f
most-ly 76
mother-hood-ly 9, 162f
moucheron (F) 43
mount-ain-eer-ous 69
mountebank 69
Mounties 69

mouse-y 210f
mouth 69
mouton (FE) 43
*mr-otos 157
much-ness 226f
multilingual 112
multiple-y-er 166f
mungūs (Mahr) 210f
municipal-ity 135f
murder-er-ous 158
murrain 158
murus (L) 29
*mūs 210f
mūs (AS) 210f
musa-angusa (Sk) 210f
muscatel 210f
muscle-ular 210f
musculus (L) 210f
muscus (L) 210f
mushk (OPers) 210f
mushroom 43
musk-melon-ox-rat 210f
muska (Sk) 210f
musle (AS) 210f
mus montanus (L) 69, 210f
mussel 210f
mutton 43
mycel (AS) 226f
mycge (AS) 34
myo-tic-tomy-carditis-sotis (GkE) 210f
myopia (GkE) 183
myortvy (Rus) 158
myrthrian (AS) 158
mys (Gk) 210f

N

nā (AS) 154f
naft (Pers) 72
Naiad 177
naïf-ve (FE) 205f
naïveté (FE) 205f
nama (AS) 164f
name-less-ly-sake 164f
nancior (L) 91
nanciscor (L) 91
nao (Gk) 177
naphtha-lene-ol 72
Naples 175f, 230f

napta (Av) 72
narrate-ion-ive-or 207
narro (L) 207
nascent 205f
nascor (L) 204ff
natal, Natal 205f
natant-tory-tion 177
natio (L) 205f
nation-al-ize-ism-ality 205f
native-ity 205f
nativus (L) 205f
nato (L) 177
natura (L) 205f
nature-al-ize-ation-ist 205f
natus (L) 205f
naus (Gk) 177
nausea 177
nautical 177
nautilus 177
navaja (Sp) 175
naval 177
nave 177
navicert 177
navigate-able-or 177
navis (L) 177
navvy 177
navy 177
nay 154f
n. b. 206f
*ṇdheri 104
*ṇdhos 104
ne (It) 161
né(e) (FE) 205f
neaht (AS) 34, 103f
Neapolis-tan 175f, 230f
Nebel (G) 72
*nebh 72
nebo (Rus) 72
nebula (L) 72
nebular-ose-ous 72
neco (L) 91
necro-logy-mancy-philia 91
necropolis 91, 230f
nectar-ine 91
nefarious 192f
nehmen (G) 11, 168
ne-homo (L) 171
*nek 91

pactus, pāctus (L) 185f
padre (ItSpE) 201f
padrone (It) 201f
pægel, pægl (AS) 214
paenitet (L) 141f
*pag 185f
pagan-ism-ize 186f
pagar (Sp) 33, 40
pagare (It) 40
page 186
page (boy) 37
pageant-ry 186f
pagella (L) 214
pagensis (L) 186f
paggio (It) 37
pagina (L) 185f
paginate-ion 186
pagus (L) 185f
paidion (Gk) 37
pail 214
pain-ful-less 142
painstaking 142
painter 194
pais (Gk) 199
*pāk 185f
pal 146f
pala (L) 185f
palabra (Sp) 52f
palace 186f
paladin 186f
palate 186f
palatial 186f
Palatine-ate 186f
Palatinus (L) 185f
palatium (L) 185f
palatum (L) 185f
palaver 52f
palavra (Pt) 52f
palefroi (F) 75
palette (FE) 186f
palfrey 75
palindrome 81f
palingenesis (GkE) 204f
palisade 186f
palm 5, 230f
palma (L) 230f
palmer 230f
palmetto 231f
palmiped 194f, 230f
palmist-ry 230f
palmito (Sp) 231f

palpable 230f
palpate-ion 230f
palpebral 230f
palpitate-ion 230f
palpo (L) 230f
palsgrave 186f
paltsgraaf (Du) 186f
palus (L) 185f
panache (FE) 200f
panada (Sp) 140
pañca (Sk) 149, 209f
Pancatantra 209f
pancratium 217f
pancreas-tic 184
panegyric 155f
panel 140f
paneterie (F) 140
pango (L) 185f
panification 140f
panis (L) 140f
Panjab 209f
pannus (L) 140
pansy 194
pant 80f
panteier (OF) 80f
pantry 140
papa 201f
papacy 201f
papal-ish 201f
Papeline 201f
papilio (L) 230f
papillon (F) 230f
pappas (Gk) 201f
pappy 201f
par 202
para, para- (GkE) 52f, 75
parable 43; 52f
parabolare (VL) 52f
parabole-a (GkL) 40, 43, 52f
paradeictic 189f
paradigm-atic 189f
paradox-ical 99f
paramount 68f
paraola, paraula (VL) 40, 52f
parasol 176
paraveredus (L) 75
pardon-able 100f
parish-ioner 93f
parlance 52f

parlando (ItE) 52f
parlare (It) 52
parlement (F) 52f
parler (F) 52f
parley 52f
parliament-ary-arian 52f
parlor 52f
parochial-ism 93f
paroisse (F) 93
parola (It) 52f
parole (FE) 40, 43, 52f
parricide 201f
parterre (FE) 120
participate-ion 1, 135f
participle 135f
pasco (L) 140f
passible-ve 141f
passion-ate 141f
passus (L) 141f
pasta (asciutta) (It) 140f
paste-board 140f
pastel 140f
Pasteur 140f
pasteurize-ation 140f
pasticcio (ItE) 140f
pastiche (FE) 140f
pastille (FE) 140f
pastor-al 140f
pastourelle (FE) 140f
pastry 140f
pasture 140f
pastus (L) 140f
pasty 140f
Pat 201f
pâté (FE) 140f
patella (L) 214
pater (LE) 5, 21, 40, 201f
pater (Gk) 201f
pater familias, patriae (LE) 201f
Pater Noster 201f
paternal-ism-istic 201f
paternity 201f
path-o- 73
pathetic 73
pathos-logical 73
patient-ce 141f
patior (L) 141f
pâtisserie (FE) 140f
patrare (VL) 201f
patria (LIt) 201f

*spek 32, 202ff
spencer, Spencer 194f
*(s)pend 193ff
spend-er-thrift 193f
speornan (AS) 153f
sperno (L) 153
*sp(h)er 153f
sphaira (Gk) 153
sphere-ical-oid 153
spice-y-ery 203
spicio (L) 32, 203
spider 193f
spin-dle-ster-dly 193f
spinel (AS) 193f
spinnan (AS) 193f
spione (It) 202f
spiritus (L) 41
spite-ful 203f
spithre (AS) 193f
split 10
*(s)pond 193ff
spond- (L) 193f
sponde (Gk) 193f
spondee-aic 193f
spondeo (L) 33, 193f
sponsor 193f
sponsus-a (L) 38, 193f
spont- (L) 193f
spontaneous-ity 193f
spoor (DuE) 153f
sporettan (AS) 153f
spouse 38, 193f
spuma (L) 102f
spumante (It) 102f
spume-y 102f
spur 153f
spura (AS) 153f
spurn 153f
spurnan (AS) 153f
spy-glass 32, 202f
sravati (Sk) 33
sreda (Sl) 182
*sreu 79f
*(s)roum 33
stabulum (L) 33
stall (ASE) 33
stand 9
standard-ize 217
star-ry-fish-let 158f, 170
starve 110
statum (L) 41

steall (AS) 33
*(s)teg 173
*stel 59f
stella (L) 38, 158f
stellar-ate 158f
*stelna (L) 38
steorfan (AS) 110
steorra (AS) 158f
stepmother 163
*ster 158f
stereoscope 202f
sterling 158f, 170
sterre (ME) 158f
stethoscope 202f
stipend 193f
*stlātus 59f
sto (Sl) 22
stone 9
story-ey 227f
strata (L) 38
strēam (AS) 33, 79f
stream-er 33, 79f
street 11, 38
strike 10
strom (Du) 80
Struma 80
student 14
studio (ItE) 13f
studium (L) 13
study 13
*sū 44f
suadeo (L) 159
suasion 159
sua sponte (L) 193f
suasus (L) 159
suave-ity 159
suavis (L) 159
sub (L) 221f
subdue 132
subhuman 171
subjoin 213
subjugate 213
subjunctive 213
submarine 121f
subpoena (LE) 142
subrogation 221f
subterranean 120
subtle-ty 173f
subtract-ion 133
subundare (VL) 224f
suburban 131

succor 218
sudor (L) 153
sudorific-erous 153
sueldo (Sp) 98
suffix-ation 128
Suffolk 176
sulz (OHG) 174f
sum-mary-ize 165f
summus (L) 165f
sun-shine-stroke-ny 9, 176
sundae 176
Sunday 176
sunna (AS) 176
sunnandæg (AS) 176
sunno (Goth) 176
*sūnu 45
sunu (AS) 45
super (LE) 21, 165f
superabundant-ce 224f
superanus (VL) 40, 166
superb 165f
superbus (L) 165f
supercargo 218
supererogation 221f
superfine 128
superhuman 171
superior-ity 165f
superlative 94f
supernal 165f
supernatural 205f
supernumerary 168
supervise 228f
supper 43
supplement-al-ary 230f
suppliant-cate-ion 166f
supply-er 166, 230f
supra- (LE) 165f
supreme-acy 165f
supremus (L) 165f
sur (FE) 165f
surcharge 218f
surface (FE) 165f
surfeit 165f
surge 221f
surgeon-ery-ical 84
surgo (L) 221f
surly-ness 124
surmount 68f
surname 164f
surplus 230f
surrender 101

truth-ful-ly 223
tryst 223f
tu (L) 19, 22
tūccian (AS) 131f
tūdor (AS) 131f
Tuesday 8, 211f
tug 131
tuig (Du) 132
tuile (F) 173
Tuileries 172
tulā (Sk) 94
tureen 120
turmeric 120
tusc (AS) 168f
tush 168f
tusk 168f
twelf (AS) 162
twelve-fth 162
twenty 178
twist 10
twit 228
twofold 166f
-ty 179
tycoon 13
tyge (AS) 131f
tyht (AS) 131f
tȳn (AS) 178
typhoid 227f
typhoon 13
Tȳr (ON) 211f

U

über (G) 21
*udero 87f
*udtero 87f
uisce (OIr) 224f
uisge beatha (OIr) 224f
Ulpius 152
umble pie 171
un- 56, 59
uña (Sp) 151f
unable 144
unbeknownst 206f
uncinate 151f
uncle 40, 106
uncouth 206f
uncus (L) 151f
unda (L) 24, 224f
undecim (L) 178
undecimal 178

under 10, 104
underfoot 198
undies 104
undine 224f
undulant-ate-ion-atory 224f
undying 110
unfeeling 230f
unghia (It) 151f
ungula (L) 151f
ungulate 151f
unhorse 218
unicorn 215
unilateral 59f
uninhabited 144
unkind 204f
unknown 206f
unmanageable 66
unnatural 205f
uns (OHG) 33
unsightly 79
untrue-th 223
unworldly 113f
*uper, *uperi 165f
upright 221f
ur- (G) 170
uralt (G) 170
urban-e-ity 131
urbs (L) 131
ureter 224f
urgermanisch (G) 170
uric 224f
urine-al-ate 224f
ūrohso (OHG) 224f
urus (LE) 224f
ūs (AS) 33
us 33
uter (L) 224f
uterine 87f
uterus (LE) 87f, 224f
utriform-cle 224f
utro (Sl) 170

V

vacant-cy 129
vacate-ion 129
vaco (L) 129
vacuity 129
vacuous 129
vacuum (LE) 129

vacuus (L) 129
vain-glory 129
Van Dyke 128
vanish 129
*vanitare (VL) 129
vanity 129
vanta (ON) 129
vanter (F) 129
vanus (L) 129
vapidus (L) 151, 193
vas-culum (L) 167
vast-ness-ity 129
vasto (L) 129
vastus (L) 129
Vater (G) 201
Vaterland (GE) 201
vaunt-ed 129
vector-ion 142f
vectus (L) 142f
Veda-nta-ic-s 29, 227f
Vēdas (Sk) 227f
vedette (FE) 228f
vehemens (L) 142f
vehement-ce 142f
vehicle-ular 142f
veho (L) 142f
veir (OF) 228f
veloce (ItE) 142f
velocipede 142f, 198f
velocity-drome 142f
velox (L) 142f
venaison (F) 43
venal-ity 101
vend-or-ition 101
vendetta (ItE) 189f
vendo (L) 101
vengeful 189f
venison 43
venter (L) 87f
ventral-iloquist 87f
venum-do (L) 101
veracious-ity 54
veracus (VL) 38, 54
verai (OF) 38, 43, 54
verb-al-ose-atim-iage 160
verbena (L) 172
verbero (L) 172
verbum-a (L) 52, 131, 160
Vercingetorix 163, 220f
verdict 54f, 190
veredus (L) 75